Sam
Western & American Samoa

a Lonely Planet travel survival kit

Deanna Swaney

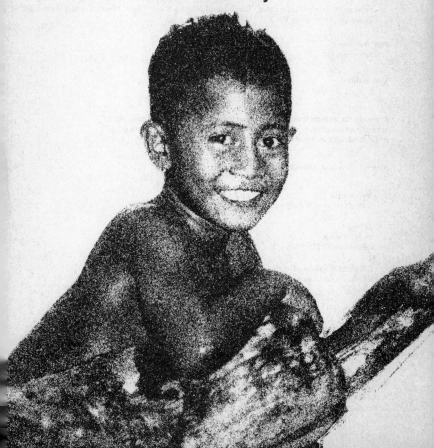

Samoa: Western & American Samoa

2nd edition

Published by
Lonely Planet Publications
Head Office: PO Box 617, Hawthorn, Vic 3122, Australia
Branches: PO Box 2001A, Berkeley, CA 94702, USA
10 Barley Mow Passage, Chiswick, London W4 4PH, UK
71 bis rue du Cardinal Lemoine, 75005 Paris, France

Printed by
McPherson's Printing Group Ltd, Australia

Photographs by
Simone Calderwood (SC)
Dr Greg Coates (GC)
Deanna Swaney (DS)

Front cover: Ancient knife dance, 'Upolu Island, Western Samoa (David Moore; Scoopix Photo Library)
Title page: Samoan boy (GC)

First Published
February 1990

This Edition
September 1994

Although the authors and publisher have tried to make the information as accurate as possible, they accept no responsibility for any loss, injury or inconvenience sustained by any person using this book.

National Library of Australia Cataloguing in Publication Data

Swaney, Deanna
Samoa : Western & American Samoa – a travel survival kit.

2nd ed.
Includes index.
ISBN 0 86442 225 3.

1. American Samoa – Guidebooks. 2. Western Samoa – Guidebooks
I. Title. (Series: Lonely Planet travel survival kit).

919.61304

text & maps © Lonely Planet 1994
photos © photographers as indicated 1994
climate charts compiled from information supplied by Patrick J Tyson, © Patrick J Tyson, 1994

Deanna Swaney

An incurable travel addict, Deanna Swaney escaped encroaching yuppiedom in the vibrant heart of mid-town Anchorage and made a break for South America to write Lonely Planet's *Bolivia – a travel survival kit*. Subsequent wanders through island paradises – Arctic and tropical – resulted in travel survival kits to *Tonga* and *Iceland, Greenland & the Faroe Islands* and to the first edition of this book.

She has also written guides to *Zimbabwe, Botswana & Namibia* (1st edition) and *Madagascar & Comoros* (2nd edition), co-authored the 2nd editions of LP's *Brazil* and *Mauritius, Réunion & Seychelles*, and contributed to shoestring guides to Africa, South America and Scandinavia.

From the Author

During my research for this update, I was fortunate enough to come in contact with a large number of people – Samoans, expats and fellow travellers – who offered their friendship, help and insights and greatly enhanced my stay. First, I'd like to thank Dieter Guschlbauer, who offered transport and photographic expertise as well as welcome company on numerous forays around the countries. I'm also especially grateful to Fuimaono Fereti Tupua of Apia, Western Samoa, who so kindly contributed his expertise to the Samoan language section and to Geoff Hyde of Apia for his assistance.

Others who made significant – and much-appreciated – contributions to my research and/or well-being include Tom at Va'oto, Ofu; Moelagi Jackson at the Safua Hotel on Savai'i; Warren Jopling, also of the Safua Hotel, Savai'i; Jo Laing at Bridge the World in London; Richard Green, UK; John David, UK; Guy Edwards, Apia; Aggie at Aggie Grey's Hotel, Apia; and Afa, Sieni, Mika, Roger and Gayle at Coconuts Beach, 'Upolu. And as always, love and thanks to Earl Swaney, Robert Strauss, Joyce Strauss, Dave Dault and Keith & Holly Hawkings for their continuing love and support.

We also received quite a few useful readers' letters, several of which were extracted for use in the book. Many thanks to Doe Risko & Andrew Weinstein (USA); Leroy Diener (USA); Sarah Vanderburg (USA); Stephen How Lum (Australia); and several people whose names were missing from the letters.

From the Publisher

This book was edited in Lonely Planet's Melbourne office by Simone Calderwwod and Miriam Cannell. Mapping, illustrations and design were handled by Sally Woodward. Thanks to Michelle Stamp and Jane Hart for assistance with mapping, and to Tamsin Wilson for the cover design.

Thanks also to the travellers who took the time to write to us about their experiences in Samoa (apologies if we have misspelt any names):

Iris Baird (USA), T P Bennett (Aus), Pauline Clayton (Aus), William de Prado (USA), LeRoy Diener, Mike Fee Lars Gotaas (N), Jim Green (USA), Stephen How Lum (Aus), Mr & Mrs Ed McCauley (USA), Martin Robinson (NZ), Donald Sheehan, T S Toalepaialii, Sarah Vanderburg Ken Waller (C), M A Whitley (UK), Alison Withey (USA) and Claire Wood.

Aus – Australia, C – Canada, NZ – New Zealand, N – Norway, UK – United Kingdom, USA – United Kingdom

Warning & Request

Things change – prices go up, schedules change, good places go bad and bad places go bankrupt – nothing stays the same. So if you find things better or worse, recently opened or long since closed, please write and tell us and help make the next edition better.

Your letters will be used to help update future editions and, where possible, important changes will also be included in a Stop Press section in reprints.

We greatly appreciate all information that is sent to us by travellers. Back at Lonely Planet we employ a hard-working readers' letters team to sort through the many letters we receive. The best ones will be rewarded with a free copy of the next edition or another Lonely Planet guide if you prefer. We give away lots of books, but, unfortunately, not every letter/postcard receives one.

Contents

AMERICAN SAMOA

Map Legend

BOUNDARIES

...International Boundary
...Internal Boundary
...Equator
...Tropics

ROUTES

...Freeway
...Highway
...Major Road
...Unsealed Road or Track
...City Road
...City Street
...Railway
...Walking Track
...Walking Tour
...Ferry Route
...Cable Car or Chairlift

AREA FEATURES

...Park, Gardens
...National Park
...Built-Up Area
...Pedestrian Mall
...Market
...Cemetery
...Reef
...Beach or Desert
...Rocks

HYDROGRAPHIC FEATURES

...Coastline
...River, Creek
...Intermittent River or Creek
...Lake, Intermittent Lake
...Canal
...Swamp

SYMBOLS

✪ CAPITAL		...National Capital
◉ Capital		...State Capital
🐾 CITY		...Major City
● City		...City
● Town		...Town
● Village		...Village
■		...Place to Stay
▼		...Place to Eat
∇		...Pub, Bar

✉	☎		...Post Office, Telephone
❶	❸		...Tourist Information, Bank
◒	₽		...Transport, Parking
⛪	✿		...Museum, Youth Hostel
⛺	⚠		Caravan Park, Camping Ground
†	✠	†	...Church, Cathedral
☪	✡		...Mosque, Synagogue
⚏			...Temple

✚	★	...Hospital, Police Station
✈	✝	...Airport, Airfield
▣	✿	...Swimming Pool, Gardens
❖	🐘	...Shopping Centre, Zoo
⚘	🎋	...Winery or Vineyard, Picnic Site
←	A25	One Way Street, Route Number
	∴	...Archaeological Site or Ruins
🏛	▲	...Stately Home, Monument
⚑	▣	...Golf Course, Tomb
⌢	⌂	...Cave, Hut or Chalet
▲	☀	...Mountain or Hill, Lookout
⛩	↘	...Lighthouse, Shipwreck
)(	⚲	...Pass, Spring
		...Ancient or City Wall
		...Rapids, Waterfalls
		...Cliff or Escarpment, Tunnel
		...Railway Station

Note: not all symbols displayed above appear in this book

Introduction

Like Korea, the Samoas are a homogeneous nation politically divided. On both sides of the 171st meridian, which divides the US territory of American Samoa and independent Western Samoa, the people speak the same language, practise essentially the same customs and to some degree, pass on the same traditions. However, because of the political disparity, the atmospheres and characters of each country remains distinct.

Western Samoa, by far the larger of the two Samoas, is a comparatively quiet and gentle country which nurtures the most traditionally Polynesian society to be found anywhere in the Pacific islands. Although it has moved lethargically into the 20th century, the rituals and tribal hierarchies have remained nearly unchanged since ancient times, despite 200 years of colonisation and disputation by several foreign powers.

Just 100 km to the east, however, is the South Pacific, American style. Fast food, souped-up cars, high-school football and 'valley girls' all feature prominently against the fading Polynesian scene. Most of American Samoa's 35,000 or so residents have been to the 'mainland' (which includes Hawaii, as far as they're concerned); most of the younger ones seem to have liked what they saw there.

The older folks however – and quite a few young American Samoans – continue to struggle to preserve the remaining vestiges of *fa'a Samoa* – the Samoan way. Thanks to restricted immigration from the USA, and regulations stating that only a small percentage of land may be leased to outsiders and

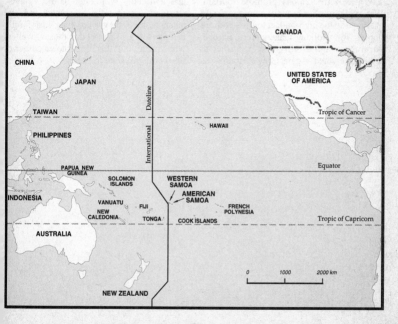

9

that North American businesses cannot compete with local ventures, it seems doubtful, at present, that their society will be as overwhelmed by materialistic US ideals and retirement condominiums as Hawaii has been.

The differences between the Samoas don't end with culture, however, and the countries provide travellers with more than an interesting social study. Although they lie within 100 km of each other, their geographies – both spectacular – are vastly different.

Western Samoa is composed mainly of two bulky islands of volcanic origin which slope gently from sparkling beaches to nondescript summits, and a few smaller islands that are little more than outcrops.

American Samoa contains four incredibly rugged volcanic peaks – dragon-like Tutuila (the main island) and the three small but wildly steep islands of the Manu'a group. It also includes the small crater island of 'Aunu'u and two coral atolls, Swains Island and Rose Atoll.

While both Samoas promote tourism, Western Samoa has been the more successful at attracting the high-budget tourists both are hoping for. Holiday-makers from Europe, Australasia and North America gather at world-renowned Aggie Grey's Hotel – as well as several other up-and-coming resorts – on the main island of 'Upolu, but rarely wander far from their swimming pool or tour bus. Travellers are rare and opportunities for exploration abound, especially on the virtually untouched island of Savai'i.

Tourism in American Samoa, on the other hand, is limited mostly to obligatory airline stopover passengers, business travellers, and yachties who stop to stock up on the cheapest groceries between Venezuela and Singapore. Few of Tutuila's visitors see any more than the congested stretch of highway between the airport and the Rainmaker Hotel. In the magnificently rugged and remote Manu'a Islands, where a US national park was created in late 1988, tourists and travellers are still a scarcity.

The people of both Western and American Samoa, like most Polynesians, welcome strangers with some of the most legendary hospitality in the world. In the larger settlements they are always prepared with a smile and a friendly word, but in the villages, strangers are proudly welcomed, fed and taken in as if they were long lost family members. It's a safe bet that those travellers who venture into this little-known corner of the world will want to return.

Facts about the Region

HISTORY

Since the Samoas are a divided nation, the histories of Western and American Samoa coincided until European partition, which occurred only at the beginning of the 20th century. There was no need to distinguish between the Samoas until contact with European powers caused them to head in different directions.

Prehistory

The Samoan people are Polynesians. The area called Polynesia, meaning 'many islands', forms a triangle with points at Hawaii, Easter Island (off the west coast of South America) and New Zealand and also includes outlying islands scattered through Fiji and the East Indies.

Polynesian peoples are presumed to have

Creation Legends

The Samoans themselves believe that their land is the 'cradle of Polynesia' – that the scientifically accepted theories that all Polynesians originally migrated to the islands from South-East Asia by way of Indonesia applies to Maoris, Hawaiians, Tongans, Rarotongans, Easter Islanders and Tahitians but not to themselves.

They tell a story of the creation by the god Tagaloa that is remarkably similar to the account given in the Bible in the Book of Genesis. Before there existed any sea, earth, sky, plants or people, Tagaloa lived in the expanse of empty space. He created a rock, commanding it to split into clay, coral, cliffs and stones. As the rock broke apart, the earth, sea and sky came into being. From a bit of the rock came a spring of fresh water.

Next, Tagaloa created man and woman, whom he named Fatu and 'Ele'ele ('heart' and 'earth'). He sent them to the region of fresh water with a command that they people that area. He ordered the sky, which was called Tu'ite'elagi, to prop itself up above the earth, and using starch and *teve*, a bitter-root plant and the only vegetation available at this early date, he made a post for it to rest upon.

The god then created Po and Ao ('night' and 'day'), who in turn bore the 'eyes of the sky', the sun and the moon. At the same time Tagaloa made the nine regions of heaven, which he peopled with all sorts of gods.

In the meantime, Fatu and 'Ele'ele were busy peopling the area of fresh water. Tagaloa, reckoning that all these earthlings needed some form of government, sent Manu'a, another son of Po and Ao, to be the chief of the people. From that time on, Samoan *tupu* (kings), were called *Tu'i Manu'a tele ma Samoa atoa*, which means 'king of Manu'a and all of Samoa'.

Next, the countries were divided into islands or groups of islands so the world consisted of Manu'a, Fiji, Tonga and Savai'i. Tagaloa went to Manu'a, apparently noticing a void between it and Savai'i, and up popped 'Upolu and then Tutuila. The final command of Tagaloa before he returned to the expanse was: 'Always respect Manu'a; anyone who fails to do so will be overtaken by catastrophe, but men are free to do as they please in their own lands.' Thus, Manu'a became the spiritual centre of the Samoan islands and, to some extent, of all Polynesia.

The name Samoa, incidentally, means literally, 'sacred chicken' which is a matter of amusement in the islands. There are several tales of how this came about, but the most interesting involves Lu, the son of Tagaloa. Father and son built a canoe which Lu put out to sea during a six-day flood caused by his mother because she found shellfish lying around homeless in the sun. Before he left, Lu caught two of the god's reserve chickens to carry on the journey.

After the flood, the vessel came to rest on Mt Malata on the eastern end of 'Upolu. Unfortunately, the chickens went missing in the village there. By chance, Lu caught the two culprits red-handed with chicken juice running down their chins and chicken bones in their hands.

Lu went to his father to complain about the demise of his sacred chickens, and ask his advice. Tagaloa replied that the country was a peaceful place and that no violence would be permitted. To appease the boy's wrath, Tagaloa granted his daughter as a wife for Lu (intra-family marriages have always been popular among deities everywhere) and the god advised his son to name the earth *Samoa* in memory of the unfortunate chickens. ∎

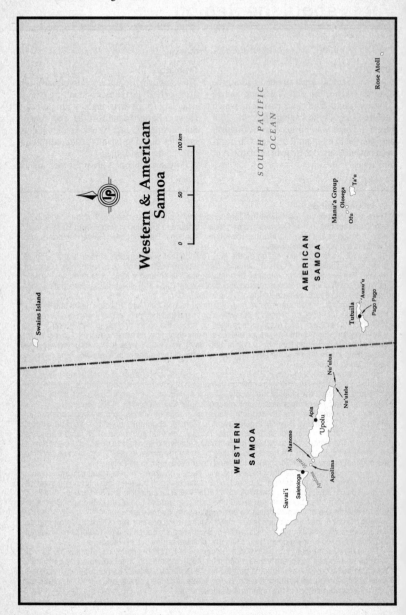

entered the Pacific from the west – the East Indies, the Malay Peninsula or the Philippines. Because lapita pottery similar to that found in the Bismarck Archipelago and New Caledonia has also been found in the Samoas and Tonga (dating from about 1500 BC to the time of Christ), and because no use of pottery was evident there at the time of European contact in the 17th century, it seems likely that those islands were the first Polynesian areas settled. It is thought that the people stopped using pottery because the local clay was unsuitable and alternatives such as coconut shells and seashells were readily available.

The theory proposed by the unconventional Norwegian anthropologist Thor Heyerdahl that the Polynesians migrated not from Asia but from the Americas is based primarily on the presence of the *'umala* (sweet potato) in the Pacific and South America but not in Asia. Interestingly, the Mormons, ubiquitous throughout the Pacific, also tell a tale of colonisation of the islands by South American mainlanders. Some members of the scientific community, however, question this theory.

Some anthropologists believe that the Samoas were initially settled by Fijians or Tongans or that the first Samoans were conquered early on by chiefs and warriors from those countries. Samoan legends which have Fijian kings and princesses as their heroes seem to support this view. In 950 AD warriors from Tonga established rule on Savai'i, the nearest island to Tonga, then moved on to 'Upolu, where they were fought back by Malietoa Savea, the chief of the Samoas, whose title was derived from the words *malie toa*, meaning 'brave warriors'. A treaty of peace between the two countries was drawn up and the Samoans were left by Tongans to pursue their own course.

The earliest known evidence of human occupation in the islands is a lapita village site partially submerged in the lagoon at Mulifanua on the island of 'Upolu, which carbon tests have tentatively dated at 1000 BC.

Nearby, and at numerous other sites on 'Upolu, Savai'i and Tutuila, archaeologists have excavated odd platforms with stone protrusions radiating from their bases which have been dubbed 'star mounds'. There are no oral traditions pertaining to the purpose of these mounds but, since they don't contain burial sites, they are generally thought to be structures used in the ancient sport of pigeon-snaring or as platforms for religious ceremonies.

On Savai'i, near the village of Palauli, is the pyramid of Pulemelei, the largest ancient structure in the Pacific, and there seems to be no tradition or speculation surrounding it.

Evidence suggests that in ancient times most Samoan settlements were located inland in the valleys and on hillsides and that villages scattered around the coasts as they are today are merely a product of European influence and trade.

European Contact

Although numerous whalers, pirates and escaped convicts had landed in the islands earlier, the first European on record to approach the Samoan islands was Dutchman Jacob Roggeveen. He sighted the Manu'a Islands in 1722 while searching for the *terra australis incognita*, the great unknown southern continent. He gave the islands Dutch names and then sailed on without landing.

In May 1768 the French explorer Captain Louis-Antoine de Bougainville also passed through Samoan waters and, upon seeing the islanders travelling about in ocean-going canoes, christened the archipelago Les Îles des Navigateurs (the Navigator Islands). He bartered with the inhabitants of the Manu'a Islands and merely sighted the more westerly islands.

Next came Bougainville's compatriot Jean-François de Galaup, Comte de La Pérouse, who landed at Fagasa on the north coast of Tutuila in 1787. The Samoans went about helping themselves to the intriguing bits of iron found aboard his ships *La Boussole* and *Astrolabe* and the French sailors made examples of a few by punishing them. Word evidently spread westward because the following day at Aasu, while they were collecting water, the locals attacked, killing 12 crewmen, including Commander Viscount de Langle. La Pérouse estimated that at least 39 Samoans also died during the encounter. The bay of Aasu was named Massacre Bay and the Europeans departed posthaste.

In 1791, the British ship HMS *Pandora*, under the command of Captain Edward Edwards, called in while in search of the Bounty mutineers, who had set their Captain Bligh and 18 crewmen adrift in Tonga two years earlier. The ship was attacked off the coast of Tutuila and as a result many Samoans were killed.

These two events dramatically introduced the Samoans to the power of European weaponry and in foreign circles, gave the Samoans a reputation for being hostile people.

The European traders, who had by this time begun plying the Pacific trade routes carrying whale products, sandalwood and bêche-de-mer to China in exchange for silk, tea and porcelain, steered clear of the Samoas until the early 1800s.

By the 1820s quite a few Europeans had settled in the islands, most of them escaped convicts and retired whalers. They were welcomed by the unsuspecting islanders because they knew the strange ways of the *palagi* (Europeans) and were willing to share the European technological expertise with them.

The Samoan population up to about 1830, when it began to grow, remained at a stable 50,000 due to the custom of only having as many children as could be adequately cared for. Natural disasters such as typhoons and droughts took their toll also, and the Europeans brought with them diseases to which the islanders had no immunity.

The Missionaries

Some of the itinerants who found themselves in the Samoas during the early 1800s – and several Christian converts from other parts of Polynesia – had introduced a form of Christianity known as the Sailors' *Lotu* (Church) to the Samoans. Given the similar-

ity of the Christian creation beliefs to Samoan legend and a prophecy by Nafanua, the war goddess, that a new religion would take root in the islands, the Samoans were well prepared to accept the message of the missionaries who arrived to convert them. The wondrous possessions of the *palagi* (Caucasians) were also used as evidence that the White man's god was more generous than the gods of the island peoples.

Peter Turner, a Wesleyan Methodist missionary based in Tonga, visited the Samoas briefly in 1828 and passed his message along to many Samoans, but he never established a mission there. In 1830, missionaries John Williams and Charles Barff of the London Missionary Society, arrived on Savai'i, and A W Murray came to Tutuila in 1836. Shortly thereafter others carried their message to Manu'a.

The *lotu Pope* (Pope's church) was brought to Falealupo on Savai'i in 1845 by French Catholic missionaries from Wallis and Futuna, who established a Marist mission. Unfortunately, this paved the way for the European rivalry between the Catholics and Protestants to extend throughout the Pacific islands.

It didn't take long for the Christian gospel to be accepted wholesale by the Samoans, and it has remained an integral part of island life to the present day. So much so, in fact, that the Samoas, along with Tonga and some neighbouring islands, have come to be called the 'bible belt of the Pacific'.

The *lotu Mamona* (Mormon church), a latecomer, was introduced by two missionaries sent by an imperialistic White politician in Hawaii named Walter M Gibson, who believed that he could use religion to help annex the Samoan islands to the Kingdom of Hawaii. By 1888 the missionaries had settled in with Samoan wives and had established an official mission in Pago Pago. Shortly thereafter, another mission was established in what is now Western Samoa. Today membership of the Mormon Church in the Samoas is less than 12,000, but there is an ornate Mormon temple just west of Apia in Western Samoa.

European Control

In 1838, the British Captain Bethune, of the HMS *Conway*, set up a code of commercial regulations that dealt with customs and ports in the Samoas. The following year, the USA sent a scientific expedition under the command of Charles Wilkes, who was charged with surveying lands and observing the natural element among the more obscure islands of the South Pacific. Wilkes made a trading treaty of sorts with the chiefs of the islands and thereby established another nation's interest in the Samoas.

The first British consul to the Samoas was G Pritchard, formerly of the London Missionary Society, who was appointed in 1847. At the time, word of Pago Pago's harbour was spreading throughout the European powers and it was becoming one of the prime whaling ports in the Pacific.

Between 1850 and 1880 many European settlers arrived in the islands, especially on 'Upolu and primarily for the purpose of trade. They established a society and minimal code of laws in Apia to govern their affairs, all with the consent of 'Upolu chiefs, who maintained sovereignty in their own villages.

One extremely important arrival in Apia was that of August Unshelm, a representative of German trade tycoon, Johann Cesar Godeffroy, who was interested in trading in Polynesia. By 1861 his firm had established stations in Fiji and Tonga. Upon the death of Unshelm, Theodor Weber took over the firm and spread the Godeffroy empire to thousands of islands around the southern, central and western Pacific. He purchased 300 sq km of land on 'Upolu and set the stage for realising his dream, the raising of the German flag over the Samoas.

Weber's plans were interrupted, however, by the bankruptcy of Godeffroy and the outbreak of the Franco-Prussian War, and the colonisation scheme was put to rest for a while. Still, quite a few German colonists remained in the Samoas and the entrepreneurial void was immediately filled by a trading company with the long-winded name of Deutsche Handels und Plantagen Gesell-schaft der Sudsee Inseln zu Hamburg (DHPG).

Squabbling Powers

There were four 'paramount' families – the equivalent of royal dynasties – in what is now Western Samoa: the Malietoa, Tupua Tamasese, Mata'afa and Tu'imaleali'ifano. During the 1870s the Samoans became involved in a civil dispute between two kings, one in the east and one in the west, contending for supreme power. Samoans sold their lands to the Europeans to acquire armaments to settle the matter.

In the meantime, Britain and the USA were struggling to attain some sort of peace in the islands. In 1872 the USA had been offered exclusive rights to a naval base in Pago Pago Harbor by the high chief of Tutuila in exchange for the protection and backing of the US government. The following year Colonel A B Steinberger, serving as an official agent of the US government, drafted a constitution and bill of rights for the Samoas and set up a government whereby the squabbling kings would serve alternate four-year terms. Steinberger ultimately became Premier of Samoa. He severed ties with the US government and began negotiations with the Germans regarding taxes, German land claims and administration of German financial interests in the Samoas.

The British and American consuls were unhappy that Steinberger had usurped power and arranged to have him deported to Fiji. As soon as he was gone, the Samoan self-government scheme collapsed, leaving a number of factions seeking political advantage. A delegation of Samoans sought protection from the British in Fiji and the Americans in Washington but both refused. Because the USA had ignored the invitation to set up a naval base on Tutuila, the Samoans made both Germany and Britain the same offer.

By the late 1880s warships of all three powers had been sent to Apia Harbour and the affair had heated sufficiently to inspire tension all around. As one Samoan author put it, they were 'like three large dogs snarling over a very small bone'.

As if nature were reprimanding the three bickering countries, on 16 March 1889, Apia Harbour was hit by one of history's worst typhoons. The Germans lost three warships – *Olga*, *Adler* and *Eber*. The Americans also lost three – *Vandalia*, *Trenton* and *Nipsic*. The British warship *Calliope* battled her way out of the harbour in time to escape destruction. There were 92 Germans and 54 American crew members killed in the storm.

All three powers mellowed a bit after the disaster and made a real effort to settle the issue by drawing up the Berlin Treaty of 1889. This stipulated that an independent Samoa would be established under the rule of a foreign-appointed Samoan king and that the consuls of Britain, Germany and the USA would be given considerable advisory powers on the island of 'Upolu.

After the Berlin Treaty the Malietoa king was given the official vote of confidence, but his hold on power was tenuous. In the years that followed, the Mata'afa king continually challenged the Malietoas' right to power. He wrote a lengthy epistle to Germany, Britain and the USA pleading for fairness in their actions regarding his country. Part of it reads as follows:

I rejoice, and my people are glad, at the prospect of a new and stable government for Samoa. If the Great Powers will send good men to take charge of the government, and not those who care only for the money they will receive, Samoa will become peaceful, happy, and prosperous.

The Samoan factions continued their struggle, and the Western powers again began to quarrel. At last the foreign rulers realised that they were going nowhere in their attempts to settle the dispute. The Berlin Treaty was declared void, and on 2 December 1899 the Tripartite Treaty was drawn up, giving control of Western Samoa to the Germans and that of eastern Samoa to the Americans. Britain stepped out of the picture altogether in exchange for renunciation of all German claims to Tonga, the Solomon Islands and Niue.

The Germans placed Mata'afa in the puppet position of paramount chief of their territory, abolishing the kingship altogether lest the Samoans be allowed too much power over the new 'German colony'. (One of the objectives of the Mau Movement (see the History section in the Facts about Western Samoa chapter) would be to increase German and, later, New Zealand respect for the nation's highest ranking native son, but until his death Mata'afa remained only a figure head.)

From this point, the histories of the Samoas diverged. The period from 1900 to the present appears in the introductory History sections for each area.

GEOGRAPHY

The Samoas are made up of mostly high but well-eroded volcanic islands that lie more or less in the heart of the South Pacific, 3700 km south-west of Hawaii. To the south lies Tonga, to the east the northern Cook Islands, and to the north the Tokelau Islands.

Western Samoa, with a total land area of 2934 sq km, consists primarily of the two large islands of Savai'i, with 1700 sq km, and 'Upolu, with 1115 sq km. Both are of volcanic origin and are much higher and newer than the islands of American Samoa. The Samoas' highest peak, Savai'i's Mt Silisili, near the centre of the island, rises to 1850 metres.

Western Samoa's other two inhabited islands, Manono and Apolima, lie in the 18-km-wide strait separating 'Upolu and Savai'i. A few other rocky islets and outcrops are found to the south-east of 'Upolu.

American Samoa, which occupies the territory east of the 171st meridian, is comprised of seven islands and a few rocky outcrops. Its land area is 197 sq km, 145 of which belong to the main island of Tutuila.

Tutuila is a narrow, dragon-like island 30 km long and up to six km wide consisting of a sharp, winding ridge and plunging valleys. The island is nearly bisected by Pago Pago Harbor, a deep indentation in its south coast. The only significant level area of Tutuila is the plain lying west of the harbour area between Pago Pago International Airport and the village of Leone.

'Aunu'u Island is a small volcanic crater off the south-east coast of Tutuila. The Manu'a group, about 100 km east, consists of the three main islands of Ta'u, Ofu and Olosega, with 39, six and five sq km, respectively. All are wildly steep and beautiful examples of volcanic remnants.

One hundred km east of Manu'a is tiny Rose Atoll, which comprises the two sandy islets of Rose and Sand. Access is restricted by the US Fish & Wildlife Service because the islets serve as nesting grounds for numerous sea birds. Swains Island, 350 km north of Tutuila, is a small, privately owned atoll which is geologically part of the Tokelau group of islands.

Darwin's theory about the life of a Pacific island can be roughly traced by travelling west to east through the Samoan islands. Savai'i, a very young island, remains volcanically active and has erupted during this century. It contains large areas of lava flow, and occasional tremors are still felt there. Just to the east, 'Upolu appears to be extinct at the moment, but its subtle peaks and ridges illustrate that it is still a fairly new island.

Tutuila and the Manu'a group, on the other hand, are wildly eroded and many of the volcanic craters they once contained are broken and submerged in the sea. Peaks and ridges are sharp and dramatic, having undergone aeons of weathering. There is, however, a still active submarine volcano lying south of the islands of Ofu and Olosega.

Rose Atoll, the easternmost island of the Samoas, has no peak of any kind. In fact, the volcano that caused it is not visible above the surface of the sea; the island is merely the result of coral polyps that have colonised its remains.

CLIMATE

Because both Samoas lie near the equator, between latitudes 13° and 16° south, the conditions are hot and humid most of the year. However, microclimates which occur in the extensive highland regions dictate that the interior portions of Savai'i and 'Upolu are likely to be cooler year-round. Similarly, the lee shores will be a bit drier, as in the area of Apia, Western Samoa. The windward shores of Western Samoa and the Manu'a Islands get about 5000 mm of precipitation each year, but Western Samoa's capital, Apia, receives only about 2900 mm. In short, the driest and most comfortable period to visit the Samoas is between May and September, but even during the rainy season, most of the precipitation falls at night and the main discomfort will be caused by the lethargy-inspiring heat and humidity.

The exception is the harbour area of Tutuila, American Samoa, where the famous Rainmaker Mountain (known as Mt Pioa by some local residents) ensures that the region receives over 5000 mm of precipitation annually. You need only read Somerset Maugham's classic tale *Rain* to get some idea of the atmosphere this casts upon the area. To best enjoy Pago Pago you should visit between April and October, when chances of fine weather are a bit better. December is normally the wettest month.

The average temperatures range from 21°C to 32°C – the warmer months being from December to April – with a year-round average temperature of 27.5°C. Year-round humidity averages about 80%, but the uncomfortable effects of this are tempered considerably by the south-easterly trade winds, which blow from April to October and intermittently at other times.

The Samoas lie squarely within the South Pacific's notorious cyclone/typhoon belt and have experienced quite a few devastating blows over the years, including two very destructive cyclones, 'Ofa and Val, in the early 1990s. Because of the risks, yachties would be wise to head for New Zealand (or elsewhere outside the cyclone zone) by the end of November at the latest. The only hurricane shelter in the Samoas is Pago Pago Harbor, which offers a little protection from stiff winds. Frequently, however, it also serves as a funnel for winds, creating hazards. In addition, the holding capacity of the harbour bottom leaves a lot to be desired,

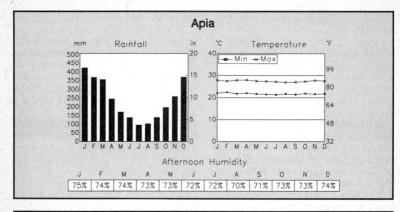

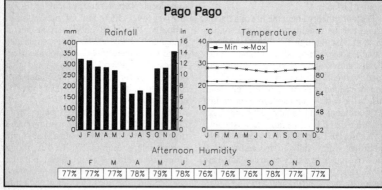

and winds stronger than 50 knots are likely to cause problems for anchored yachts.

About 60% of the time the winds are south-easterly, while north-easterly and southerly winds each occur about 10% of the time. Westerly and north-westerly winds bring the most unpleasant weather, but squalls and storms normally blow themselves out within 24 hours.

FLORA & FAUNA

On all the islands, most of the upland areas which haven't been altered by agriculture or logging are covered in lush forests. The dominant type consists of rainforest of broadleaf evergreens, vines, ferns and mosses. On the heights of Savai'i, 'Upolu, Ofu, Olosega and Ta'u one finds more temperate forest vegetation, featuring tree ferns, grasses, wild coleus and a number of epiphytic plants. Particularly on cloudy or misty days, these forested heights take on an otherworldly aspect.

Especially on Savai'i and 'Upolu is found the magnificent banyan, which dominates the landscape of the higher areas of these islands. Other parts of the Samoas are characterised by scrublands, marshes, pandanus forests and mangrove swamps.

Because the Samoas are relatively remote islands, few animal species have managed to colonise them. Apart from the flying fox, which is found in abundance in the Manu'a Islands (but has been hunted close to extinction elsewhere), the small sheath-tailed bat, and the Polynesian rat (that resides on all the islands), mammals are limited to the marine varieties. Whales, dolphins and porpoises migrate north and south through the Samoas, depending on the season but most common are the pilot whales, which are frequently seen from ships in the open seas around the islands.

Skinks *(pili)* and geckos may be seen everywhere. The Pacific boa is found only on Ta'u Island. Black and hawksbill turtles are seen rarely, only coming ashore to lay their eggs in the sand. Marine toads were introduced from Hawaii in an attempt to control insects but seem to have had little effect apart from adding the toads to the Samoas' species list.

Birds are now less plentiful in the Samoas than they once were because most were considered very good eating. The greatest variety is to be found in American Samoa, where a new US national park hopes to preserve as many native species as possible within its boundaries.

Most prominent among bird species are numerous sea birds such as petrels, tropic birds, boobies, curlews, frigate birds and terns. Other species include the nearly flightless banded rails, which are in danger from cats and other introduced predators; the barn owl, seen occasionally in the Manu'a Islands; and the beautiful blue-crowned lory, which Samoans call the *sega* or parrot. While walking in the forests, listen for the haunting calls of native doves and pigeons, which are found throughout the islands.

The beaches and reefs all over the Samoas are home to brilliant tropical fish and numerous species of shellfish, starfish and crustaceans. There are also several shark species but fortunately, they don't present much of a problem for divers because they're generally small and remain outside the reefs and lagoons.

NATIONAL PARKS

As yet, there are only two fully fledged national parks in the Samoas, as well as several national marine and forest reserves: Palolo Deep Marine Reserve, Mt Vaea Rainforest Reserve and the Aleipata Islands Marine Reserve on 'Upolu; the Tafua Peninsula Rainforest Reserve and the Falealupo Rainforest Reserve, both on Savai'i; and the Fagatele Bay Marine Sanctuary and Rose Atoll National Wildlife Refuge in American Samoa.

On the southern shore of the island of 'Upolu in Western Samoa is 'O Le Pupu-Pu'e National Park, which contains a cross section of island environments from the coastline up to the misty heights around the spine of the island. Development in the park is limited but there are a couple of walking tracks and routes as well as Western Samoa's best opportunities to observe native forest and bird life.

The development of the 12,000-hectare Falealupo Rainforest Reserve on Savai'i was through the efforts of Americans Jim Winegar and Dan Wakefield, a pair of former Mormon missionaries to Samoa who were particularly interested in traditional medicines which grew in the rainforest. The matais of the area had already signed a contract with a Japanese logging firm in order to pay for the construction of a primary school in Falealupo village. When the pair heard about the deal, they raised the US$55,000 needed to pay for the school and the logging agreement was cancelled. In effect, they bought the land and turned it over to the government as a reserve. Unfortunately, the reserve suffered serious damage during the recent cyclones; 60% of the trees were destroyed, causing bird and bat numbers to drop significantly.

American Samoa's contribution to nature conservation is American Samoa National Park, which consists of three areas: a large chunk of the upland forest and wild coastline of northern Tutuila Island; the magnificent stretch of beach and coral along the southern shore of 'Ofu; and the rugged cliffs and rainforested volcanic highlands of southern

The Coral Reef

Many of the coastlines in the Samoas are fringed by coral reefs – fragile environments of calcareous deposits secreted by tiny marine animals known as coral polyps. Furthermore, many of the glorious white-sand beaches of the Pacific Ocean are composed of dead coral, shells and marine algae. Without the reefs, many of the beaches would eventually erode and disappear. The reefs also provide shelter and habitat for a variety of fish, shellfish, crustaceans, sea urchins and other marine life which in turn provide a food source for larger fish as well as humans, both directly and indirectly.

Coral is usually stationary and often looks decidedly flowery but in fact it's an animal and a hungry carnivorous one at that. Although a 3rd century AD Greek philosopher surmised its faunal nature, coral was generally considered to be a plant up until around 250 years ago.

Corals are coelenterates, a class of animals which also includes sea anemones and jellyfish. The true reef-building corals or *Scleractinia* are distinguished by their lime skeletons. It is this relatively indestructible skeleton which actually forms the coral reef, as new coral continually builds on old dead coral and the reef gradually builds up.

Coral takes a number of forms but all are distinguished by polyps, the tiny tube-like fleshy cylinders which resemble their close relation, the anemone. The top of the cylinder is open and ringed by waving tentacles which sting any passing prey and draw it into the polyp's stomach, the open space within the cylinder. Each polyp is an individual creature but they can reproduce by splitting to form a coral colony of separate but closely related polyps. Although each polyp catches and digests its own food, the nutrition passes between the polyps to the whole colony. Most coral polyps only feed at night; during the daytime they withdraw into their hard limestone skeleton so it is only at night that a coral reef can be seen in its full, colourful glory.

Hard corals may take many forms. One of the most common and easiest to recognise is the staghorn coral which grows by budding off new branches from the tips. Brain corals are huge and round with a surface looking very much like a human brain. They grow by adding new base levels of skeletal matter and expanding outwards. Flat or sheet corals, like plate coral, expand out at their outer edges. Many corals can take different shapes depending on their environment. Staghorn coral can branch out in all directions in deeper water or form flat tables when they grow in shallow water.

Like their reef-building relatives, soft corals are made up of individual polyps, but they do not form a hard limestone skeleton. Without the skeleton which protects hard coral it would seem likely that soft coral would fall prey to fish but in fact it seems to remain relatively immune either due to toxic substances in its tissues or due to the presence of sharp limestone needles which protect the polyps. Soft corals can move around and will sometimes engulf and kill off a hard coral.

Corals catch their prey by means of stinging nematocysts. Some corals can give humans a painful sting and the fern-like stinging hydroid should be given a wide berth.

Coral Reef Symbiosis A number of reef species engage in interesting symbiotic relationships, where two unrelated species get together in some activity for their mutual good.

The best recorded and, to the casual onlooker, most visible of these relationships is probably that of the anemone fish and the anemone. The brightly coloured anemone fish is a type of damselfish which has become acclimatised to living amongst the stinging tentacles of anemones. The bright orange clown anemone fish with its white vertical stripes edged with black is one of the most instantly recognisable fishes on the reef. A typical group of anemone fish will consist of several males and one larger female fish. They spend their entire life around the anemone, emerging briefly to feed then diving back into the protective tentacles at the first sign of danger. Anemone fish are not naturally immune to the anemone's sting, it is thought they gradually acquire immunity by repeatedly brushing themselves against the tentacles. Possibly they coat themselves with a layer of the anemone's mucus and the anemone does not sting the fish, just as its tentacles avoid stinging one another.

The relationship between anemone fish and the anemone is probably somewhat one-sided. While the anemone fish may attract other fish within the anemone's grasp, an anemone can survive without the anemone fish; however, anemone fish are never seen without a protective anemone nearby.

Cleaner fish present another interesting reef relationship. The small cleaner wrasse performs a service job on larger fish. They set themselves up at 'cleaner stations' and wait for customers. The cleaners perform a small 'dance' to indicate they're ready for action and then zip around the larger fish nibbling off fungal growth, dead scales, parasites and the like. They will actually swim right into the mouth of larger fish to clean their teeth! Obviously this must be a tempting opportunity to get a quick free meal but cleaner fish are not threatened while they're at work.

The cleaner stations are an important part of reef life; some fish regularly travel considerable distances for a clean and brush up and experimental removal of the cleaner fish from a section of reef has resulted in an increase in diseased and unhealthy fish and a fall in the general fish population. Certain varieties of shrimps also act as fish cleaners but in nature every situation presents an opportunity for some other creature and the reef also has false cleaners. These tiny fish masquerade as cleaners and then quickly take a bite out of the deceived larger fish. They've been known to take a nip at swimmers!

Even coral itself takes part in a symbiotic relationship. Within the cells of coral polyps are tiny single-cell plants known as *Zoocanthellae*. Like other plants they utilise sunlight to create energy and they also consume carbon dioxide produced by the coral. Their presence enables coral to grow much faster.

Sex & Coral For the coral, sex may be infrequent (it only happens once a year) but when the time comes, it's certainly spectacular. Some colonies of coral polyps are all male or all female while polyps of other colonies are hermaphrodite, that is both male and female. In a few types of coral, hermaphrodite polyps can produce their own young which are released at various times over the year. In most cases, however, the sperm of these polyps cannot fertilise its own eggs or other eggs from the same colony.

Although the mass spawning which creates new coral only takes place once a year, the build up to the big night lasts for six months or more. During that time the polyps ripen their eggs which are initially white but later turn pink, red, orange and other bright colours. At the same time, male coral develops testes and produces sperm.

The big event comes in late spring or early summer beginning a night or two after a full moon and building to a crescendo on the fourth, fifth and sixth nights. At this time water temperatures are ideal and there's a minimum of tidal variation. Within the coral, the eggs and sperm from the hermaphrodite coral are bundled together and a half hour prior to spawning time, the bundles are 'set'. That is they are held ready at the mouth of the polyp, clearly visible through the thin tissue. Suddenly, all across the reef these tiny bundles are released and are allowed to float upward towards the surface.

Remarkably, all over the reef this spawning takes place simultaneously. Different colonies release their egg and sperm bundles; single sex polyps eject their sperm or their eggs; and everything floats upward. The egg and sperm bundles, large enough to be seen with the naked eye, appear spectacular. The release has been described as a fireworks display or an inverted snowstorm. Since the event can be so accurately predicted divers are often able to witness it.

Once at the surface the bundles break up and the sperm swim off in search of eggs of the same coral species. Obviously corals of the same species must spawn at the same time in order to unite sperm and eggs of different colonies. Amid the swarm, it's obviously not easy for an individual sperm to find the right egg but biologists believe that by spawning all at once they reduce the risk of being consumed by the numerous marine creatures which would prey on them. By spawning soon after the full moon the reduced tidal variation means there is more time for fertilisation to take place before waves and currents sweep them away.

Once fertilisation has occurred, the egg cells begin to divide and within a day have become swimming coral larvae known as *Planulae*. These are swept along by the current but after several days the planulae sink to the bottom and if the right spot is found, the tiny larvae become coral polyps and a new coral colony is begun.

Coral Reef Conservation In the interest of preserving this complex and vital environment, visitors may want to consider the following recommendations:

- Avoid touching or breaking coral branches, whether or not they appear to be dead.
- Don't practice sailboarding or boating in shallow lagoons where coral is present.
- Leave shells, starfish, sea urchins and other creatures where you find them.
- If at all possible, avoid walking on coral beds; swim or stick to the sandy bottoms.
- Don't fish in reef areas; hooks, harpoons, nets, anchors and other fishing apparatus are deadly to coral.
- Avoid throwing rubbish or trash into the sea from either the shore or from boats. It winds up fouling reefs and beaches.
- Resist buying shells, coral jewellery and other marine products, regardless of their origin. By avoiding this largely illegal trade, you're preserving the reefs in other parts of the world. ■

Ta'u Island. Combined, these areas encompass the largest tracts of wilderness in the Samoas, with most of the island environments represented.

American Samoa National Park also contains the greatest collection of indigenous plant and animal species in the Samoas. However, organisation and development of the park for recreational purposes (eg campsites, hiking tracks, etc) have been held up by ongoing disputes over land rights and compensation. What will come of it is anyone's guess. For park information, contact the national park superintendent (☎ 633-7082) on the 2nd floor of Pago Plaza shopping centre in Pago Pago.

POPULATION & PEOPLE

The indigenous people of both Samoas are Samoan – large and robust folk of Polynesian origin. As of December 1992, the population of Western Samoa was 161,298, the majority Polynesian. 'Upolu is home to over 115,000, and of these 35,000 live in urban Apia. Savai'i has fewer than 50,000 residents, and Manono and Apolima combined are home to only about 2000. Although nearly half the population is under the age of 15, the rate of growth is surprisingly low at .1% annually. This is mainly due to a massive rate of emigration to New Zealand, Australia and the USA. However, that outlet valve is now closing as those countries revise their immigration policies and crack down more heavily on illegal immigrants and those who overstay their visas.

Western Samoa has a substantial Chinese Samoan community, which is centred in Apia but there is relatively little immigration due to strict statutes and limited job opportunities. Most of the Europeans and Asians residing in the country are involved in UN development projects, business investment or volunteer aid organisations, such as the Peace Corps or VSO.

The population of American Samoa is about 35,000, most of which is concentrated on the main island of Tutuila, while about 2000 are scattered about the remaining islands. The easternmost island, Rose Atoll, is uninhabited. There is free migration between Western and American Samoa and a large percentage of American Samoa's population is comprised of Western Samoan citizens residing legally in the territory. A lot of American Samoa's drudgery work – especially that associated with the canneries – is done by Western Samoans and Tongans.

In addition, there are about 1500 foreigners residing in American Samoa, most of whom are Koreans or Chinese involved in the tuna industry. About one third of this number are Europeans, Australians or North Americans, most of whom hold teaching, health care or government jobs.

The Western Samoans are citizens of an independent country, while the American Samoans are nationals of the USA. The latter may not vote in presidential elections until they opt to become US citizens, which they are free to do at any time. US citizens residing in American Samoa, however, must vote absentee. In addition, there are nearly 100,000 ethnic Samoans from both sides of the border living in New Zealand, Australia and the USA (especially Hawaii). Many of these people were born outside the Samoas.

ARTS
Music

Like most people, Samoans love music, and it seems that the percentage of musically talented people in the Samoas is high – relative to that in most other countries. Their ability to harmonise and play musical instruments seems to be almost a birthright of the Polynesian islanders. One need only attend a choir practice or church service to hear the magnificent blend of voices raised in apparently heartfelt devotion.

Traditional music is quite beautiful and is normally sung in Samoan. Songs are written to tell stories or commemorate events, most of which are sad and stirring. Love songs are the most popular, followed by patriotic songs extolling the virtues of the Samoas. Others tell depressing or joyous tales of traditional life in the country.

Another highly respected institution is the brass band, and musical competitions between villages are common. The most prominent brass band in the Samoas is the Police Band of Western Samoa, which performs daily at 7.50 am as the flag is raised in front of the prime minister's office in Apia. (However, when the new government offices are opened and occupied, the ceremony is likely to shift to that location.)

Dancing & Fiafia

Originally the *fiafia* was a village play or musical presentation in which participants would dress in a variety of costumes and accept money or other donations given in amounts based upon the value of the performances. These days the term 'fiafia night' refers to a lavish presentation of Samoan dancing and singing staged at tourist hotels for tourists exclusively, usually accompanied by a huge *umu* feast (see under Food in the following chapter). For more information on fiafia, see the Entertainment section in the Facts for the Visitor chapter.

Most of the dancing, including the *sa sa*, is performed by groups to the rhythm of a beating wooden mallet. The popular *siva* is a slow and fluid dance performed by one or two women acting out impromptu stories and expressions with their hands.

Traditionally, the final dance of the evening was called the *taualuga*, which is also the word for the finishing touch on the roof of a fale. It was normally a siva danced by the *taupou* (ceremonial virgin), who performed dressed only in *siapo* (artistically decorated tapa cloth, see Tapa later in this section) and with her body oiled seductively. It goes without saying that the missionaries made quick work of putting an end to such a 'disgusting' practice.

Today the dance usually performed as the grand finale is the dramatic fire knife dance, the favourite of most visitors. Dancers, who are always men, gyrate, leap and spin while juggling flaming torches in time to a rapid and primaeval drum beat.

Tapa

Although handicrafts and material arts aren't as emphasised in the Samoas as in nearby

Taupou taking part in an 'ava ceremony

Tonga, some traditions continue. Siapo, also known as tapa, is made from the bark of the *Broussonetia papyrifera*, the paper mulberry tree *(u'a)*, and provides a medium for some of the loveliest artwork in the Samoas. The mature trees are cut near their base, normally measuring only three cm or so in diameter, and the bark is stripped off. After a day or two of drying, the rough outer bark is peeled away, leaving only the soft, fibrous inner bark. This is then beaten with a wooden mallet on a long wooden anvil to separate and spread the individual fibres. When it is

45 cm or so in width, it is folded with another piece and pounded further. When ready, these strips are placed side by side and pasted together using sticky starch from half-cooked roots of the taro or cassava.

A traditional family design, or one of the artist's own creation, is made with coconut frond and sewn to a wooden tablet with coconut sennit. The strips of tapa are placed over the tablet and rubbed with a ruddy vegetable dye in order to transfer the design squares to the material.

After it has been allowed to dry, the stencilled designs are painted by hand in black and rich earthy reds and browns, derived from candlenuts and mangrove bark. Vegetable paints are called *o'a* and colours from clay and earth are known as *'ele*.

Architecture

The most prevalent manifestation of traditional – and practical – Samoan architecture is the *fale*. A fale is a traditional Samoan home or meeting house, but the word is also used to connote a business, a European-style dwelling or even a bus shelter, due to the lack of words for such things in the Samoan language.

The fale is an oval structure without walls. The thatched coconut-frond roof is supported by wooden poles and the floor consists of a platform of coral rock. The entire building is constructed without nails, the rafters and joints being tied with strong coconut fibres called *'ofa*. Blinds made of woven pandanus mats are lowered to keep out wind and rain. In American Samoa and in a few places in Western Samoa, the fales are being replaced by fale-shaped European constructions with concrete slab floors, metal poles and tin roofs.

Fales are normally sparsely furnished, but they nearly always contain a clothes chest and a store of sleeping and sitting mats. Lately, however, 'palagi' furniture, kitchen appliances, TVs and video machines have become more and more common. There is often a smaller kitchen fale near the main home used for meal preparation.

Western-style square homes with walls,

Samoan fale

windows and doors, though uncomfortable and impractical given the climate of the Samoas, are becoming very popular. They are considered a symbol of wealth and status and offer a measure of privacy previously impossible to find.

Every village has one prominently elevated fale, the *fale talimalo*, in which the village council meets. It is the responsibility of the village women's committee to keep it clean and brightly decorated. They skewer hibiscus, frangipani and ginger flowers on little pales to decorate the surrounding grounds and hang strings of these flowers all through the building. Coconut fronds are plaited around all the posts in preparation for a council meeting.

The committee is also responsible for making inspections of village homes. They insure that homes are clean and in order and that kitchens and toilets measure up to village health standards. Those families whose homes are deemed below standard must pay a fine. The government of Western Samoa holds an annual competition and awards a prize to the village judged to be the most orderly and well cared for.

CULTURE

More than any other Polynesian people, Samoans are tradition-oriented and follow closely the social hierarchies, customs and courtesies established long before the arrival of Europeans. Many visitors sense correctly that below the surface lies a complex code of traditional ethics and behaviour and, feeling awkwardly ignorant, may often become frustrated in their dealings with the locals.

At times, sensitive visitors to the Samoas are overwhelmed by the aura of mystery that surrounds the outwardly friendly and responsive Samoan people. The fa'a Samoa ('Samoan way') is closely guarded and preserved, especially in remote villages where European influences are minimal, but visitors should not become discouraged: the people are understanding and most will be willing to answer questions you may have regarding their customs. What most people won't readily divulge is their personal feelings about the system and the effects it has on their lives.

Matai System

The *fa'amatai* (matai system of government) is in effect throughout the islands of the Samoas and has its roots in ancient Polynesian culture. Each village *(nu'u)* comprises a group of *aiga* (extended families) which include as many relatives as can be claimed. The larger an aiga, the more powerful it can become, and to be part of a powerful aiga is the goal of nearly every traditionally-minded Samoan.

The aiga is headed by a chief, called a *matai*, who represents the family on the *fono* (village council). Matais, who can be male or female, are normally elected by all adult members of the aiga, but most candidates already hold titles of some description and many inherit office automatically. The position may, however, be granted to a non-family member whose relatives the family would like to bring into its sphere of influence.

Although matais hold title to all assets of the aiga they represent, many matais in

---

Tragedy in Lona

In 1993, Western Samoa suffered a cultural clash that shocked the entire Pacific region and threatened to undermine the uneasy harmony that had existed between the Western-based national government and the traditional matai system.

In September, 1993, Fatiala Nuutai Mafulu, who was a matai in the Fagaloa Bay village of Lona, on the north-eastern coast of 'Upolu, incurred the wrath of other local matais and was condemned to ostracism by the village and the council. According to the council, his 'crimes' included refusing to contribute to village affairs, resisting council decisions, playing cricket for Uafato (a rival village) and allowing his wife to wear shorts in the village. It has been speculated that the central cause of the animosity, however, was his comparative wealth (he'd recently returned after working for 20 years in New Zealand), which invoked envy among villagers. The last straw, however, was his refusal to allow the sa curfew bell to be rung near his home.

After the bell incident, retaliation was swift. On Saturday, 25 September, the mob burned his shop, bus and Suzuki jeep and killed all his animals. They then showered stones on his house, dragged him out and while he begged for mercy, they shot him in the head and killed him in front of his wife and children. The order went out to tie up his wife, Lauitaila, and beat her, but fears that it would invite retaliation from her own village kept her from physical harm. The only person who could have intervened, the Roman Catholic priest, was away in another village.

The incident attracted international media attention and resulted in murder charges against Sesela Mateo Afoa, who was accused of the shooting, and most of the village council. Charges of arson, wilful damage and stoning were brought against 42 villagers. Of these, 36 pleaded guilty while six refuted the charges. In the end, 12 villagers were sentenced to 20 months in prison (18 of which were suspended); a fine of WS$209 each, to be paid to the deceased's family; and 100 hours of community service. Five men received lesser sentences and 11 other people, mostly young children, received two years' probation and were required to perform 350 hours of community service. The murder charges haven't yet been resolved and it will probably be quite a long while before the issue is settled.

The whole matter is especially significant in Western Samoa because it raises the issue of individual rights versus the traditional matai rule, as well as the authority of matai law versus European law. Understandably, the government is happy with the matai system, which oversees village affairs and minimises the responsibility (and cost) of providing police protection in scattered villages. ∎

smaller villages live remarkably austere lives. The matais are responsible for law enforcement and punishment of infractions that may occur in their village. Social protocol is taken extremely seriously and crimes such as manslaughter, adultery, violence, insubordination and even defiant cheekiness are punishable by all sorts of unpleasant rulings. (For evidence of how extreme this can become – and how seriously it clashes with the Western-style system followed by the national government, see the Tragedy in Lona section under History in the Facts about Western Samoa chapter.)

The most serious crimes require the offender to endure the humiliating but face-saving ritual of *fa'asifoga* (often just *ifoga*), the begging of forgiveness of the offended party. The guilty person and his or her matai, covered in fine mats, must carry gifts and food to the victims' fale and kneel before the door awaiting an invitation to enter. This must be done day after day until the wronged party feels that the offence has been atoned for by the humility of its perpetrator. It is interesting that in the Catholic church the penitent sinner appears before the priest and begs forgiveness in much the same way, thus making peace with God.

The fono consists of the matais of all aiga associated with the village. The highest chief of the village, or *ali'i*, sits at the head of the fono. In addition, each village has one *pulenu'u* (a combination of mayor and police chief), and one or more *tulafale* (talking chiefs). The pulenu'u is elected every three years and acts as an intermediary between the village and the national (or territorial, in the case of American Samoa) government. The tulafale is an orator who carries out ceremonial duties, engages in ritual debates and liaises between the ali'i and outside entities.

The symbol of the tulafale's office is the *fue* (fly whisk), a four kg mop of sennit that represents wisdom and must be carried when the tulafale speaks in an official capacity. He also carries a *to'oto'o*, a staff representing chiefly authority. Both items are handed down from father to son.

Meetings are held in a fale talimalo, a traditional open hut with a roof supported by posts, and all participants in the meetings are seated according to rank, the ali'i at one end and the chief of next highest rank at the other.

When a chief dies, villages effectively close down; at such times travellers are unwelcome. The sea around the village is also closed during the period of mourning and no fishing or swimming is permitted. In extreme cases, villagers cut off their hair, pigs are slaughtered, boats are smashed, and village treasures are destroyed to illustrate the villagers' grief at the loss of their leader.

The commoners of the village are divided into four categories. The wives of matais and the pulenu'u are called *faletua ma tausi*. Untitled men belong to the group called *aumaga* or *taulele'a* and unmarried women are *tama'ita'i*. School children belong to the group called *tamaiti*. Close social interaction among commoners is generally restricted to members of one's own group.

Avoiding Offence

Although many visitors to the Samoas wish to see traditional villages, such visits can be extremely disruptive in such traditional societies. This is not to say that visitors are not welcome. They are, and to a degree unmatched in any Western country you'd care to name. A few guidelines, however, will go a long way towards keeping things on an even keel.

Certain rules of etiquette have their origins in ancient Samoa, while others are the direct results of the emergence of Christianity. While special allowances are made for visitors, especially in American Samoa where many of the locals ignore established traditions, those who learn and respect traditions will endear themselves to the people and will be more readily accepted in rural areas.

Although guidelines are quoted in nearly every tourist publication in the islands, I'll repeat some of them here for the benefit of intending visitors who may want to prepare themselves:

- It's best not to arrive in a village on a Sunday. The presence of a foreigner unknown to the village will interrupt the smooth customary flow of religious and family activities, and on occasion village elders have been known to become visibly upset.

- Don't swim near a village or perform any manual labour on a Sunday. Excessive noise on the Sabbath is also deemed sacrilegious, so uninhibited raging on Sundays should be confined to hotel rooms or remote beaches and mountainsides.

- If you're staying with a village family, politely refuse invitations to stay with other village families, since this will bring shame upon your hosts. Be prepared to repay your hosts with some token of your esteem, such as cash, 'store-bought' foods or small gifts representative of your home country; anything that is difficult to obtain in a village will usually be graciously received. If your gift is politely refused, you may have to resort to some sort of harmless trickery to get it into the proper hands! Gifts should more or less reflect the value of the services the visitor has received from his or her hosts. If you've taken photos of the family, they would treasure any copies you may send them later; such photos may well become family heirlooms.

- There are no real beggars in Samoa (Samoan society would never permit anyone to reach such a state!) so avoid indiscriminately distributing gifts. This applies especially to children who have taken to begging foreigners for sweets, pens and money (thanks, no doubt, to earlier visitors who believed their largess constituted a good deed). Not only can it lead them to believe something can be had for nothing, it also sends misleading signals regarding foreign cultures in general. It can also be a real nuisance (and embarrassment) for the children's parents, relatives and village, as well as for travellers that follow.

- Although fashion and dress are becoming increasingly liberal (and Western) among Samoan youth on both sides of the border, many middle-aged and older people are still quite sensitive to it. Therefore, visitors would still do well to be particularly mindful of their appearance, especially in villages and remote areas. Throughout the Samoas, women should avoid wearing shorts or bathing gear away from the beach no matter what the temperature, and men should always wear shirts while walking in the streets.

- Shoes should be removed when entering a fale. When invited into a fale, sit cross-legged or cover your legs. Never enter during prayers or meetings and don't make noise or commotion in the area while prayers are being said. If you inadvertently enter a village during *sa* (see under Religion later in this chapter), sit down and wait quietly until the all clear is sounded.

- Try not to address people or eat while standing or strolling through a village. Don't eat while walking through a village or town and don't pass a meeting of chiefs while carrying a load on your shoulders or with an open umbrella.

- If you'd like to swim at a village beach, climb a mountain, take photos or merely have a look around, be sure to ask permission beforehand of the pulenu'u in the appropriate village. (More will be said about this in a later discussion of custom fees.)

- When walking in front of someone, lower your head and say '*tulou*' or 'excuse me'.

- Most importantly, avoid becoming visibly frustrated or angry when things don't happen as they would at home. Things rarely go according to plan in the Samoas, and inflexibility on your part will make for a miserable visit.

Customs

In theory, all wealth and property in the Samoas are owned communally by the aigas; European concepts of property and wealth are lost on the most traditional Samoans and looked upon with varying degrees of suspicion by others. Although materialism is rapidly encroaching on American Samoa and also making inroads into Western Samoa, visitors who can reconcile themselves to existence in a communal situation will be far happier in the Samoas. Changes that have been in evidence of late are having profound effects upon the young as regards their aiga, villages and roles in society, but in the villages, the old standard remains in effect for the time being.

Despite this communal attitude within the aiga, competition between aiga is enthusiastically accepted and the best matai is the one who can bring home the most bacon for the clan. A matai who fails in this calling may be stripped of his or her title, lands and esteem.

Perhaps the most important aspect of traditional Samoan life is respect, even veneration, for those perceived to be higher than oneself. Children show respect for their parents, women for their husbands, aiga for their matai, and matais and tulafale for the ali'i. Teachers, doctors, politicians, ministers and priests are also held in great esteem.

As a foreigner, you will also be considered worthy of respect as long as you behave appropriately as far as the locals are concerned. This can be frustrating at times. Samoans will often keep themselves at arm's length in order to avoid the possibility of making you unhappy. They will often answer your questions with the response they suppose you'd like to hear rather than with the truth, which they believe may upset you. And usually they will not show emotion in your presence even though they will openly weep at weddings and funerals and laugh, sing and dance on festive occasions – times that they perceive to be appropriate for such behaviour. The better you become acquainted with the people, of course, the more relaxed they will become.

It is perfectly normal in the Samoas for members of the same sex to hold hands and display friendship in public, but open displays of affection between men and women, married or not, will be met with disapproval. Samoan men are required to obtain the approval of a woman's brothers before showing admiring interest in her, and regardless of what Margaret Mead wrote on the issue, the Samoas are not playgrounds of free and available love.

While sexual indiscretions are not taken quite as seriously as they would be in many parts of the Christian world, young women are expected to protect their bodies from the advances of young suitors.

And along these lines, it is interesting to note that, particularly in Western Samoa, people see marriageable foreigners as tickets out of the Samoas as much as foreigners see marriageable Samoans as tickets in. Marriage to a Samoan – or any Polynesian – will provide you not only with a spouse but also with the responsibility to provide for his or her aiga. Family members will probably be ecstatic to see one of their aiga joining up with someone whom they perceive to be rich. Those who cannot be dissuaded should at least be prepared! As a caveat, keep in mind also that a local marriage does not always guarantee a foreigner the right to remain in paradise (although Americans in American Samoa will probably encounter few problems).

Another concept that causes breakdowns in communications between Samoans and foreigners is *musu*, which may be roughly translated as 'moodiness'. An otherwise pleasant and vivacious person may inexplicably become quiet and sullen. If this happens, don't worry – you haven't committed some unforgivable faux pas so don't react with apologies or questions. Your friend is just experiencing musu and will usually get over it soon.

Traditional Medicine

Traditional Samoan medicine has been handed down through the generations for 200 years and nearly every Samoan family will have some knowledge of traditional folk remedies. As a profession, however, traditional healing is now a dying art and more and more people are looking to Western medicine.

Traditional healers are typically women who learn their methods from a long apprenticeship. Normally, their training begins in early childhood when a girl assists her mother or a close female relative in her craft. During this apprenticeship, they must learn to recognize several hundred species of rainforest plants, each of which has its own specific medicinal value. Modern healers are taught to take notes and keep a close and accurate record of each patient's symptoms, diagnosis, treatment and response.

Many healers specialise in particular diseases and come to be known for their expertise. As a general rule, there are four types of Samoan healers: the *fa'atosaga* or midwives; the *fofo* or massage therapists; the *fofogau*, or orthopedists (who are normally men capable of setting broken bones); and the *taulasea*, who are herbalists who utilise the diversity of Samoan rainforest flora in their treatment of disease. Other related types of healers include those who effect love potions or banish troublesome *aitu* (spirits).

A typical taulasea can diagnose and treat over 200 different diseases, many of which have no Western equivalent, with a combination of 120 or more rainforest plants. Such complaints can range from stomach upset to tension to personal hostility. Whenever an illness is diagnosed, the healer must visit the forest (or send her apprentice to do so) to collect the required combination of herbal remedies. Most of the treatments are applied externally with the aid of an oil base, although some are burned and inhaled while others are taken internally with water.

If you're interested in Samoan herbal healing, the Land Grant Program of American Samoa publishes a free booklet entitled *Samoan Medicinal Plants & their Usage*. To get a copy, ask for it by name from ADAP Project, Pacific Agricultural Development Office (☎ (808) 956-8140; fax (808) 956-6967), Tropical Energy House, University of Hawaii, Honolulu, HI 96822, USA.

The Fa'afafine

By traditional definition, a *fa'afafine* is a male child who opts to dress and behave as a female for whatever reason. The word translated means simply 'like a woman', but one senses that there's more to the custom than that. They dress as females, play female roles and get away with promiscuity on a scale forbidden to biological females.

Although often there is great sport made of teasing and tormenting them, there is no social stigma attached to their open flaunting of transvestitism or sexual preference. Therefore, it is difficult not to suspect that some are simply normal homosexuals hiding behind the title fa'afafine in order to be readily accepted by society. Interestingly, some revert to traditional male roles upon reaching adulthood.

The American Samoan fa'afafine dress more distinctively than those in Western Samoa, and every year in October they hold a territory-wide drag queen contest in which the local transvestites dance, sing, play musical instruments and strut around on stage in lavish finery. It's attended by the cream of American Samoan society and is one of the social events of the year. Less elaborate drag queen competitions are held in both Samoas throughout the year.

Sport

Samoans seem to excel in sports. On weekday afternoons after school or work, young Samoans (mainly Western Samoans) gather on a *malae* (village green) to play rugby, volleyball and a unique brand of cricket, *kirikiti*.

American Samoan secondary schools sponsor football teams, and high school matches are among the most spirited and well-attended entertainment in the South Pacific. The dream of many young men in American Samoa is to play American football professionally or for a university team – and there are many success stories.

In Western Samoa, basketball and soccer are both growing in popularity but at present, the main item is rugby which is enthusiastically followed, played and supported. The main season runs from February to July, with an international competition hosted by St Joseph's college in mid-February. Between July and November, Rugby League games are held at Apia Stadium.

With the new Japanese ownership of the Hotel Kitano Tusitala and the opening of the Royal Samoa Country Club at Fagali'i, golf has also arrived in Western Samoa. The 18-hole Lava Golf Course in American Samoa is at Ili'ili, just west of Tafuna Airport on Tutuila.

Among women, the most popular sport is netball; the Western Samoan women's team is currently gaining outside recognition and has competed in several international tournaments. The main season is between late March and late May.

Kirikiti Any discussion of Western Samoan sporting tradition wouldn't be complete without a mention of the national game, which is taken quite seriously by Western Samoan sports fans. A bizarre version of cricket, kirikiti is played by apparently flexible rules known only to the players and probably only marginally recognisable to aficionados from elsewhere.

The balls are handmade of rubber and wrapped with pandanus. The three-sided bat also keeps things interesting – no one, not even the batter, has a clue where the ball will go. Lack of pads and face protection adds to the element of risk – disputed calls have resulted in death by cricket bat. This certainly isn't Lords!

Since everyone in the village will normally want to be involved in a typical afternoon game, Samoans don't limit participation to 22. Serious competitions go on for days, and once a team has lost, it can buy its way back into the match by paying a fee to the hosting village, which is responsible for catering for the entire tournament.

The game is played year-round, with frequent Saturday matches throughout the year and practice games held practically every day. The main season for inter-village matches is from April to June, while the national play-offs are held in August in preparation for the national championships. These take place during the Teuila Festival during the second week of September.

If you'd like to have a look at cricket Samoan-style or even participate in a game, wander through the rural villages of 'Upolu or Savai'i in the mid-afternoon. You'd be hard-pressed to find a malae where a game is not in progress (if not kirikiti, then volleyball or rugby), and since teams aren't limited to a specific number of participants and women are as welcome to play as men, the players will be happy to explain the rules and be honoured to let you join the game.

Dress

Western dress is becoming more or less the norm among the younger people of both Samoas, but many Samoans (and tourists) wear a *lavalava*, a wraparound unisex piece of brightly coloured material normally decorated with palm trees, outrigger canoes, fales, Polynesian dancers, and the printed names of myriad Pacific islands. Less kitsch lavalava are available, but they're few and far between. Many women wear a *puletasi*, a long skirt under a tunic.

The Samoan equivalent of the business suit is the *ie faitaga*, an undecorated lavalava of suit-coat material worn with a plain European-style white shirt. This outfit is always accompanied by a briefcase and a rotund physique resulting from high social status.

Tattooing

The *pe'a* (Samoan tattoo) is not merely a drunken sailor's whim or a mark of the individuality of its wearer but a centuries-old tradition that identifies the tattooed person as a proud and courageous Samoan.

Although the missionaries considered tattoos to be evil, pagan personal adornments and tried to discourage the perpetuation of the practice, the Samoans weren't interested in giving it up. Although many young men of late have opted not to undergo the painful procedure, growing numbers, especially in Western Samoa, are choosing to be tattooed, possibly in defiance of encroaching Western ideals and as a mark of manhood and Samoan identity.

There are currently 18 tattooists, or *tufuga*, in Western Samoa, each with his own designs. Male tattoos *(tatau)* normally cover the man's body from the waist to the knees with such artistic density that they resemble a pair of trousers. On occasion, women also elect to be tattooed, but their designs, which are known as *malu*, cover only the thighs.

The women's tattoos are never to be shown in public except on community occasions, such as the mixing of *kava* for a ceremony. Most traditional Samoans believe that male tattoos should also be kept hidden and considered only as a personal mark of courage and accomplishment. Although boys as young as nine have received tattoos, most people agree that it's better to wait until the mid-teens, so the design will not be distorted by growth.

The man receiving the tattoo lies on the floor while the artist works through the painful process of tattooing the intricate design. The artist uses sharpened sharks' teeth or boars' tusks and a dye made of charcoal from the candlenut. Another man wipes away blood and excess dye. Once begun, the tattoo should be completed or the young man will bring shame upon himself and his aiga. In most cases the entire procedure will take a month to complete.

'Ava Ceremony

'Ava, sometimes known as kava, is a drink derived from the ground root of the pepper plant *Piper methysticum* and the active ingredients include 12 or 14 chemicals of an alkaloidal nature. It is both an anaesthetic and an analgesic, high in fibre, low in calories, and serves as a mild tranquilliser, an antibacterial and antifungal agent, a pain killer, a diuretic, an appetite suppressant and a soporific. It is legal in North America and Europe, and Samoans habitually send packages of it to family member overseas.

Visitors who try 'ava will often report that it tastes like dishwater – it certainly looks like well-used dishwater – but dishwater probably tastes better since it may contain residue of foodstuffs while 'ava is just murky and almost tasteless. Nevertheless, it does grow on you and many foreigners actually come to enjoy it.

The 'ava ceremony is ritual in the Samoas. Every meeting of matai and all government gatherings are preceded by an 'ava ceremony. Originally the village taupou, a ceremonial virgin who was often the daughter of an ali'i, was responsible for serving the drink but now the job is often performed by a tulafale (the talking chief).

The ground root is mixed with water in a carved multi-legged bowl. Men seat themselves in an oval with the bowl, called a *tanoa*, at one end. When the 'ava is ready, the tulafale calls out the names of the participants in order of rank. He then dips the drink into half a coconut shell with a wad of coconut sennit and passes it to the recipient, who drips a few drops on the ground and says *'manuia lava'*, the Samoan equivalent of 'cheers', before drinking it. Visitors who find the taste objectionable can merely pour the remainder onto the ground without causing offence.

'Ava bowl

A good place to observe 'ava drinking without participating is the Maketi Fou (New Market) in Apia, Western Samoa.

RELIGION

The Christian missionaries did their job thoroughly, succeeding in turning both Samoas into overwhelmingly Christian entities. The official motto of Western Samoa is *Fa'avae i le Atua Samoa*, meaning 'Samoa is founded on God'. American Samoa's is *Samoa, ia muamua le Atua* – 'Samoa, let God be first'. There seems to be a consensus between the two about what is important, anyway.

It is significant that some of the early 19th-century adventurers who found their way to the Samoa islands brought with them a form of Christianity that, on a limited scale, would catch on there. In addition, converted islanders from other Pacific countries arrived from time to time and spread the message they had accepted from the palagi.

Perhaps the most important factor leading to wholesale acceptance of the new religion in the islands, however, was a legendary prophecy made by the war goddess, Nafanua, that a new religion would arrive from the sky and be embraced by the people, bringing peace and prosperity to the land. The Samoan word 'palagi', which is used to identify all Caucasian peoples, means 'those who break the sky'. Where else could these odd beings have originated?

In 1830 the Reverend John Williams of the London Missionary Society landed in western Savai'i in his crude ship the *Messenger of Peace*, which had been hastily constructed in Rarotonga. Given the turbulent situation in Savai'i at the time of his arrival, any suggestion of peace would have been appropriate. When the internal war ended, Williams was successful in converting the chief of the winning side, Malietoa Vainu'upo, to Christianity, and the rest is history. The chief accepted eight teachers assigned to the task by Williams, and matais and villagers joined the new church en masse. The message spread quickly around the islands.

In nearby Tahiti and the Cook Islands, conversion to Christianity involved the tearing down of Polynesian idols and temples. The Samoans, having none of these things, were required to go through a different ritual. All Samoans had a personal *aitu* – a fish, bird or other animal that was sacred to them. To prove the sincerity of their conversions, the Samoans were required to eat their aitu, which the missionaries regarded as symbols of paganism. Interestingly, aitu are still going strong in Samoa, but these days the word refers to any mischievous or wandering spirit.

The Wesleyan Methodists came to the Samoas under the direction of Peter Turner. Many Samoans who had connections with Tonga awaited the formation of a Wesleyan mission in Samoa similar to the one that had taken over the nearby archipelago. Turner had originally visited the Samoas in 1828 but hadn't established a mission because of an informal agreement with the London Missionary Society that the Samoas would be left to them in exchange for the Wesleyans' free reign in Tonga and Fiji. Although Turner found many Samoans awaiting his message in the mid to late 1830s, the Wesleyan Church chose to honour the agreement and withdrew Turner.

The Catholics arrived on the scene in 1845, a little late to take part in the fury of conversion and dispute that had characterised the previous decade, but they still managed to win quite a few adherents. In the latter part of the century came the Mormons, who continue to entice the islanders away from other sects with opulence, emigration and educational opportunities,

and a tale that all Polynesians are directly descended from the lost tribes of Israel.

These days, half of all Samoans belong to the Congregational Church, derived from the London Missionary Society. About one quarter are Catholics, 12% are Methodists and most of the remainder are Mormons.

The pastor's house is normally the largest in every village, and in most cases, it is provided by the villagers themselves. Quite a few villages contain multiple churches, and it becomes a matter of competition to determine which church is the best maintained. Many of the buildings are imaginatively designed and creatively coloured (with the exception of the ubiquitous Mormon churches, which are all the same drab beige colour surrounded by athletic courts and sturdy chain-link fences).

The Mormons have a large and striking temple on the outskirts of Apia surrounded by an extensive educational compound. The Baha'is, although not particularly well represented in the Samoas, have a beautiful temple in the highlands of 'Upolu, one of only seven in the world. (The Samoan one closely resembles the US Football Hall of Fame in Canton, Ohio, for those familiar with such things!)

Burials

Samoan burials are of interest to visitors. Chiefs get large multi-tiered tombs – the more tiers, the higher the chief buried there. Family graves are rarely in a formal cemetery. Instead, people are buried in a place of honour in the front yard and their graves covered with an elaborate monument, which is usually well-cared for as a mark of respect to those buried there. This explains the revered nature of traditionally held aiga lands and the Samoans' reluctance to part with them.

Sa

Sa, which literally means 'sacred', is the nightly vespers or devotional and it is taken very seriously in the Samoas. Sometime between 6 and 7 pm, or thereabouts, a village gong (most often made of an empty propane tank) sounds, signifying that the village should prepare for sa. All activity comes to an abrupt halt and automobile and foot traffic stops. When the second gong is sounded, sa has begun.

This time is used for devotionals and prayers in individual family homes and should not be interrupted under any circumstances. Samoan villagers who ignore the regulations of sa will incur fines and the ridicule of neighbours.

When a third gong is sounded, usually after about 10 or 15 minutes, sa is over and activities may be resumed. If you're caught out in a village during sa, stop what you're doing, sit down and quietly wait for the third gong to sound. These rules do not apply in Apia or the Pago Pago Harbor area.

LANGUAGE

The main language spoken in both Samoas is Samoan, although nearly everyone in American Samoa and the majority of people in Western Samoa speak English as a second language. Except in remote villages on Savai'i, those who don't speak the indigenous language should have few problems communicating.

Samoan is a Polynesian language similar to Maori, Tongan, Hawaiian and Tahitian. All of these belong to the Austronesian or Malayo-European family of languages (which includes Malay, Malagasy and Melanesian dialects), and many words are strikingly similar to Malay, providing evidence of Polynesian migrations to the islands from South-East Asia. It is likely that Samoan is the earliest of all the Polynesian languages.

Pronunciation

Samoan uses only 14 letters – five vowels and nine consonants. The five vowels may be long or short, depending on whether or not they are stressed, but the actual difference in sound between them is very slight to the untrained ear. A long vowel is conventionally indicated by a superscribed bar, and is pronounced the same, only lengthened. Stress is normally placed on the next to last

syllable. A glottal stop, represented by an apostrophe, is equivalent to the space between the syllables of 'oh-oh'. Diphthongs, or combinations of vowels, are pronounced by producing their component sounds in rapid succession. They may be broken up by the insertion of a glottal stop.

Vowels

a	as the 'a' in 'and'
e	as the 'e' in 'set'
i	as the 'i' in 'sing'
o	as the 'o' in 'hot'
u	as the 'u' in 'full'

Consonants

f	as the 'f' in 'far'
g	as the 'ng' in 'longing'
l	as the 'l' in 'love'
m	as the 'm' in 'may'
n	as the 'n' in 'now'
p	as the 'p' in 'pear'
r	as the 'r' in 'ring' (the tongue is only slightly flapped against the the roof of the mouth)
s	as the 's' in 'Samoa'
t	as the 't' in 'time'
v	as the 'v' in 'very'

Since their language is spoken only in the Samoas, the Samoans are both pleased and surprised when foreigners make an attempt to use it. The following are a few useful words and phrases to get you started:

Greetings & Civilities

hello	malo
goodbye	tofa
goodbye and farewell	tofa soifua
good morning	talofa
good evening	talofa
good night	manuia le po
please	fa'amolemole
thank you (very much)	faafetai (tele)
welcome	afio mai
yes	ioe
no	leai
maybe	masalo

excuse me	*fa'amolemole lava*
pardon me	*tulou*
I am sorry	*ua ou sese*
forgive me	*malie*
How are you?	*O a mai oe?*
I'm fine, thanks.	*Manuia, faafetai.*

Essentials

Please write it down.
  Fa'amolemole tusi i lalo.
Where are you going?
  Alu i fea?
Please show me on the map.
  Fa'amolemole faasino mai ia te au i le fa'afanua
I understand.
  Ua ou Malamalama.
I don't understand.
  Ou te le malamalama.
I don't speak...
  Ou te le tautala...
Do you speak English?
  E i ai se isi e Nanu?
Where/what country are you from?
  Fea/O ai lou atunu'u?

American Samoa	*Amerika Samoa*
Australia	*Ausetalia*
Canada	*Kanata*
France	*Falani*
Germany	*Siamani*
Great Britain	*Peretania*
Holland	*Holani*
Italy	*Italia*
Japan	*Iapani*
New Zealand	*Niu Sila*
Switzerland	*Suisilani*
USA	*Iuanaite Setete o Amerika*
Western Samoa	*Samoa i Sisifo*

How old are you?	*Fia ou tausaga?*
I am...years old.	*Ua...o'u tausaga.*
I have a visa/permit.	*E iai lo'u visa/ pemita.*
surname	*igoa faai'u*
given name	*igoa masani*
date of birth/place of birth	*aso fanau/nu'u na fanau ai*
nationality	*tagatanu'u*
age	*matua*

male/female	*tane/fafine*
passport	*tusi folau*

Small Talk

What is your name?
  O ai lo'u igoa?
My name is...
  O lo'u igoa o...
I'm a tourist/student.
  O a'u o le turisi/tama aoga.
Are you married?
  Ua fai se aiga?
How many children do you have?
  E to'afia tama'iti?
Do you like...?
  E te manao i le...?
I like it very much.
  O lo'u vaisu.
Just a minute.
  Fa'atali mai lava.
May I?
  E mafai?
It's all right/no problem.
  Ua lelei.
How do you say...?
  E faapefea ona...?

Social Terms

foreigner	*palagi*
boy	*tama*
boyfriend	*ma'amusa*
family	*aiga*
girl	*teine*
girlfriend	*ma'amusa*
little boy	*tama'iti'iti*
little girl	*teine'iti'iti*
father	*tama*
man	*tamaloa*
mother	*tina*
woman	*fafine*

Getting Around

I want to go to...
  Ou te fia alu i...
I want to book a seat for...
  E fia totogi i lo'u pasese i le...
What time does it leave/arrive?
  O le a le taimi e alu ese ai/taunuu ai le?
What time is it?
  Ua ta le fia?

Where does...leave from?
O fea e alu ese mai ai le...?

bus	*pasi*
train	*nofoa-afi*
boat/ferry	*va'a/va'a lau pasese*
yacht	*va'afaila*
canoe	*paopao*
longboat	*fautasi*
aeroplane	*va'alele*

How long does the trip take?
O le a le umi a le malaga?
Where do I catch the bus?
O fea e fa'atali ai le pasi?
Do I need to change buses?
E tatau ona ou sui pasi?
You must change buses.
E tatau ona sui pasi.

ticket	*pepa o le pasese*
ticket office	*ofisa tusi pasese*
timetable	*fa'asologa o malaga*

I'd like to hire a...
E fia togipau se...

car	*ta'avale*
guide	*taiala*
horse	*solofanua*
petrol/gas	*penisini*
bicycle/motorbike	*uila vili vae/uila-afi*

Directions

How do I get to...?
Fa'apefe'a ona ou ali i...?

Where is...?	*O fea...?*
street/road	*maga'ala/au'ala*
street number	*numera o le maga'ala*
suburb	*fuai'ala*
town	*taulaga*

Is it near/far?
E latalata/mamao?
(Go) straight ahead.
Alu (sa'o lava).
(Turn) left.
(Liliu) itu tauagavale.
(Turn) right.
(Liliu) taumatau.

at the traffic lights
i moli auala
at the next/second/third corner
i le isi tulimanu/lona lua/lona tolu
up/down
luga/lalo
behind/opposite
tua/fa'afeagai
east/west
sasae/sisifo
north/south
matu/saute
here/there/everywhere
i/io/soo se me'a

Useful Signs

campground	*fanua e tolauapi ai*
entrance	*ulufale*
exit	*ulufafo*
full	*tumu*
gents/ladies	*tane/fafine*
guesthouse	*fale mo malo*
hotel	*fale talimalo*
information	*fa'amatalaga*
open/closed	*tatala/tapuni*
police	*leoleo*
police station	*ofisa o leoleo*
prohibited	*fa'asa*
do not enter	*ua sa*
rooms available	*potu avanoa*
toilets	*fale'ese*
youth hostel	*fale nofo tumau*

Around Town

Where is the/a...?	*O fea le/se...?*
bank	*faletupe*
exchange office	*ofisa suitupe*
city centre	*nofoaga autu o le a'ai*
embassy	*ofisa o le amapasa*
entrance/exit	*ulufale/ulufafo*
hospital	*falemai*
market	*maketi*
police	*leoleo*
post office	*falemeli*
public toilet	*fale'ese faitele*
restaurant	*fale'aiga*
store	*faleoloa*

telephone office	*ofisi telefoni*
tourist information office	*ofisa a fa'amatalaga tau turisi*

I want to make a telephone call.
E fia fai la'u telefoni.
I'd like to change some...
e Fia sui a'u...
money/travellers' cheques
tupe/siaki malaga

beach	*matafaga*
bridge	*ala laupapa*
cathedral	*malumalu*
church	*falesa*
hospital	*falemai*
island	*motu*
lake	*vaituloto*
laundry	*tagamea*
sea	*sami*

Accommodation

I'm looking for...
O lo'o tau su'e...

the campground	*nofoaga e tolauapi ai*
a hotel	*fale talimalo*
a guesthouse	*fale e mautotogi ai*
the manager/owner	*le pule/po'o le ona*

What is the address?
O le a le tuatusi?
Do you have a...available?
O i ai sau...o avanoa?

bed	*moega*
cheap room	*potu taugofie*
single/double room	*potu toatasi/toalua*
for one/two nights	*mo le tasi/lua po*

How much is it per night/person?
E fia i le po/tagata?
Is service/breakfast included?
O aofia ai mea uma/taumafataga o le taeao?
Can I see the room?
E mafai ona ou va'ai i le potu?
Where is the toilet?
Fea le fale'ese?
It is dirty/noisy/expensive.
E palapala/pisa/taugata.
I am/We are leaving now.
O le a/matou o nei.

Do you have...?	*E i ai sau...?*
a clean sheet	*le afu mama*
hot water	*vai vevela*
the key	*le ki*
a shower	*fale taele*

Plants & Animals

bird	*manulele*
chicken	*moa*
fish	*ia*
flower	*fuamatala*
mosquito	*namu*
pig	*pua'a*

Food & Drink

food	*mea taumafa*
I am hungry/thirsty.	*Ua ou fia ai/fia inu.*
breakfast	*aiga o le taeao*
lunch	*aiga o le aoauli*
dinner	*aiga o le po*
set menu	*mea'ai masani*
food stall	*fale'aiga fa'atau*
grocery store	*fale'oloa o mea'ai*
market	*maketi*
restaurant	*fale'aiga*

I would like the set lunch, please.
Aumai se aiga masani o le aoauli fa'amolemole.
I am a vegetarian.
Ou te le ai i aano o manu.
I would like some...
Aumai sau...ma.
Another, please.
Se isi fa'amolemole.

I don't eat...	*Ou te le 'ai...*
beer	*pia*
bread	*fala'oa*
chicken	*moa*
coffee	*kofe*
eggs	*fuamoa*
fish	*ia*
fruit	*fuala'au aina*
liquor	*ava malosi*
meat	*fasi povi*
milk	*susu*
mineral water	*vai mama*
pepper	*pepa fai mea'ai*
pork	*fasi pua'a*
salt	*masima*

soup	*supo*
sugar	*suka*
tea	*ti*
vegetables	*fuala'au fai mea'ai*
water	*vai*
wine	*uaina*
hot/cold	*vevela/malulu*
with/without	*i ai fa'atasi/e leai se*

Shopping

How much does it cost?
E fia le tau?
I would like to buy it.
Ou te fia fa'atauina.
It's too expensive for me.
Taugata mo a'u.
Can I look at it?
E mafai ona ou va'ai i ai?

I'm just looking.	*Sei ou matamata.*
I'm looking for...	*O lo'o su'e...*
the chemist	*fale talavai*
clothing	*lavalava*
souvenirs	*mea fa'amanatu*

Do you have another colour/size?
E i ai se isi lanu/lapoa?

big/bigger	*lapo'a/lapo'a atu*
small/smaller	*laititi/laititi teisi*
more/less	*tele/iti'iti*
cheap/cheaper	*taugofie/taugofie atu*

Other Useful Words & Phrases

bad	*leaga*
beautiful	*manaia*
fine	*Manuia*
good	*lelei*
happy	*fiafia*
house	*fale*
journey	*malaga*
love	*alofa*
rain	*timu*
sun	*la*
village	*nu'u*
wind	*savili*

Health & Emergencies

Help!
Fia'ola
Go away!
Alu ese

Call a doctor/the police.
Vili se foma'i/leoleo.
I'm allergic to penicillin/antiobiotics.
Ele aoga ia te a'u tui penisini/vaila'au.
I'm diabetic/epileptic/asthmatic.
Ou te ma'i suka/ma'i maliu/ma'i sela.

antiseptic	*vaila'au*
aspirin	*fuala'au aspirin*
condoms	*pa'u fai aiga*
contraceptive	*faiga e le ma'ito ai*
diarrhoea	*manava tata*
medicine	*vaila'au*
nausea	*fa'afaufau*
sunblock cream	*kulimi mo le vevela o le la*
tampons	*to'o o fafine*

Times & Dates

Sunday	*Aso Sa*
Monday	*Aso Gafua*
Tuesday	*Aso Lua*
Wednesday	*Aso Lulu*
Thursday	*Aso Tofi*
Friday	*Aso Faraile*
Saturday	*Aso Toana'i*
January	*Ianuari*
February	*Fepuari*
March	*Mati*
April	*Aperila*
May	*Me*
June	*Iuni*
July	*Iulai*
August	*Aukuso*
September	*Setema*
October	*Oketopa*
November	*Novema*
December	*Tesema*
What time is it?	*Ua ta le fia?*
It's...	*Ua ta le...*
in the morning	*i le tae'ao*
in the evening	*i le afi'afi*
1.15	*kuata e te'a ai le tasi*
1.30	*afa le tasi*
1.45	*kuata i le lua*

Numbers

1	*tasi*
2	*lua*

3	*tolu*	21	*lua sefulu-tasi*
4	*fa*	30	*tolu sefulu*
5	*lima*	40	*fa sefulu*
6	*ono*	100	*selau*
7	*fitu*	101	*selau tasi*
8	*valu*	110	*selau sefulu*
9	*iva*	111	*selau sefulu-tasi*
10	*sefulu*	200	*lua selau*
11	*sefulu-tasi*	1000	*afe*
12	*sefulu-lua*	10,000	*sefulu afe*
13	*sefulu-tolu*	100,000	*selau afe*
20	*lua sefulu*	1,000,000	*tasi le miliona*

Facts for the Visitor

This chapter contains information relevant to both Samoas. For information specific to one or the other, such as details about visas, customs, money, etc, see the Facts for the Visitor chapter relating to the country or territory concerned.

TIME

Time really doesn't move more slowly in the South Pacific, but it certainly seems that way. Sometimes – on Sundays for instance – it can even appear to grind to a halt.

Visitors will need to get accustomed to an entirely different set of rules regarding punctuality. If a Samoan agrees to meet you at 9 am, you may be waiting until noon, three hours being a perfectly acceptable margin of lateness in the islands. Nothing is so pressing, they reason, that one should become flustered or inconvenienced by it. If it's worth doing, it can wait until later, or even until tomorrow. If not worth doing, it can be conveniently forgotten.

The Samoas lie just east of the International Dateline, which means their dates are the same as those of North America. The local time is GMT/UTC minus 11 hours. Therefore, noon in the Samoas is 11 pm the same day in London, 3 pm the same day in Los Angeles and 9 am the following day in Sydney.

BUSINESS HOURS & HOLIDAYS

As a general rule, banks are open Monday to Friday from 9 am to 4 pm. In Western Samoa, government offices open from 8 am to noon and 1 to 4.30 pm. In American Samoa, they're more likely to open at 9 am and close at 5 pm. Shops in both countries remain open from 8 am to noon and from 1.30 or 2 pm to 4.30 pm. Restaurants and takeaway shops operate between 8 am and 4 pm if they serve breakfast and lunch or from 6 to 10 pm if they serve only the evening meal. Saturday shopping hours are from 8 am to 12.30 pm. On Sunday, everything not directly related to the tourist industry is closed, although dribbles of activity appear around evening.

Markets normally get underway by about 6 am. In American Samoa they close at about 3 pm, but the Maketi Fou in Apia is active 24 hours a day. The big market day in the Samoas is Saturday.

The following list outlines public holidays in the Samoas. Those holidays celebrated only in Western Samoa are followed by (W). Those unique to American Samoa have an (A) beside them.

1 January
   New Year's Day
2 January
   Day after New Year's Day (W)
Third Monday in January
   Martin Luther King Day (A)
Third Monday in February
   President's Day (A)
17 April
   Flag Day (A)
25 April
   ANZAC Day (W)
April
   Good Friday (A & W), *Easter* (A & W)
   & *Easter Monday* (W)
First Monday in May
   Aso o Tina or *Mothers' Day* (W)
Last Monday in May
   Memorial Day (A)
1 to 3 June
   Independence Celebrations (W)
4 July
   Independence Day (A)
First Monday in September
   Labor Day (A)
Second Sunday in October
   White Sunday
Second Monday in October
   White Monday (W)
Second Monday in October
   Columbus Day (A)
October or November
   Palolo Day (W)
11 November
   Veteran's Day (A)
November
   Arbor Day (AS)
25 December
   Christmas Day

26 December
  Boxing Day (W)

CULTURAL EVENTS

In American Samoa, the territorial holiday is Flag Day, which falls on 17 April. It commemorates the raising of the US flag over eastern Samoa on that day in 1900 and features an art festival, performing arts and visual arts exhibits, and long-winded speeches by political figures. Accompanying the celebration are *fautasi* (longboat races), singing, dancing and traditional sports and skills competitions – coconut husking, basket weaving and fire building.

Western Samoan independence, celebrated on the first three days of June, features a number of well-attended events including fautasi and outrigger races, horse races, dancing, feasting and more of the traditional

competitions mentioned in the discussion of Flag Day (yes, even the long-winded speeches by tulafale, the aptly named talking chiefs). Everything in Western Samoa closes down for five days during this celebration, so don't be caught needing to transact business during this time!

The actual independence of Western Samoa was gained on 1 January 1962. However, as New Year's Day is already a cause for merriment, Western Samoans celebrate independence in June and thereby extract another holiday from it.

White Sunday, the second Sunday in October, is anxiously awaited by children of both Samoas as this day is dedicated to honouring children. They dress in their finest whites and parade to church and sing and lead church services. Afterwards the children are guests of honour at a feast that is prepared and served to them by adults.

A newly instituted annual event is the Teuila Festival, which takes place from the first to the second week of September. The original objective of this lively festival, which combines a variety of cultural and sporting events, was to draw more tourists to Western Samoa. However, it has also caught on with locals and is now quite a popular event, featuring choir, marching, dancing and brass band competitions; a mini-Olympic competition; traditional sports matches; *paopao* (canoe) races; arts and crafts demonstrations; Samoan cooking demonstrations; musical entertainment; talent shows; art exhibitions; a beauty pageant; and a number of tourism-related seminars and workshops. The festival is named after the *teuila* or red ginger *(Alpinia purpurata)*, which is Western Samoa's national floral emblem.

A similar but lower-key festival, Tourism Week, takes place in American Samoa in early July. The highlight of the event seems to be the crowning of Miss American Samoa.

Palolo Day isn't really a holiday but it is an event and occurs sometime in October or November, on the seventh day after the full moon. This is the day the *palolo* reefworm, or more technically, *Polychaete annelid (eunice viridis)*, emerges from the coral reefs to mate.

The blue-green vermicelli-shaped worms, rich in calcium, iron and protein, are a prized delicacy in much of the South Pacific, although once you've seen them, it may require more fortitude than I have to partake. Parties and musical festivities take place on the beaches while villagers anxiously anticipate the big event. When the worms finally appear, Samoans carrying nets and lanterns, some in paopao (canoes), frantically scoop them up.

And new events are cropping up all the time:

A new public holiday was created in 1992 – *Aso o Tina* – a celebration of Mothers' Day. It occurs the Monday following Mothering Sunday. All banks and shops are closed for the whole day. Women's groups from all over Samoa parade in Apia, displaying their woven mats. They all gather between Beach Rd and Apia harbour. Traffic comes to a complete standstill while bands and marchers congregate to be addressed by the prime minister.

Mrs M A Whitley

WEIGHTS & MEASURES

While Western Samoa uses the standard metric system, American Samoa uses the American version of the Imperial system, including miles, feet, inches for distances and measurements; the Fahrenheit scale for temperatures; and US pints, quarts and gallons for volume. For conversion information, see the table inside the back cover of this book.

BOOKS

For information about bookshops and libraries, refer to the Western Samoa and American Samoa Facts for the Visitor chapters.

Fiction

The Trembling of a Leaf (Mutual Publishing, Honolulu, 1985), by W Somerset Maugham, is a collection of Maugham's South Pacific short stories, including *Mackintosh*, *Red*, *The Pool* and the most famous, *Rain*, all of which take place in the Samoas. The protagonist of *Rain* is the infamous Sadie Thompson, whom residents of Pago Pago claim was an historical character.

Leaves of the Banyan Tree, *Flying Fox in a Freedom Tree*, *Pouliuli*, *Birth and Death of the Miracle Man*, *Inside Us the Dead*, *Shaman of Visions* and *Sons for the Return Home*, are novels by Albert Wendt. They are fictional and poetic treatments of a serious and controversial social issue facing Western Samoa: how to accommodate the encroachment of Western technology and ideals (and

---

Albert Wendt

Along with Tongan Epeli Hau'ofa, Albert Wendt is one of the best known contemporary Pacific authors. He was born in Western Samoa but was educated in New Zealand at New Plymouth Boys' High School, Ardmore Teachers' College and Victoria University, spending a total of 13 years in that country. When an overwhelming sense of exile took hold of him, even though his foreign education had effectively removed him from his Samoan roots, he decided to return.

Armed with a Master of Arts degree, he went home in 1965 to serve as the principal of Samoa College and discovered a changing society that was finding it difficult to reconcile and assimilate encroaching industrial values with age-old Samoan ideals.

He realises that the issue is not unique to Samoa, however, and so, apparently, does the literary community. One reviewer has described Wendt's Samoa as a microcosm of the modern world. His growing list of novels and volumes of poetry, which tend to reflect this theme above all others, has been highly acclaimed by critics. In 1980 his third novel, *Leaves of the Banyan Tree*, won the New Zealand Wattie Book of the Year Award.

In 1974 Albert Wendt accepted a professorship at the University of the South Pacific in Suva, where he teaches Pacific literature. His books are available in paperback in Apia, but being scarce there and in considerable demand, they command high prices and most readers will be content to wait until they get home to buy them. ■

the Samoas' place in the world scheme) while maintaining to some degree the values of fa'a Samoa and its related social structures. Wendt is Western Samoa's most renowned scholar and author.

Tales of the South Pacific, Rascals in Paradise and *Return to Paradise*, by James Michener, are collections of short stories dealing with life in, and observations of, the South Pacific from WW II onward.

The Beach at Falesá, The Ebb-Tide and *The Wrecker*, by Robert Louis Stevenson, were all written at the Vailima estate above Apia during the last four years of the Tusitala's (meaning teller of tales) life, and they reflect well his attitudes toward the islands.

Anthropology
Coming of Age in Samoa (Morrow Quill, 1928), by Margaret Mead, is perhaps the most famous work ever written about the Samoas. This controversial study was made on the island of Ta'u in the Manu'a group. Her theory was that cultural values determine adolescents' attitudes towards, and their abilities to face, the pressures of impending adulthood, particularly as they relate to sexuality, hypocrisy, education and authoritarian expectations. Although some claim that the study was tailored to fit the hypothesis, Mead found that casual attitudes toward life in Polynesian society fostered a healthy and stress-free transition from childhood to adulthood and promoted European acceptance of the age-old 'Polynesian myth' as regards sexuality in the South Sea islands.

Margaret Mead and Samoa: The Making and Unmaking of an Anthropological Myth (Harvard University Press, 1983), by Derek Freeman, refutes Mead's study. While Freeman accuses Mead of employing flawed methods of data collection and discredits her findings on the basis of his own study, he is unable to formulate any convincing conclusions. Thanks to the dynamic nature of the world during the 50-odd years between the two studies, it is unlikely that the dispute, regarding the Samoas, will ever be settled to anyone's satisfaction.

Man's Conquest of the Pacific (Collins, 1979), by Peter Bellwood, discusses the arrival and migration of the Polynesian islanders from South-East Asia through the islands. Bellwood is the foremost authority on the subject.

History & Biography
The Fatal Impact (Penguin, 1968), by Alan Moorehead, critically assesses the havoc wreaked on the Pacific by early European explorers and fortune-seekers. Although it doesn't deal with the Samoas directly, the issues are certainly relevant.

Slavers in Paradise (University of the South Pacific, 1986), by H E Maude, gives an enlightening account of the tragic events surrounding the kidnapping of Pacific islanders by the Peruvian slave traders in the early 1860s.

A Dream of Islands (Jacaranda Press, 1980), by Gavan Dawes, deals with the lives and perspectives of island-inspired authors and artists, including Robert Louis Stevenson, who loved the Samoas and settled on 'Upolu during the final years of his life.

Queen Emma (Pacific Publications, 1965), by R W Robson, is an interesting biography of the daughter of a Samoan mother and an American father, who left the Samoas for New Britain Island in Papua New Guinea and there became an entrepreneur, landowner and pillar of high society, thus earning the title of 'Queen'.

Samoa – A Hundred Years Ago and Long Before (University of the South Pacific Press, 1984), by George Turner, was first printed in Britain in 1884 and gives an interesting rundown of the myths, legends and social structure of the Samoan islands before the onslaught of outside influences.

Aggie Grey of Samoa (Hobby Investments Pty Ltd, 1979), by Nelson Eustis, is a biography of the woman often called the 'first lady of Samoa' and the inspiration for Michener's 'Bloody Mary' in *Tales of the South Pacific*. This book, written in large print and short sentences, also includes a great deal of the history of Western Samoa.

Tusitala of the South Seas (Hastings

House, 1953), by Joseph W Ellison, is the story of Robert Louis Stevenson, the Tusitala (teller of tales), and his time in the Samoas and the South Pacific.

Lagaga – A Short History of Western Samoa (University of the South Pacific, 1987), by Malama Meleisea and other contributors, is the definitive work and the best available source of information about the history of Western Samoa, made even more credible by its Samoan authorship. It covers in detail the legend and prehistory of the country as well as the period of European influence.

The War in Samoa, 1892: A Footnote to History (Cassells, London), by R L Stevenson, is the author's observations of the political unrest in Western Samoa in the early 1890s.

My Samoan Chief (University of Hawaii Press, 1971), by Faye Calkins Alailima, recounts the experiences of a California woman who married a Samoan man and returned with him to live in Samoa. The same author has also written *Aggie Grey – a Samoan Saga*, a thoughtful biography on the 'first lady of Samoa'.

Travelogues

Over the past several years, there has emerged a trio of South Pacific travelogues, each with its own angle and appeal.

First came *The Pacific* by Simon Winchester, an entertaining but rather hastily assembled account of his journalistic journeys around the great ocean. It would be excellent reading on a similar trip of your own.

Next is *Transit of Venus – Travels in the Pacific* (Minerva, 1992) by Julian Evans. This well-written account chronicles the author's shoestring travels around the Pacific by boat and ship. It includes a very entertaining chapter on the Samoas and is probably the best modern travelogue about the Pacific.

Last is the book travellers love to hate, *The Happy Isles of Oceania – Paddling the Pacific* (Penguin, 1992) by Paul Theroux. This time, the perpetually miserable Theroux finds himself kayaking around in the South Pacific islands. Because his brother had served as a Peace Corps volunteer on Savai'i, the Samoas get particularly high billing. Cynics will love the amusingly downbeat prose; Theroux's observations all seem to have been made through grey-coloured glasses and he utterly fails to notice any of the Samoas' favourable aspects. Just as well – in the end he concludes that thoroughly American Hawaii is the only real paradise on earth and he goes home.

A slightly earlier account of travel through the South Seas is *Slow Boats Home* (Hutchinson, 1985), by Gavin Young. This book is the sequel to his earlier book *Slow Boats to China*. Combined, they recount the author's 1979 around-the-world voyage aboard a wide range of maritime transport. His witty and well-observed chapter on the Samoas is especially worthwhile.

Guidebooks

South Pacific Handbook (Moon Publications, 4th edition, 1993), by David Stanley, is a thorough guidebook that covers adequately everything between the Galápagos and the Solomons. As yet, it's by far the best overall guide to the islands.

Exploring Tropical Islands and Seas (Prentice-Hall, 1984)' by Fredric Martini, contains only bare-bones information about island groups. The real emphasis is on the natural history and environmental aspects of tropical islands in the Atlantic and Pacific. It is highly recommended.

Adventuring in the Pacific (Sierra Club Books, 1988), by Susana Margolis, isn't Sierra Club's best publication, containing very little of the meaty practical information about 'adventuring'. In fact, the wild island of Savai'i seems to merit only a third of a page.

If you'll be wandering beyond the Samoas in the Pacific, Lonely Planet also publishes travel survival kits to Tahiti & French Polynesia, Fiji, Rarotonga & the Cook Islands, Vanuatu, New Caledonia, Tonga, Micronesia, the Solomon Islands, Papua New Guinea and New Zealand. The Galápagos Islands and Easter Island are covered in detail in the guides to Ecuador and Chile, respectively.

Other Books

Pacific Islands Yearbook, edited by John Carter (Pacific Publications, 1981), provides facts and figures in brief.

Pacific Tourism as Islanders See It (University of the South Pacific, 1980), by various authors, contains essays by islanders regarding the increase in tourism and, consequently, in outside influences on their cultures and lifestyles.

Samoa Sketchbook (Hobby Investments Pty Ltd, 1979), by Nelson Eustis & A J Peake, includes sketches and background information about the various points of interest around Apia and Pago Pago.

American Samoa in the South Seas (Robert Boom Company, 1973), by Chris Christensen, consists mostly of nice colour photos and brief explanatory text; it has good souvenir value.

Periodicals

If you want to keep up with the issues in the Samoas and all around the Pacific, your best source will be the *Pacific Islands Monthly*, PO Box 1167, Suva, Fiji. Although it's available in Apia bookshops, copies are scarce in American Samoa. Overseas subscriptions are available; write for information.

MAPS

Maps of Western Samoa can be purchased at the Department of Lands & Surveys near the government building in Apia. They will provide as concise topographic sheets as are available for WS$5 each. If you ask them to wrap up the map, however, they'll sometimes roll another map around it: two for the price of one.

Although it's now outdated, the best general map of both Samoas is the one published by the University of Hawaii. In Apia, you can sometimes buy it at *Aggie's Gift Shop* and at *Kava & Kavings*.

The new map *Western Samoa* by South Pacific Maps, Pty Ltd was first published in 1992 and is currently the most up-to-date map of the country. It is distributed worldwide. For information, contact Hema Maps, PO Box 724, Springwood 4127, Queensland, Australia.

The US Geological Survey (USGS) mapping for American Samoa is available through the USGS, PO Box 25286, Denver Federal Bldg, Denver, CO 80225, USA. For a catalogue of US government nautical mapping available for American Samoa, contact the National Ocean Service, Distribution N-CG33, Riverdale, MD 20737, USA.

FILM & PHOTOGRAPHY

Points worth remembering include the heat, humidity, very fine sand, tropical sunlight, equatorial shadows and the great opportunities for underwater photography. Don't leave your camera for long in direct sunlight and don't store used film for long in the humid conditions, as it will fade.

The best times to take photographs on sunny days are the first two hours after sunrise and the last two before sunset. This brings out the best colours and takes advantage of the colour-enhancing long red rays cast by a low sun. At other times, colours will be washed out by harsh sunlight and glare, although it's possible to counter this by using a polarising (UV) filter. If you're shooting on beaches, it's important to adjust for glare from water or sand; and keep your photographic equipment well away from sand and salt water.

When photographing out of doors, take light readings on the subject and not the brilliant background or your shots will all turn out underexposed. Likewise for people shots: dark faces will appear featureless if you set the exposure for background light.

Film & Equipment

Film is normally more expensive in Samoa than it is in Europe, North America and Australasia so stock up before you leave home. There are photographic and processing shops only in the capitals. Remember to take spare batteries for cameras and flash units since they're quite expensive in Samoa.

If you're shooting transparencies, you'll probably get the best results with Fujichrome 100, Velvia or Kodachrome 64. The cost of the film normally includes processing and you can mail the rolls to the labs in the envelopes provided. Rewrap the package to disguise it and send it registered if you don't trust the post. (it's quite reliable in the Samoas, although in 1986, Apia's post office did burn down under suspicious circumstances).

Useful accessories would include a small flash, a cable release, a polarising filter, a lens-cleaning kit (fluid, tissue, aerosol), and silica-gel packs to protect against humidity. Also, remember to take spare batteries for cameras and flash units and make sure your equipment is insured.

Photographing People

As in most places, the quest for the perfect 'people shot' will prove a photographer's greatest challenge. While many Samoans will enjoy being photographed, others will be put off and some people may be superstitious about your camera, suspicious of your motives or simply interested in whatever economic advantage they can gain from your desire to photograph them. The main point is that you must respect the wishes of the locals, however photogenic, who may be camera shy for whatever reason. Ask permission to photograph if a candid shot can't be made and don't insist or snap a picture anyway if permission is denied.

Often, people will allow you to photograph them provided you give them a photo for themselves, a real treasure in these countries. Understandably, people are sometimes disappointed not to see the photograph immediately materialise. If you don't carry a Polaroid camera, make it clear that you'll have to take their address and send the photo by post once it's processed.

Photographing people, particularly dark-skinned people, requires more skill than snapping landscapes. Make sure you take the light reading from the subject's face, not the background. It also requires more patience and politeness.

HEALTH

In the Samoas, health is traditionally determined by the location of the to'ala (life essence). In a healthy individual, its proper place is in the upper abdomen; in the case of displacement, sickness is the inevitable result. Prior to the arrival of Western medicine, many types of illness were treated with directional massage aimed at returning the to'ala to its proper place. For a brief discussion of traditional medicine, see under Culture in the Facts about the Region chapter.

For the visitor these days, there are few health risks in the Samoas that will require great concern, apart from the 'Polynesian paralysis' that seems to affect everyone, including Samoans. Those who spend too much time feasting, relaxing in the shade and napping on sandy white beaches will begin to notice the classic symptoms of this incapacitating disease – lack of motivation, excessive weight gain, increased appetite and general lethargy. The only cure is evacuation to a stressed-out industrial country combined with massive doses of noise, work, traffic and TV.

There is a chance of contracting hepatitis, and bacterial infections can be caught from swimming in the sea with open wounds. Food poisoning is also a possibility. Otherwise, the Samoas have a fairly healthy population and environment.

Predeparture Preparations

Make sure you're healthy before embarking on a long journey, have your teeth checked and if you wear glasses or contacts, bring a spare pair and a copy of your optical prescription.

At least one pair of good-quality sunglasses is essential, as the glare is terrific and dust and sand can get into the corners of your eyes. A hat, sunscreen lotion (15+) and lip protection are also important.

If you require a particular medication, take an adequate supply as it may not be available locally. Take the prescription with the generic rather than brand name so it will be universally recognisable. It's also wise to carry a copy of the prescription to prove you're using the medication legally. Customs and immigration officers may get excited at the sight of syringes or mysterious powdery preparations. The organisations listed under Travel Health Information can provide medical supplies such as syringes, together with multilingual customs documentation.

Health Insurance A travel insurance policy to cover theft, loss and medical problems is a wise idea. Before heading abroad travellers should get up-to-date information. There is a wide variety of policies; contact your travel agent for further information. When buying a policy, it's important to check the small print:

Some policies specifically exclude 'dangerous activities' which can include scuba diving, motorcycling or even trekking. If these activities are on your agenda, such a policy would be of limited value.

You may prefer a policy which pays doctors or hospitals directly rather than requiring you to pay first and claim later. If you must claim after the fact, however, be sure you keep all documentation. Some policies ask you to phone (reverse charges) to a centre in your home country where an immediate assessment of the problem will be made.

Check on the policy's coverage of emergency transport or evacuation back to your home country. If you have to stretch out across several airline seats, someone has to pay for it!

Travel Health Information In the US you can contact the Overseas Citizens Emergency Center and request a health and safety information bulletin on the countries of the Pacific Ocean by writing to the Bureau of Consular Affairs Office, State Department, Washington, DC 20520. This office also has a special telephone number for emergencies while abroad, (☎ (202) 632-5525).

Read the Center for Disease Control's *Health Information for International Travel* supplement of the ominously titled *Morbidity & Mortality Weekly Report*, or the World Health Organisation's *Vaccination Certificate Requirements for International Travel*

& Health Advice to Travellers. Both of these sources (CDC and WHO) are superior to the Travel Information Manual published by the International Air Transport Association.

International Association for Medical Assistance to Travelers (IAMAT) at 417 Center Street, Lewiston, New York, NY 14092 can provide you with a list of English-speaking physicians in the Pacific.

In the UK, contact *Medical Advisory Services for Travellers Abroad (MASTA)*, Keppel Street, London WC1E 7HT (☎ (071) 631-4408). MASTA provides a wide range of services including a choice of concise or comprehensive 'Health Briefs' and a range of medical supplies. Another source of medical information and supplies is the *British Airways Travel Clinic* (☎ (071) 831-5333). The Department of Health publishes leaflets SA40/41 on travellers' health requirements, and operates a phone service Freephone (☎ (0800) 555777).

In Australia, contact the Traveller's Medical & Vaccination Centre in Sydney (☎ (02) 221-7133) and Melbourne (☎ (03) 602-5788) for health information pertaining to South Pacific countries.

Medical Kit It's a good idea to carry a small, straightforward medical kit which may include:

1. Aspirin or paracetamol – for pain or fever
2. Antihistamine (such as Benadryl) – useful as a decongestant for colds and allergies, to ease itching from insect bites, or to prevent motion sickness
3. Antibiotics – useful if you're travelling off the beaten track. Most antibiotics are prescription medicines. *
4. Kaolin and pectin preparation such as Pepto-Bismol for stomach upsets, and Imodium or Lomotil to bung things up in case of emergencies during long-distance travel
5. Rehydration mixture – for treatment of severe diarrhoea. This is particularly important when travelling with children.
6. Antiseptic liquid or cream and antibiotic powder for minor injuries
7. Calamine lotion – to ease irritation from bites and stings
8. Bandages and Band-aids

9. Scissors, tweezers, and a thermometer – but remember that you cannot transport mercury thermometers on airlines
10. Insect repellent, sunblock, suntan lotion (15+), chapstick and water purification tablets (or iodine).

* Ideally, antibiotics should be administered only under medical supervision and should never be taken indiscriminately. Overuse of antibiotics can weaken your immune system and reduce the drug's efficacy in the future. Take only the recommended dosage at the prescribed intervals and continue using the antibiotic for the prescribed period, even if you're feeling better sooner. Antibiotics are quite specific to the infections they will react with so if you're in doubt about a drug's effects or suffer any unexpected reactions, discontinue use immediately.

Immunisations Vaccinations provide protection against diseases you may encounter along the way. A yellow fever vaccination and related documentation is only necessary if you arrive in the Samoas from Africa or South America (and note that vaccination is contraindicated during pregnancy). Otherwise, the only recommended jabs for travel to the Samoas are tetanus DPT (in case you're bitten by a dog), polio and gamma globulin or a hepatitis vaccine.

For your information, the following is a rundown of some of the more common vaccines offered by travellers' health clinics:

Cholera Although some countries require this vaccine, it lasts only six months and is not recommended for pregnant women.
Gamma globulin Gamma globulin is not a vaccination but a ready-made antibody which has proven successful in reducing the chances of contracting infectious hepatitis (hepatitis A). Because it may interfere with the development of immunity, it should not be given until at least 10 days after administration of the last vaccine needed and as near as possible to departure due to its relatively short-lived effectiveness – normally about six months.
Hepatitis A A new hepatitis A vaccine (administered as a course of two doses one month apart) has recently become available. The long term protection offered by this vaccine should prove particularly useful for frequent or long-term travellers.

Polio This vaccine is normally given in the form of droplets on the tongue. In most Western countries, it is given to children as a matter of course, but travellers are still advised to have a booster every few years.
Tetanus DPT Boosters are necessary at least every 10 years and are highly recommended as a matter of course.
Typhoid Protection lasts for three years and is useful if you are travelling for longer periods in rural tropical areas. The most common side effects from this vaccine are pain at the injection site, fever, headache and a general unwell feeling.

Medical Care
Not surprisingly, medical care is limited in the Samoas and the type of care and standards of sanitation you're probably accustomed to in your home country simply aren't available. The LBJ Tropical Medical Center in Faga'alu, American Samoa, was once highly regarded as the finest facility in the tropical Pacific but unfortunately, staffing problems and illicit diversion of hospital funds have taken their toll and it can now provide only marginal service. If you come down with anything really serious, you should make arrangements to get to Hawaii, Australia or New Zealand.

In Western Samoa, there is the large National Hospital in Apia and a fairly extensive system of rural hospitals, but sadly, they lack the staff and medications to treat anything but minor injuries and illnesses.

If you need to visit the hospital in Western Samoa, bear in mind that the facilities are well used and allow the better part of a day waiting in the queue. Western Samoa has a national health scheme but nonresidents are required to pay a charge of WS$15 per visit. Medicines are free for Samoans, but foreigners are required to pay the full price. There are private physicians in Apia who will normally provide more extensive and timely care but they charge more than the hospital clinics.

For more information, see under Health in the individual country Facts for the Visitor chapters.

Pharmacies & Medicines
Some Western pharmaceutical companies

sell their expired stock to places like Western Samoa, which means that some medications you receive here could be ineffectual (although local medical workers maintain that medical supplies are dated very conservatively for litigation-plagued Western markets and that the risk of problems is negligible). Furthermore, many rural hospitals lack doctors or only receive a visit from an Apia doctor every couple of weeks, and personnel may refuse to provide medicines without a doctor's prescription. Occasionally, rural hospitals in the Samoas may hesitate to dispense medical supplies to foreigners lest they deplete their stocks.

Therefore, if you come down with a potentially dangerous bacterial infection requiring antibiotic treatment, you may be faced with a problem. Those travelling in Western Samoa away from Apia (especially on Savai'i) may want to carry a cycle of a range of antibiotics – talk to your doctor or to a travellers' medical clinic before you leave home and ask to be prescribed treatments for the ailments described later in this section. Ideally, antibiotics should be administered only under medical supervision and should never be taken indiscriminately. Overuse can weaken your body's natural ability to deal with infections and can reduce the drug's efficacy in the future. Take only the recommended dosage at the prescribed intervals and continue using the antibiotic for the prescribed period, even if the illness seems to be cured and you're feeling better. Antibiotics are quite specific to the infections they treat; stop immediately if you have any serious reactions, and don't use an antibiotic if you are unsure that you have the correct one.

In addition, all travellers should be aware of any drug allergies they may have and avoid using them or their derivatives while travelling in the Samoas. Since common names of prescription medicines in the Pacific islands are likely to be different from the ones you're used to, ask a pharmacist before taking anything you're not sure about.

Basic Rules
Care in what you eat and drink is the most

important health rule; stomach upsets are the most common travel health problem but the majority of these upsets will be minor. Don't be paranoid about sampling local foods – it's all part of the travel experience and shouldn't be missed.

Diseases of Insanitation
Diarrhoea & Samoa Stomach The most common complaint of visitors could be called 'Samoa stomach', which is just a South Seas variation of Montezuma's revenge. The bacteria found naturally in food and water will be different from those you are accustomed to at home. Your stomach will probably notice this and the resulting discomfort and diarrhoea will be its response to the problem. A few rushed trips to the toilet with no other symptoms does not indicate a serious problem.

Moderate diarrhoea, involving half a dozen loose movements in a day, is more of a nuisance. (Make sure you bring some soft loo paper from home.) Dehydration is the main danger with any diarrhoea, particularly for children, so fluid replenishment is the number one treatment. Weak black tea with a little sugar and flat soft drinks, particularly lemonade and diluted 50% with water or soda water are good. With severe diarrhoea a rehydrating solution is necessary to replace minerals and salts. You should stick to a bland diet as you recover. Chewing a small pellet of paregoric, a stronger version of milk of magnesia, will relieve the pain of the cramps.

Lomotil or Imodium can be used to bring relief from the symptoms, although they do not actually cure the complaint. Only use these drugs if absolutely necessary – if you *must* travel, for example. For children, Imodium is preferable. Do not use other drug if the patient has a high fever or is severely dehydrated. Antibiotics can be very useful in treating severe diarrhoea, especially if it is accompanied by nausea, vomiting, stomach cramps or mild fever. Three days' treatment should be sufficient and an improvement should occur within 24 hours.

In order to prevent more serious stomach ailments such as amoebic dysentery, wash vegetables and fruits with rainwater and boil any questionable drinking water before use. The water that emerges from Samoan taps sometimes tastes foul and briny. Most people prefer rainwater, which is collected in tanks and is available in some places. Special care should be taken immediately following a cyclone or other bad storm.

The simplest way to purify suspect water is to boil it for eight to 10 minutes. Simple filtering won't remove all dangerous organisms so if you can't boil suspect water, it should be treated chemically. Chlorine tablets (Puritabs, Steritabs and other brand names) will kill many but not all pathogens. Iodine is very effective and is available in tablet form (such as Potable Aqua) but follow the directions carefully and remember that too much iodine is harmful.

If you can't find tablets, tincture of iodine (2%) or iodine crystals may be used. Add two drops of tincture of iodine per litre or quart of water and let stand for 30 minutes. Iodine crystals can also be used to purify water but this is a more complicated and dangerous process since you first must prepare a saturated iodine solution. Iodine loses its effectiveness if exposed to air or damp so keep it in a tightly sealed container. Flavoured powder will disguise the normally foul taste of iodine-treated water and is an especially good idea for those travelling with children.

When it's hot, be sure to drink lots of liquids. Excessive sweating can lead to loss of salt and cause muscle cramping. Failure to urinate or dark yellow urine is a sign of dehydration. Always carry a bottle of water on long trips.

Once you're headed towards recovery, try some yoghurt but stay away from other dairy products, sweets and fruit. If you don't recover after a couple of days, it would be wise to visit a doctor to be tested for other problems which could include giardiasis, dysentery or cholera.

Giardiasis This is first characterised by a swelling of the stomach, pale-coloured faeces, diarrhoea, frequent gas, headache and later by nausea and depression. Many doctors recommend Flagyl (metronidazole) tablets (250 mg) twice daily for three days. Flagyl, however, can cause side effects and some doctors prefer to treat giardiasis with two grams of Tinaba (tinadozole), taken all at once to knock the bug out hard and fast. If it doesn't work the first time, the treatment can be repeated for up to three days.

Dysentery This serious illness is caused by contaminated food or water and is characterised by severe diarrhoea, often with blood or mucus in the stool, and painful stomach cramps. There are two types: bacillary dysentery, which is uncomfortable but not enduring; and amoebic dysentery which, as its name suggests, is caused by amoebas. This variety is much more difficult to treat and is more persistent.

Bacillary dysentery hits quickly and because it's caused by bacteria it responds well to antibiotics and is usually treated symptomatically with a kaolin and pectin or a bismuth compound. On the other hand, since the symptoms themselves are actually the best treatment – diarrhoea and fever are both trying to rid the body of the infection – it may be best to just hole up for a few days and let it run its course. If activity or travel is absolutely necessary during the infection, you can take either Imodium or Lomotil until reaching a more convenient location to R & R (rest and run).

Amoebic dysentery, or amoebiasis, is a much more serious variety. It is caused by protozoans, or amoebic parasites, called *Entamoeba histolytica* which are also transmitted through contaminated food or water. Once they've invaded, they live in the lower intestinal tract and cause heavy and often bloody diarrhoea, fever, tenderness in the liver area and intense abdominal pain.

If left untreated, ulceration and inflammation of the colon and rectum can become very serious. If you see blood in your faeces over two or three days, seek medical attention. If that's not possible, try the antiparasitic

Flagyl (metronidazole). You'll need three tablets three or four times daily for 10 days to rid yourself of the condition. Flagyl should not be taken by pregnant women.

The best method of preventing dysentery is, of course, to avoid eating or drinking contaminated items.

Viral Gastroenteritis This is not caused by bacteria but, as the name implies, is a virus. It is characterised by stomach cramps, diarrhoea, vomiting and slight fever. All you can do is rest and keep drinking as much water as possible.

Hepatitis This incapacitating disease is caused by a virus which attacks the liver. Type A, which is the most common strain in the Pacific, can be caught by eating food, drinking water or using cutlery, crockery or toilets contaminated by an infected person. The victim's eyes and skin turn a sickly yellow and urine orange or brown. An infected person will also experience tenderness in the right side of the abdomen and a loss of appetite.

If you contract infectious hepatitis (hepatitis A) during a short trip to the Samoas, you probably should make arrangements to go home. If you can afford the time, however, and have a reliable travelling companion who can bring food and water, the best cure is to stay where you are, find a few good books and only leave bed to go to the toilet. After a month of so, you should feel like living again. Drink lots of fluids and keep to a diet high in proteins and vitamins. Avoid alcohol and cigarettes absolutely.

The best preventative measures available are either the recently introduced long-term hepatitis A vaccine; or a gamma globulin jab before departure from home and booster shots every three or four months thereafter while you're away (beware of unsanitary needles!) A jab is also in order if you come into contact with any infected person; and if *you* come down with hepatitis, anyone who has been in recent contact with you should take the shot too.

Hepatitis B, formerly known as serum hepatitis, can only be caught by having sex with an infected person or by skin penetration such as tattooing or using the same syringe. If type B is diagnosed, fatal liver failure is a real possibility and the victim should be sent home and/or hospitalised immediately. Gamma globulin is not effective against hepatitis B.

A vaccine does exist for hepatitis B, but it's very expensive. It consists of a course of three shots over a period of six months.

A variant of the B strain, called hepatitis C, now also exists. Transmission and symptoms are similar to hepatitis B; but, care is presently no vaccine against hepatitis C. However, it is rare and should not be of too much concern to travellers.

Typhoid In mid-1993, four villages in Western Samoa were reported as having been contaminated with typhoid-causing bacteria, with at least 110 confirmed cases. Appropriate precautions are advised (see under Immunisations earlier in this section).

Contaminated food and water are responsible for typhoid fever, another stomach infection that travels the faecal-oral route. Vaccination against typhoid isn't 100% effective. Since it can be very serious, medical attention is necessary.

Early symptoms are like those of many other travellers' illnesses – you may feel as though you have a bad cold or the flu combined with a headache, sore throat and fever. The fever rises slowly until it exceeds 40°C while the pulse slowly drops. These symptoms may be accompanied by nausea, diarrhoea or constipation.

In the second week, the fever and slow pulse continue and a few pink spots may appear on the body. Trembling, delirium, weakness, weight loss and dehydration set in. If there are no further complications, the fever and symptoms will slowly fade during the third week. Medical attention is essential, however, since typhoid is extremely infectious and possible complications include pneumonia or peritonitis (burst appendix).

When feverish, the victim should be kept cool. Watch for dehydration. The recommended antibiotic is chloramphenicol but ampicillin causes fewer side effects.

Cuts, Bites, & Stings

Cuts & Scratches The warm, moist conditions of the tropics lowlands invite and promote the growth of 'wee beasties' that would be thwarted in more temperate climates. Because of this, even a small cut or scratch can become painfully infected and lead to more serious problems, so even tiny cuts should be treated immediately with soap, water and a disinfectant such as peroxide or alcohol. Since the waters around the Samoas are full of staphylococcus bacteria, it is best not to swim with an open wound. Staph infections are miserable and are very difficult to treat. Sadly, many villagers in the Samoas die of such infections that have ulcerated and spread to vital organs.

Your immune system cannot fight such an infection once it has taken hold. The variety of staph found in the Samoas reacts to an artificial penicillin called flucloxicillin, so request a prescription from your doctor at home and if you have a painfully infected or ulcerated cut or boil accompanied by fever and/or headache, begin treatment as directed immediately. One cycle may not be enough; once again, discuss with your doctor the possibility of needing a second course – you don't want to risk a return of the infection. If it does return, it will be in a stronger form and consequently even more dangerous and difficult to treat.

Since bacterial immunity to certain antibiotics can build up, it's not wise to take these medicines indiscriminately or as a preventative measure. The best treatment for cuts is to frequently cleanse the affected area with soap and water and apply mercurachrome or an antiseptic cream. Where possible, avoid using bandages, which keep wounds moist and encourage the growth of bacteria. If, despite this, the wound becomes tender and inflamed then use of a mild, broad-spectrum antibiotic may be warranted.

Insects & Animals Ants, gnats, mosquitoes, bees and flies are just as annoying in Samoa as they are at home. Cover yourself well with clothing and use insect repellent on exposed skin. Burning incense and sleeping under mosquito nets in air-conditioned rooms or under fans also lowers the risk of being bitten. If you're going walking in humid or densely-foliated areas, wear light cotton trousers and shoes, not shorts and sandals or thongs. Regardless of temperature, never wear shorts or thongs in the forest and remember to carry an effective insect repellent.

Unless you're allergic to them, bee and wasp stings are more painful than dangerous. Calamine lotion offers some relief and ice packs will reduce pain and swelling.

The good news is that the Samoas are free of both malaria and rabies at present. Buzzing mosquitoes may drive you to insanity at night and the fierce barking dogs may appear threatening, but they are not carriers of insidious diseases. Mosquito repellent and nets will usually protect you from the insects, while a few well-aimed stones should keep aggressive dogs at bay. If you are bitten by a dog, you should have a tetanus vaccination within a few hours if you haven't had one during the past three years.

In the sea, however, there are some serious hazards. Coral is sharp and can cause nasty cuts that may become infected. Several species of jellyfish deliver an excruciating sting and stings from the inhabitants of cone shells can be deadly. Learn which ones are dangerous before collecting them and don't handle them.

The agony caused by the poison of the stonefish is legendary, and although they are not common, utmost care should be taken to avoid accidentally treading on one. Always wear reef shoes or sneakers while walking through the water and don't touch anything unfamiliar while snorkelling.

Sun, Heat & Exertion

Travellers from the middle and high latitudes, especially those who are fair-skinned, will need to exercise caution in tropical countries such as the Samoas. The rays of the sun are more direct here than in temperate countries and so their burning capacity is much greater – twice as great, for instance, as in Sydney or Los Angeles. Even in the cooler highland areas, everyone will be susceptible to hazardous UV rays. A good, strong sunblock and possibly even a dab of zinc oxide will prevent a painful and potentially dangerous burn. A sunblock with a protection factor of at least 15 is normally recommended under such conditions. In addition, a hat will serve to shade your face and protect your scalp. Sunglasses will prevent eye irritation (especially if you wear contact lenses).

A few people may find that they are allergic to prolonged exposure to the sun's rays. This problem will manifest itself in an itchy rash, most often on the arms, neck and face. In any area but the face it is treated with cortisone cream. Ask the chemist to recommend a milder cream for use on the face.

Fungal infections caused by humid conditions are also common in Polynesia. Loose-fitting and light-coloured clothing will go a long way towards preventing problems, but those who are susceptible to yeast infections and athlete's foot should come prepared with their usual treatments.

Those spending a lot of time in the sun should take care to prevent dehydration. Before setting out on any walk or visit to the beach, be sure you are carrying sufficient drinking water.

Prickly Heat Prickly heat is an itchy rash caused by excessive perspiration trapped under the skin. It usually strikes those newly arrived in a hot climate whose pores have not opened enough to accommodate profuse sweating. Frequent baths and application of talcum powder will help relieve the itch.

Heat Exhaustion Heat combined with humidity and exposure to the sun can be oppressive and leave you feeling lethargic, irritable and dazed. A cool swim or lazy afternoon in the shade will do wonders to improve your mood. You'll also need to drink lots of liquids and eat salty foods in order to replenish your supply of these products lost during sweating.

Serious dehydration or salt deficiency can lead to heat exhaustion. Take time to acclimatise to high temperature and again, be sure to drink sufficient liquids. Salt deficiency, which can be brought on by diarrhoea or nausea, is characterised by fatigue, lethargy, headaches, giddiness and muscle cramps. Salt tablets will probably solve the problem. Anhidrotic heat exhaustion, caused by inability to sweat, is quite rare but can strike even those who have spent some time in hot climates.

Heatstroke This serious, sometimes fatal, condition can occur if the body's thermostat breaks down and body temperature rises to dangerous levels. Continuous exposure to high temperatures can leave you vulnerable to heatstroke. Alcohol intake and strenuous activity can increase chances of heatstroke, especially in those who've recently arrived in a hot climate.

Symptoms include minimal sweating, a high body temperature (39 to 40°C), and a general feeling of unwellness. The skin may become flushed and red. Severe throbbing headaches, decreased coordination, and aggressive or confused behaviour may be signs of heatstroke. Eventually, the victim will become delirious and go into convulsions. Get the victim out of the sun, if possible, remove clothing, cover with a wet towel and fan continually. Seek medical help as soon as possible.

Motion Sickness If you're susceptible to motion sickness, you should be prepared because the ferry trips in the Samoas aren't always smooth sailing. If Dramamine works for you, take some along. Eating very lightly before and during a trip will reduce the chances of motion sickness. Try to find a place that minimises disturbance, near the wing on aircraft or near the centre on ferries. Fresh air almost always helps but reading or cigarette smoking (or even being around someone else's smoke) normally makes matters worse.

To be effective, commercial motion sickness preparations, which can cause drowsiness, must be taken before the trip. After you've begun feeling ill, it's too late. Dramamine tablets should be taken three hours before departure and scopolamine patches (which are available only by prescription in most places) should be applied 10 to 12 hours before departure. Scopolamine will dilate the pupils if it accidentally comes in contact with the eyes and has been known to cause drowsiness, so caution should be exercised. Ginger can be used as a natural preventative and is available in capsule form.

Sexually Transmitted Diseases
Gonorrhoea & Syphilis Sexual contact with an infected partner can spread a number of unpleasant diseases. While abstinence is 100% effective, use of a condom will lessen your risk considerably. The most common of these diseases are gonorrhoea and syphilis which in men first appear as sores, blisters or rashes around the genitals and pain or discharge when urinating. Symptoms may be less marked or not evident at all in women. The symptoms of syphilis eventually disappear completely but the disease continues and may cause severe problems in later years. Antibiotics are used to treat both syphilis and gonorrhoea.

HIV/AIDS HIV/AIDS is another issue and everyone should be aware of the seriousness of this disease. It is now a serious problem worldwide. HIV (human immunodeficiency virus) may develop into AIDS or acquired immune deficiency syndrome. Although in the West it is most commonly spread through intravenous drug abuse and male homosexual activity, it is increasingly being transmitted through heterosexual activity as well.

Most people affected by the HIV virus are not aware they have it and hospitals are likely to diagnose their symptoms as something more mundane. The obvious way to best avoid the disease is to remain celibate while travelling. Not everyone can – or is inclined to be – but without a blood test, it is impossible to detect the seropositivity (HIV-positive status) of an otherwise healthy-looking person. Always practising safe sex – using condoms is the most effective preventative.

HIV/AIDS can also be spread through blood transfusions and most developing countries cannot afford to screen blood used for transfusions. It is also possible to contract the virus through injection with an unsterilised needle so vaccinations, acupuncture, tattooing and ear or nose piercing can potentially be as dangerous as intravenous drug use if the equipment is not sufficiently sterile. If you must have an injection, it's a good idea to provide a new sterilised syringe (either bought from the pharmacy or one which you have carried from home) and ask the doctor to use it.

Interestingly, a suspected AIDS inhibitor has recently been discovered in the Falealupo Rainforest Reserve on Savai'i. This substance, known as prostratin, comes from the trunk of the tree *Homolanthus nutans*, which has shiny green leaves and pale yellow flowers. It has long been used by traditional Samoan healers as a remedy for such viral diseases as yellow fever.

Women's Health
Gynaecological Problems Poor diet, lowered resistance due to the use of antibiotics, and even contraceptive pills can lead to vaginal infections when travelling in hot climates. To prevent the worst of it, keep the genital area clean, wear cotton underwear and skirts or loose-fitting trousers.

Yeast infections, characterised by a rash, itch and discharge, can be treated with a vinegar or lemon juice douche or with yoghurt. Nystatin suppositories are the usual medical prescription. Trichomoniasis is a more serious infection which causes a discharge and a burning sensation when urinating. Male sexual partners must also be treated and if a vinegar and water douche is not effective, medical attention should be sought. Flagyl is the most frequently prescribed drug.

Pregnancy Most miscarriages occur during the first trimester of pregnancy so this is the most risky time to be travelling. The last three months should also be spent within reasonable reach of good medical care since serious problems can develop at this stage as well.

Pregnant women should avoid all unnecessary medication but vaccinations and malarial prophylactics should still be taken where possible. Additional care should be taken to prevent illness and particular attention to diet and proper nutrition will significantly lessen the chances of complications.

Back Home

Remain aware of illness after you return; take note of odd or persistent symptoms of any kind, get a check-up and remember to give your physician a complete travel history. Most doctors in temperate climates will not suspect unusual tropical diseases. If you feel ill and have been travelling in malarial areas, have yourself tested for the disease.

WOMEN TRAVELLERS

Thanks to Western and Asian videos, which are extremely popular in the Samoas, foreign women have a reputation for easy availability, whether or not they are single. Polite refusal by a non-Samoan woman of sexual attention will probably be taken to mean 'keep trying' by a hopeful Samoan man who may have difficulty imagining why you wouldn't be interested, given the European, Oriental, African, etc, promiscuity he sees portrayed on the screen (sort of the Polynesian myth working in reverse).

The Samoan word for 'no' is 'leai' and it should be used firmly (of course, only if that's what you want to say). While frequent advances will be annoying, sober Samoans are unlikely to physically force the issue.

To avoid some measure of attention that a lone foreign woman is likely to attract, modest dress is recommended. See how young Samoan women dress and do likewise. Don't turn up at a pub or disco alone unless you're expecting advances, and

ignore the inane remarks of adolescents who'll try to chat you up. Samoan custom requires men to ask permission of your male escort before requesting a dance so unwanted attention can be screened that way. Most of all, however, don't be paranoid or you'll miss out on some very pleasant (and platonic) friendships.

DANGERS & ANNOYANCES
Security

Violent crime and alcohol-related incidents seem to be more prevalent in American Samoa than in Western Samoa, although the latter has been experiencing its share of minor crime and mischief lately, most of it perpetrated by bored juveniles. Theft isn't really a problem in the Samoas and you and your personal belongings are probably safer than in your home country, but it's best not to strain the honesty of the people by leaving things lying around unattended.

Actually, it's not really honesty that's the issue here. As mentioned under Culture in the Facts about the Region chapter, Samoan society is traditionally communal. This means that an article belonging to one person also belongs to others who may have need of it. 'Borrowing' your possessions or absconding with them altogether (essentially the same thing) will not violate any real social restrictions and will not cause severe strain on the Samoan conscience.

Visitors may also notice another practice that may become irritating at times but is perfectly innocent. There are really no beggars, per se, in the Samoas, but Samoans will habitually make requests of their well-off aiga members who are responsible for the welfare of the family. They also like to approach foreigners, whom they imagine to be inconceivably wealthy, and help them voluntarily part with some of their endless means before someone else does. They're not always after money, though some are. Many would be just as happy to get the book you're reading, your sunglasses or the shirt off your back. A polite explanation that you've already promised the item in question to someone is a good way to refuse.

If you suffer from guilt pangs for having so much cash and technology at your disposal, you could be cleaned out very quickly. Bear in mind that the Samoas are not poor, and lack of monetary affluence and electronic gadgetry does not necessarily constitute poverty.

Quite a few Samoans who migrate to other countries get caught up in Western materialism, but many others return to the Samoas complaining foreigners are required to work too hard, that everyone abroad is in a big hurry and that good food is too difficult to come by. Many say they also miss contact with their traditions and the protection provided by their aiga.

Officials

Police and government officials in the Samoas seem to be fairly friendly and straightforward, although the arrogance and superficiality of some officials in American Samoa can astound you. For what it's worth, I've never heard of a tourist running afoul of the law unless they've overstayed their visas or been caught carrying illicit substances.

Custom Fees

Each village in the Samoas is separately governed by a village council (the hierarchy of which is explained in the section on culture) responsible for affairs of associated aiga and for furthering the cause of the village as a whole. Outsiders, both foreigners and residents of other communities, are required to pay a fee to use resources 'belonging' to one village or another.

Such resources include beaches, mountains, caves and so on, and while this seems a fairly good way to supplement village coffers, there are a few scams involved. Sometimes, custom fees are prominently signposted, or a collection booth is set up near the entrance to the attraction. On other occasions, however, visitors will merely be approached and requested to pay.

Sometimes this is legitimate, but often, individuals who are in no way related to the village council get away with collecting money, sometimes in extortionate amounts,

from unwary or foolish travellers. Even authorised charges can be unrealistic; in the Savai'i village of A'opo, travellers are being asked to pay extortionate amounts to use the northern approach to Mt Silisili, the Samoas' highest peak. Rather than face unpleasant scenes, most walking groups now resort to the more difficult access route from the other side of the island.

If you are in doubt about a particular fee, ask to see the pulenu'u (mayor) before paying. Never pay children and never pay after the fact unless there was no one around to collect a valid fee when you arrived. Standard custom fees range from WS$1 to WS$2 per person in Western Samoa and US$2 in American Samoa. In many places, charges are made per vehicle. All legitimate custom fees in force at the time of writing are outlined in this book, but that doesn't mean prices won't change or new fees won't be introduced. Keep your wits about you and don't pay anything until you're certain it's legitimate; if you are charged unfairly, report the incident to the Western Samoa Visitors' Bureau in Apia or the American Samoa Office of Tourism in Fagatogo.

Children

Visitors to remote villages in both Samoas will find the children gregarious and charming, begging to be photographed, crowding around and following foreigners, and yelling 'what's your name' and 'bye-bye, palagi' unceasingly. Their motivation seems to be an odd mixture of friendliness, curiosity and the desire to provoke some sort of reaction from what they consider an exotic creature.

For those with a mellow attitude, this can be one of the most enchanting aspects of the islands, but there is also a dark side to such attention. Foreigners walking, cycling or riding motorbikes through villages will frequently be considered moving targets by village children and stones will fly. They will often surround you mockingly and demand money or sweets and will make great sport of trying to upset you.

Given the typically warm and friendly reception given by adult Samoans, visitors

may find such behaviour incongruous and rather disturbing by Western reckoning. Although some foreigners have postulated that it's due to the envy of tourists' perceived material wealth, this explanation sounds like Western guilt combined with patronising indulgence. The fact is, wealthy Samoans are treated with respect.

According to several Samoan friends, the key to this problem lies in the blanket of protection afforded every Samoan by his or her aiga. Just as Western children often torment small dogs, grasshoppers or other creatures they may consider helpless, so do Samoan children try to take the mickey out of those who lack the protection of this all-pervasive support system. If that seems disagreeable or insensitive, bear in mind that Samoa is Polynesia's most traditional society and that Western notions simply don't apply, especially in the rural villages of Western Samoa.

When faced with mischief, resist losing your temper. Instead, report cases of stoning to the pulenu'u of the village, who will take appropriate action. In other cases, either ignore the kids and keep going or try to turn the irritation into a joke. If a child merely demands sweets or money, perhaps hold out your hand and demand something of him or her, smiling or laughing all the while.

HIGHLIGHTS

The following items get my vote for Samoa's top attractions for visitors. These are, of course, in addition to the traditional Samoan hospitality that so pleasantly pervades all the islands:

Aleipata Beaches, 'Upolu, Western Samoa – the place to go for the whitest sand and clearest water in the Samoas.

Aunu'u Island, American Samoa – a beautiful and unusual island which presents a different face of American Samoa, just a few minutes by boat from Tutuila. Don't miss the lake of red quicksand, the crater lake full of eels and Ma'ama'a Cove, a wild cauldron of surf.

Falealupo Peninsula, Savai'i, Western Samoa – a remote area combining lovely wild beaches with a beautiful rainforest reserve, which protects Samoa's unique vegetation as well as flying foxes and a variety of birds. Unfortunately, this area was the hardest hit by recent cyclones and much evidence remains of the destruction.

Fatumea Pool, Piula, 'Upolu, Western Samoa – a clean freshwater cave pool full of fish; it offers a cool and refreshing break on a hot day.

Mt Matavanu, Savai'i, Western Samoa – a gaping crater, which made its debut in 1911, and makes a wonderful and impressive day walk.

Mulivai Waterways, 'Upolu, Western Samoa – where an exotic tangle of freshwater streams meets the salt water and creates a unique region of rainforest and mangrove wetlands.

Palolo Deep Marine Reserve, 'Upolu, Western Samoa – a favourite with snorkellers, right on Apia's doorstep.

Papase'a Sliding Rock, 'Upolu, Western Samoa – an all-natural slippery slide which is better than Disneyland and just minutes from central Apia.

Pulemelei Mound & Olemoe Falls, Savai'i, Western Samoa – Polynesia's largest ancient monument and Samoa's most beautiful waterfall and tropical pool are to be found on the Letolo plantation on Savai'i.

South Ofu Beach, Manu'a, American Samoa – part of American Samoa National Park, it offers the finest snorkelling in the territory. Some judge it to be the most beautiful beach in the world and it certainly is a contender.

Tafua Savai'i Rainforest Reserve, Savai'i, Western Samoa – a new reserve which shelters a large colony of flying foxes and is also the last stronghold of the Samoan tooth-billed pigeon. There are several walking tracks which are ideal for day hikes.

Taga Blowholes, Savai'i, Western Samoa – among the world's largest and most impressive marine blowholes.

Vailima Estate & Stevenson Graves, 'Upolu, Western Samoa – on the summit of Mt Vaea, this is a great place for a picnic or to soak up the sun, surrounded by forest and great views down to Apia.

ACCOMMODATION
Bottom End & Middle

The only real budget accommodation available in the Samoas is in Apia, where WS$15 will get you a reasonable place to crash, or around Aleipata, where the same amount will allow you to sleep in one of an increasing number of open fales on the beach. The least expensive places on Savai'i are still relatively highly priced, and in American Samoa, you won't get by paying much less than US$35 per night for a relatively grotty room. If you'd like to spend a bit of time in Pago Pago, you might consider hiring a room or a flat, which will cost as little as US$150 or so per month.

Camping There are quite a few places in the Samoas, especially in the interiors of islands or on remote beaches, where no formal accommodation and not even village accommodation will be available. For those who'd like to spend a few days climbing Mt Silisili, wandering around the crater lands of Savai'i or exploring the remoter reaches of the Manu'a Islands, the only option will be to camp.

In most cases, surface water will not be available and you'll have to carry water or be sure that coconuts are available. (Don't drink anyone's plantation coconuts without permission.) If you opt for the latter, carry a hefty bush knife to open them – Swiss Army knives are ineffective for removing tough green coconut husks unless you are prepared to mutilate the knife, the nut and your hands in the process.

In Western Samoa, there are four official camping areas: O Le Satapuala Resort (WS$5 per site), Tafatafa Beach (WS$5), Lotofaga Beach (WS$10) and Return-to-Paradise Beach (WS$10) all on 'Upolu. Hotels and guesthouses will often allow campers to set up a tent on their grounds and use their facilities for a small fee. In other populated areas, you may be required to pay a custom fee to camp within the jurisdiction of a village. It is unlikely, however, that you will be permitted to do so, thanks to the hospitality of the Samoan people, who will insist that you stay in a home as guests of the village.

It won't help much to explain that you'd like to sleep outside, close to nature – Samoan fales are as close to nature as you're likely to get! Telling them that you'd like to spend some time alone won't get you too far, either. You'll rarely see a Samoan alone, and the concept of privacy has only recently started to take hold. Indeed, the people actually feel sorry for those required to spend time alone for one reason or another: hence, those walking by themselves in the streets are often joined by total strangers who feel it their obligation to keep you company. For those who'd still like to have a go at camping out, good luck.

In American Samoa, camping is not permitted in public parks.

Staying in Villages Samoan hospitality is legendary, and sometime during their visit, travellers will probably be invited to stay in the home of a Samoan family. Not only will this provide the outsiders with invaluable insights into the extremely complex culture of the islands, it will reflect a degree of honour upon the host in the eyes of other villagers. No one in the Samoas, foreigner or otherwise, will ever be required to spend a night without a roof over their head. Those who would choose to do so – to camp outside, for instance, especially within sight of a village – might inadvertently cast shame upon the village for failing to invite the strangers in.

Be warned, however, that the hospitality of the people should not be construed as a cheap means of 'doing' the islands. Even the most welcome guest eventually becomes a strain on a family's resources, and though no complaints will ever be heard by the guests, considerate travellers should assess from time to time the impact they're having. It's probably best to move on after a few days, but of course that will depend upon the individual situation.

When it's time to leave, gather the family together and offer your sincerest thanks for their hospitality, then leave a *mea alofa* (gift) as a token of your esteem. Don't call it 'payment' or your hosts may be offended that you may consider them guilty of selling their kindness and friendship. Perhaps you can say something like: 'Your kindness and hospitality are greatly appreciated. Please accept this gift as a symbol of my respect for you and of our mutual friendship.'

The best gifts will be those that can't normally be obtained without money. Samoans love *pisupo*. This is tinned corned beef, and before you say 'yuck' you should know that, years ago, palagis turned it into a national institution in the islands. It must be bought from a store and is considered quite a treat. Clothing such as T-shirts printed with kitsch sayings will also be enthusiastically accepted, as will photographs of the family, postcards or picture books, simple toys for the children or any type of gadgetry unavailable or expensive in the islands. As much as possible, try to choose a gift that reflects the value of food and accommodation you've enjoyed with them and the individual personalities of your friends.

The following letter by two readers offers a personal view about accepting Samoan hospitality:

Western Samoa has grown more dependent on the values of Western civilisation over the past few years, specifically regarding the awareness of and the reliance upon money. We heard that more foreigners have begun to stay in Samoan villages without considering the cost to the family and the severe economic impact on the village. This has created an undercurrent of resentment in Western Samoans, particularly those who have been to New Zealand and worked in a money-based society.

The Western Samoans are awakening to the fact that their hospitality is being abused, even though foreigners are still honoured guests in most villages. It is wise to return their graciousness. We thought that Western Samoan villages should be compensated for housing and feeding guests, since the number of visitors has grown considerably. One Samoan woman suggested about US$5 or 10 per day. While money is not the perfect answer, it is worth mentioning that some form of compensation is appropriate, whereas no compensation may contribute to the destruction of a wonderful tradition.

Doe Risko & Andrew Weinstein, USA

Home-Stay Programs In American Samoa, the Office of Tourism has now set up an official home-stay program known as *Fale, fala ma ti*, which means 'House, mat and tea'. In theory, it provides the option of staying with Samoan host families for US$25 to US$45 per night. For information and the most current listings of participants, contact American Samoa Office of Tourism, P O Box 1147, Pago Pago, American Samoa 96799.

In Western Samoa, home and village stays may be most easily organised through the Safua Hotel (☎ 51271; fax 51272) in Lalomalava on the island of Savai'i. They charge WS$30 per person.

Top End

For those on an unlimited budget there are four 'resort' hotels on 'Upolu (two in Apia), one in Pago Pago and one at Vaisala on Savai'i. These offer varying degrees of luxury, so don't expect the Ritz, but be prepared to shell out US$70 or so per day for the privilege of isolating yourself from the Polynesia you came to see. While a night or two of relative luxury may be welcome as a change, to spend all your time in such places would be to rob yourself of the best of the Samoas – the natural, down-to-earth, easygoing essence of the islands.

FOOD

Traditional Samoan food, for the most part, is very good, and some excellent dishes are derived from tropical crops. Meals consist mostly of such items as root vegetables, coconut products *(niu* and *popo)*, taro *(talo)*, fresh fruit, pork (pua'a), chicken (moa), corned beef (pisupo) and fish (i'a).

Unfortunately, the situation in the Samoas is getting fairly grim food-wise. The health of the people, especially in American Samoa, is suffering as junk foods and expensive supermarket items invade and replace the healthy diet to which Samoans have long been accustomed. The ultimate blasphemy is the availability and status attached to the use of products such as tinned vegetables, fish and fruit, and as white bread, greasy meat products and artificial snack foods, while traditional items lie rotting on the ground.

Breakfast

Breakfast in the Samoas isn't terribly different from other meals. A hearty breakfast will normally include some type of root vegetable (yam, *'umala* (sweet potato), taro, etc), a piece of fish, and coffee or *koko Samoa*, a delicious chocolate drink made with locally grown roasted cocoa beans, sugar and water. Such a meal can be had at the market stalls in Apia or Salelologa (Savai'i) for about WS$2. In American Samoa, it will be harder to come by inexpensive traditional fare. Also popular are Samoan pancakes, greasy deep-fried dough balls sometimes containing a bit of mashed banana. They are reminiscent of doughnuts but quite heavy on the stomach and most people won't be able to get down more than two.

Western breakfasts of cereal, eggs, pancakes and the like are available in American Samoa at a variety of places and in Apia, Western Samoa, at the big hotels and a couple of Western-style restaurants.

Real brewed coffee can be found in quite a few places around the islands and delicious local coffee is available at the big hotels and a couple of selected coffee shops in Apia.

Lunch

Rural Samoans eat pretty much the same thing for lunch as they do for breakfast: some kind of root vegetable, cooked banana or breadfruit, and fish or chicken. Those who work will normally pick up some sort of fast food – curry, fried chicken or fish, chop suey, a hamburger, a hot dog or the like – at a take-away. While this isn't terribly exciting fare, it is inexpensive and life-sustaining to a degree.

Those who have a bit more to spend can find European-style luncheons in up-market restaurants and hotel dining rooms in both Pago Pago and Apia. In Pago Pago, excellent Mexican and Korean food is also available.

Dinner

A variety of cuisines – Chinese, Korean, Thai, Mexican, German, North American and even Samoan – can be eaten in one or both of the capital cities. All of these are quite reasonably priced when compared to similar quality food in North America or Australia but the atmosphere of most places is less than elegant. The best eating establishments in the Samoas, I've found, are certainly not those with the finest appearance.

Some resort hotels offer 'Samoan feasts' and European buffets that are quite good, but since they cater primarily for tourists, prices are relatively high. Similarly, there are several atmospheric restaurants in both capitals which serve up small portions of gourmet food and fine wines for budget-crunching prices. After a month of market fare and fast food, however, such frivolities will probably be appreciated.

Umu Feasts An umu is a traditional Polynesian earth oven. Unlike umu constructed in the rest of Polynesia, the Samoan variety is above ground and some of the most interesting and delicious traditional concoctions are prepared in it. Feasts are normally held in honour of a festive event, such as a wedding, a birthday, an investiture of title, a holiday or the arrival of visitors, but feasts in the Samoas rarely reach the proportions they do in nearby Tonga; travellers will either have to attend one staged especially for tourists or stumble upon one.

Typical feast foods include the ubiquitous chicken and fish, roast suckling pig and a variety of root vegetables, sweets and concoctions derived from coconut cream, such as *palusami* (baked coconut cream in taro leaves and banana leaf), *oka* (raw fish marinated in coconut cream, lemon juice, chili and onions), *supo esi* (papaya pudding) and *fa'ausi talo* (taro in coconut cream). No one should leave the Samoas without trying some of these wonderful creations.

DRINKS

The most refreshing drink available is the juice of the immature coconut, which is naturally carbonated and is quite delicious. Green coconuts are collected by climbing coconut trees, and rural Samoans are usually happy to scramble up a tree in order to secure drinking nuts for visitors. (Visitors are often impressed at the agility and gracefulness of these climbers.)

If you want to collect and drink coconuts while walking in rural Samoa, carry a bush knife to hack away the tough green husk. The more mature nuts can be opened (with some difficulty) with a pointed stick and a bit of elbow strain. The meat of the green coconut is soft and pliable and some people prefer it to the crunchy meat of the mature brown nut. Picking up fallen nuts is normally not a problem but before collecting nuts from trees, be sure to seek permission of home or plantation owners.

Despite the variety of fruit available, fresh

Making a Samoan Umu

For those who would like to try their luck at making a Samoan umu, it's fairly easy and is an effective way to prepare large quantities of food.

Find four logs of wood, each measuring one to 1½ metres long, and lay them in a square. Arrange a layer of fist-size stones inside. Place tinder wood atop them in a mound, leaving space around the edges, then place larger pieces of firewood around the central mound. Light the mound to start the fire, and after it's going well, place more stones atop the wood. As the wood burns down, the stones will heat up and retain enough heat to cook your meal. Remove any wood still burning and smooth down the layer of stones, making a slight depression in the centre. Fan ashes away from the stones with a large banana or taro leaf. Arrange root vegetables, breadfruit, meat, packets of palusami and so on in the centre of the rock pile and place some other rocks on top. Cover completely, firstly with banana leaves and then with burlap sacks, to keep the heat in.

If you've included a whole suckling pig, you will need to leave it in the umu for three or four hours. Otherwise, your meal should be ready in an hour or less. ■

juices aren't terribly popular so those who enjoy them (who doesn't?) will have to do the extracting themselves. Inexplicably, most restaurants serve tinned juices.

Sweet and syrupy foreign soft drinks – Coca Cola, Pepsi and Fanta – are available almost everywhere. Alternatively, there's a range of locally produced soft drinks but most of them are so insipid that they shouldn't be given a passing thought.

Alcoholic Beverages

Alcoholic beverages are very popular in the Samoas, and especially in the capital cities you'll never be lacking a place to buy a drink (except on Sunday, of course). In American Samoa you must be at least 21 years of age to purchase alcohol, although they don't seem to check as closely as on the US mainland.

In American Samoa you can buy a range

Samoan Recipes
If you'd like to try Samoan cuisine, the following are some of the best traditional recipes.

Fa'ausi Talo
1 cup coconut cream
2 cups grated taro root
1 cup sugar
1 banana leaf

To make coconut cream, grate the meat of three to four mature coconuts and add one cup of hot water for each two cups of meat. Let stand for a quarter of an hour or so then pass through a cheesecloth or coconut sennit to extract the cream. Wring well. Mix the coconut cream (reserving about one quarter of it for use later) and grated taro root, wrap in a banana leaf and bake in an umu (or an oven). Remove the banana leaf and cut the taro into cubes three or four cm in diameter. Make a caramel syrup from the sugar and remaining coconut cream. Pour the syrup over the taro cubes and serve hot.

Oka
1 kg raw fish
⅓ cup lemon juice
⅓ cup diced onion
¼ cup diced tomatoes
1 tsp chopped chili peppers
⅓ cup diced cucumbers
1½ cups coconut cream
salt

Prepare coconut cream as described in the previous recipe. Cut fish into three cm squares and rinse with cold water. Place in a bowl and add lemon juice, onion and salt to taste. Mix well and marinate in the refrigerator for a few hours. Add diced vegies and chili pepper. Serve cold.

Palusami
36 young taro leaves
1 medium onion
2 cups coconut cream
1 tsp curry powder (optional)
6 wilted banana leaves
salt
6 breadfruit leaves

Prepare coconut cream as described in the Fa'ausi Talo recipe but use six or seven coconuts. Add salt, finely diced onion and curry (if desired) to coconut cream. Take a bunch of six taro leaves and form them into a cup. Pour about half a cup of the cream mixture into the bowl, wrap it in a banana leaf and then in a breadfruit leaf. Repeat with remaining leaves. Bake in an umu (or an oven) for half an hour. ■

of American beers – Budweiser, Coors, Stroh's and the like – as well as Aussie Fosters and New Zealand Steinlager. Western Samoa's contribution to the lager market is Vailima, an excellent beer brewed by a German brewmaster on the outskirts of Apia. Samoa Lager, a lesser and cheaper brew, is also bottled in Apia; it has a sweetish taste reminiscent of bubble gum, but it does grow on you.

Talofa wine – actually more like a wine cooler – is brewed by Island Styles in the hills above Apia. It's made from local fruit products and is a cool and refreshing way to enjoy a drink.

The ceremonial drink, 'ava, is discussed in the Culture section of the earlier Facts about the Region chapter.

ENTERTAINMENT
Bars & Nightclubs

Bars and nightclubs are immensely popular with urbanised Samoans and many foreigners enjoy getting in and partying with them or seeking out quiet places to meet expats or have a quiet conversation over a tropical drink. By law, in Western Samoa, bars and night clubs must close at midnight and at the more energetic clubs, the police arrive to make sure that the music is turned off and send the patrons home. Night owls shouldn't despair at this point; 15 minutes after the police have gone, the music normally resumes and carries on for at least another hour.

Foreign women who don't relish constant and persistent attention – whether or not they're with a date – should avoid the more rollicking places. Samoans are normally courteous but sometimes a combination of alcohol, loud music and pre-conceived notions about foreign women can bring about misunderstandings. If you're in a dance venue, the assumption is that you want to dance. Samoan men normally ask men for permission to dance with their female companions but if your date agrees or says that it's up to you, you're pretty much obligated as far as the Samoan is concerned. At this stage, your refusal of his invitation will

amount to a personal insult and if he's had more than a few beers, this sense of rejection could be taken very badly.

Men, on the other hand, should keep in mind that while Samoan women normally love to dance, they're not all looking to be picked up (although quite a few are and in most local bars, Western men will have no lack of attention in that department). Also, bear in mind that Samoan women are normally attached to a very large Christian family and that your innocent fling could open an immense can of worms for all concerned. For the best results, use a heavy dose of discretion.

As a final caveat, under certain circumstances (such as in a disco or night club) alcohol-induced disputes can readily escalate into full-blown fisticuffs. These altercations rarely involve foreigners, but if you're in a bar and troubles erupt, keep a low profile until the bouncer arrives or things have blown over.

Gays and lesbians will probably have to remain discreet in the Samoas. The obvious presence of fa'afafine belies the fact that homosexuality is technically illegal and is not openly accepted in Samoan society (this is just another of many Samoan paradoxes). Furthermore, there are no specifically gay bars in the Samoas; although your chances are slim, the best hope of finding like-minded people will be at the Mt Vaea Club in Apia.

Fiafia

The original fiafia was a local play or music program which amounted to a fund-raising effort for the performers; the better their performance, the more money they were able to collect. Nowadays, the 'fiafia night' is a presentation of Samoan dancing and singing staged at tourist hotels for tourists exclusively. It is sometimes accompanied by a huge *umu* feast (see the earlier Food section).

The fiafia is all the contact that many visitors have with Samoans, but that doesn't mean they aren't worthwhile. The dancing and music are normally colourfully superb and good-value entertainment. It is also apparent that the participants are caught up in the joy of artistic expression and that they appreciate the opportunity to perpetuate their traditional arts, even on a superficial level.

The best fiafia programmes will be found at Aggie Grey's Hotel, the Kitano Tusitala Hotel, the Beachcomber Bar and Coconuts Beach Club Resort, all on the island of 'Upolu in Western Samoa.

THINGS TO BUY

Although the emphasis on handicrafts in the Samoas is visibly less than in nearby Tonga, there are practical items and articles of artistic expression to be found and appreciated, particularly in Western Samoa. Siapo, also known as tapa, is made from the pounded bark of the *Broussonetia papyrifera*, the paper mulberry tree *(u'a)*, and one of the most typically Polynesian souvenirs you can buy. Samoan siapos are small in comparision to their their Tongan counterparts, reaching only a few square metres in size. Consequently, they're more portable. The best place to find good work is on Savai'i where a few individuals keep the art alive; for expert advice, consult Moelagi Jackson at the Safua Hotel.

Woven mats of dried and treated pandanus are made by women in their spare time and serve as beds and carpeting in traditional fales. The *fala moe* (bedroll mats) are stored in the fale and used for sleeping. The *papa laufala* cover the floors of Samoan dwellings. The much more intricate *ie toga*, or fine mat, is made of pandanus leaves split into widths of just a couple of mm and when completed has the sheen and appearance of fine silk. An average one will take hundreds or even thousands of hours to weave, and the finest ones will merit heirloom value. Ie toga are given as gifts on important occasions such as weddings, births and investitures of title.

Baskets and other articles of woven pandanus are beautiful, inexpensive and make excellent souvenirs. Likewise, carved wooden 'ava bowls are popular with visitors and are actually used in the islands. The many-legged Samoan bowls come in more imaginative shapes than their counterparts in other South Pacific countries.

Samoan carvings, jewellery and trinkets, which can be bought all over the islands, may be beautiful but they are not traditional. Be sure to check import restrictions and consider environmental impact before buying any whalebone or black coral.

Finally, the latest trend in Western Samoa fashion seems to be in T-shirts depicting huge, shirtless (odd, considering the medium involved!), muscle-bound brutes with coconut-sized biceps and a scowl that would avert a charging bull (or even Hulk Hogan). These seem to be the favoured attire of teenage boys of any size. Typically, the intimidation factor is enhanced by a clarifying slogan: Fa'a Samoa; Samoa Strength; Matai – Symbol of Power; Ocean Warrior; Samoa Super Power; Samoa Shark Tamer and so on. Their popularity probably has something to do with kitty cats and tigers, Chihuahuas and wolves and dreams of being big and dangerous.

WHAT TO BRING

Given the consistently warm temperatures of the Samoas, the variety of clothing you'll need to bring can be kept to a minimum. Shorts for men and cotton skirts for women, light cotton shirts and trousers, a beach towel, a hat, flip-flops (thongs), walking shoes, a swimsuit and a jumper, flannel shirt or light jacket will be about all anyone will need. This wardrobe can be supplemented as necessary at the Korean shops in Pago Pago or several inexpensive clothing shops around Apia.

Personal items such as sunblock cream, tampons, toothpaste, contraceptives, mosquito repellent and shampoos should probably be brought from home since the availability, quality and price of such things may be unpredictable. Film and camera equipment is also best brought from home, although US prices on some items are available in Pago Pago.

A few paperbacks to read on the beach, a torch for exploring caves, a Swiss Army Knife, a universal-type drain plug, snorkelling gear and rain gear will also be useful.

If you're planning to camp out or travel by ferry between Apia and Pago Pago, a sleeping bag and ground cover will be essential, while a tent will allow you freedom to stay overnight at a particularly appealing beach, forest or mountain.

Music fans may also want to carry a tape recorder in order to immortalise some of the magnificent Samoan voices and musical talent they'll be hearing. Bring your own batteries, however, as they're quite expensive, especially in Western Samoa.

Getting There & Away

The South Pacific is relatively expensive transport-wise and unless you have unlimited funds to allow you the luxury of whim-to-whim travel, some careful route-planning will be in order. Remember that all visitors arriving in the Samoas need onward air tickets or a yacht-owner's guarantee that they will be departing on the same boat they arrived on.

AIR

The majority of the Samoas' visitors arrive on scheduled flights at Pago Pago International Airport at Tafuna on Tutuila in American Samoa or at Faleolo International Airport 35 km west of Apia on 'Upolo in Western Samoa. (Faleolo was only opened to large trans-oceanic jets in 1985.) While the Samoas aren't exactly as remote or obscure a destination as Tuvalu or Kiribati, neither are they as popular as Fiji or Tahiti and airfares often reflect that.

From New Zealand, Australia, Fiji, Tonga, Hawaii and Los Angeles, access to Samoa is fairly straightforward. From anywhere else, travelling to the Samoas will entail first reaching one of these connecting points. Auckland and Nadi/Suva seem to be the most convenient and best served runs. The major carriers are Air New Zealand, Air Pacific and Polynesian Airways. Samoa Air connects Western and American Samoa as well as Niue and Nuku'alofa and the Vava'u group in Tonga.

Buying a Plane Ticket

Your plane ticket will probably be the single most expensive item in your budget, and buying it can be an intimidating business. There is likely to be a multitude of airlines and travel agents hoping to separate you from your money, and it is always worth putting aside a few hours to research the current state of the market. Start early: some of the cheapest tickets have to be bought months in advance, and some popular flights sell out early. Talk to other recent travellers – they may be able to stop you making some of the same old mistakes. Look at the ads in newspapers and magazines, consult reference books and watch for special offers. Then phone round travel agents for bargains. (Airlines can supply information on routes and timetables; however, except at times of inter-airline war, they do not supply the cheapest tickets.) Find out the fare, the route, the duration of the journey and any restrictions on the ticket. Then sit back and decide which one is the best for you.

You may discover that those impossibly cheap flights are 'fully booked, but we have another one that costs a bit more...' Or the flight is on an airline notorious for its poor safety standards and leaves you in the world's least favourite airport in mid-journey for 14 hours. Or they claim only to have the last two seats available for that country for the whole of July, which they will hold for you for a maximum of two hours. Don't panic – keep ringing around.

Use the fares quoted in this book as a guide only. They are approximate and based on the rates advertised by travel agents at the time of going to press. Quoted airfares do not necessarily constitute a recommendation for the carrier.

If you are travelling from the UK or the USA, you will probably find that the cheapest flights are being advertised by obscure bucket shops whose names haven't yet reached the telephone directory. Many such firms are honest and solvent, but there are a few rogues who will take your money and disappear, to reopen elsewhere a month or two later under a new name. If you are suspicious about a firm, don't give them all the money at once – leave a deposit of 20% or so and pay the balance when you get the ticket. If they insist on cash in advance, go somewhere else. And once you have the ticket, ring the airline to confirm that you are actually booked on the flight.

You may decide to pay more than the rock-bottom fare by opting for the safety of a better known travel agent. Firms such as STA, who have offices worldwide, Council Travel in the USA or Travel CUTS in Canada are not going to disappear overnight, leaving you clutching a receipt for a nonexistent ticket, but they do offer good prices to most destinations.

Once you have your ticket, write its number down, together with the flight number and other details, and keep the information somewhere separate. If the ticket is lost or stolen, this will help you get a replacement.

It's sensible to buy travel insurance as early as possible. If you buy it the week before you fly, you may find, for example, that you're not covered for delays to your flight caused by industrial action.

Air Travellers with Special Needs

If you have special needs of any sort – you've broken a leg, you're vegetarian, travelling in a wheelchair, taking the baby, terrified of flying – you should let the airline know as soon as possible so that they can make arrangements accordingly. You should remind them when you reconfirm your booking (at least 72 hours before departure) and again when you check in at the airport. It may also be worth ringing round the airlines before you make your booking to find out how they can handle your particular needs.

Airports and airlines can be surprisingly helpful, but they do need advance warning. Most international airports will provide escorts from check-in desk to plane where needed, and there should be ramps, lifts, accessible toilets and reachable phones. Aircraft toilets, on the other hand, are likely to present a problem; travellers should discuss this with the airline at an early stage and, if necessary, with their doctor.

Guide dogs for the blind will often have to travel in a specially pressurised baggage compartment with other animals, away from their owner, though smaller guide dogs may be admitted to the cabin. All guide dogs will be subject to the same quarantine laws (six months in isolation, etc) as any other animal when entering or returning to countries currently free of rabies such as the UK or Australia.

Deaf travellers can ask for airport and in-flight announcements to be written down for them.

Airlines will usually carry babies up to two years of age at 10% of the relevant adult fare, and some carry them free of charge. Reputable international airlines usually provide nappies (diapers), tissues, talcum and all the other paraphernalia needed to keep babies clean, dry and half-happy. For children between two and 12 years of age, the fare on international flights is usually 50% of the regular fare or 67% of a discounted fare. These days, most fares are considered to be discounted. 'Skycots' should be provided for infants by the airline if requested in advance; these will take a child weighing up to about 10 kg. Push chairs can often be taken as hand luggage.

Discounted Fare Deals

Polypass Polynesian Airlines' Polypass is a popular option open to those who don't mind limited time in a number of South Pacific destinations. It is good for 30 days and includes travel on Polynesian Airlines' flights to Western Samoa, American Samoa, Tonga, Fiji, New Caledonia, French Polynesia, Niue and the Cook Islands as well as a return trip to both New Zealand and Australia.

This is a good way to fill up your passport with stamps but actually see very little. If you're planning to visit more than one Pacific destination from Australia, the Polypass will actually work out cheaper than a combination of individual flights. From Honolulu, Australia or New Zealand, the adult Polypass costs US$999; from Los Angeles, it's US$1299. Discounts are available for children under 12 years of age.

A much more leisurely Polypass option is the Triangle Fare, which includes one circuit of the classic 'triangle' of Fiji, Tonga and

Western Samoa. It's valid for one year and costs US$414.

Round-the-World Tickets Round-the-world (RTW) tickets have become quite popular in recent years and are often very good value. Since Samoa is pretty much on the opposite side of the world from Europe and the North American east coast, it can work out no more expensive or even cheaper to keep going in the same direction right around the world rather than backtrack on your return.

The official airline RTW tickets are usually put together by a combination of two airlines and permit you to fly anywhere you want on those airlines' routes as long as you do not backtrack. For example, Air New Zealand can normally get you from London to New Zealand or Australia, allowing up to three free stopovers en route (Los Angeles, Honolulu, Samoa, Tonga, Fiji, Cook Islands, etc), for as little as UK£470 one way or UK£850 return. The one-way option can be used in conjunction with a special fare on Thai, Malaysian or another Asian airline for the return route via Asia (currently less than UK£450).

Restrictions are that you (usually) must book the first sector in advance and cancellation penalties then apply. The Air New Zealand ticket allows a 75% refund only if no sector of the route has been flown. Alternative RTW routings may be put together by speciality travel agents using a combination of discounted tickets.

For some suggestions, see Finding a Discounted Ticket under To/From Europe later in this chapter.

Circle Pacific Fares Circle Pacific fares are similar to RTW tickets, and use a combination of airlines to formulate a circle route through the Pacific, including the Samoas and a combination of other countries. As with RTW tickets, there are advance purchase restrictions and limits to the number of stopovers allowed. Typically fares range between US$1500 and US$2000. Your best bet will be to organise your itinerary through an agency which specialises in independent travel.

Student Travel Worldwide, there are a number of student travel organisations which offer bargain-basement airfares to out-of-the-way destinations the world over, including the Pacific. Organisations which offer student services include:

Australia
    STA Travel, 224 Faraday St, Carlton, Victoria, 3056 (☎ (03) 347-6911)
    STA Travel, 1st Floor, 732 Harris St, Ultimo, Sydney 2007, NSW (☎ (02) 212-1255; fax (02) 281-4183)
Canada
    Travel CUTS, 187 College St, Toronto, Ontario M5T 1P7 (☎ (416) 979-2406)
France
    CTS Voyages, 20 Rue des Carmes, 75005 Paris (☎ (01) 43-25-00-76; fax (01) 43-54-48-98)
Germany
    Council Travel, 18 Graf Adolfstrasse, D-4000 Düsseldorf 1 (☎ (211) 329-088)
    SRID Reisen, Bergerstrasse 118, 60316 Frankfurt/Main (☎ (69) 430191; fax (69) 439858)
    SPS Reisen, Marienstrasse 25, 10117 Berlin (☎ (30) 281-6741; fax (30) 281-5133)
Italy
    CTS Torino, Via Camerana 3E, 10128 Torino (☎ (011) 535966)
Japan
    STA Travel, 4th Floor, Nukariya Bldg, 1-16-20 Minami-Ikebukoro, Toshima-Ku, Tokyo 171 (☎ (03) 5391-2889; fax (03) 5391-2923)
    Council Travel, Sanno Grand Bldg, Rm 102, 0-14-2 Nagata-cho 2 chome, Chiyoda-ku, Tokyo 100 (☎ (03) 358- 5517)
New Zealand
    STA Travel, 10 High St, Auckland (☎ (09) 309-9995; fax (09) 309-9829)
    STA Travel, 223 High St, Christchurch (☎ (03) 379-9098)
    STA Travel, 233 Cuba St, Wellington (☎ (04) 385-0561)
UK
    Council Travel, 28A Poland St, London W1 (☎ (071) 437-7767)
    STA, 74 Old Brompton Rd, London SW7 3LQ (☎ (071) 937-9971)
    STA Travel, Priory House, Wrights Lane, London W8 6TA (☎ (071) 938-4711; fax (071) 938-4321)

USA
Council on International Educational Exchange, 205 East 42nd St, New York, NY 10017 (☎ (212) 661-1450)
Council Travel, 1093 Broxton Ave, Los Angeles, CA 90024 (☎ (310) 208-3551)
STA Travel, 48 East 11th St, New York, NY 10003 (☎ (212) 477-7166; fax (212) 477-7348)
STA Travel, 51 Grant St, San Francisco, CA 94108 (☎ (415) 391-8407; fax (415) 391-4105)
STA Travel, 5900 Wilshire Blvd, Suite 2100, Los Angeles, CA 90036 (☎ (213) 937-1150; fax (213) 937-2739)

To/From the USA

The main hub for travel between North America and the Pacific is Honolulu and most travellers to the Pacific islands (the notable exception is those on Polynesian Airlines' direct Los Angeles-Apia routing) will have to pass through here.

In the USA, the best way to find cheap flights is by checking the Sunday travel sections in major newspapers such as the *Los Angeles Times*, *San Francisco Examiner* or *Chronicle* on the west coast and the *New York Times* on the east coast. The student travel bureau – STA or Council Travel – are also worth a go but in the USA you'll have to produce proof of student status and in some cases be under 26 years of age to qualify for their discounted fares.

North America is a relative newcomer to the bucket-shop traditions of Europe and Asia, so ticket availability and the restrictions attached to them need to be weighed against what is offered on the standard Apex or full economy (coach) tickets. Do some homework before setting off. The magazines specialising in bucket-shop advertisements in London (see the discussion under To/From Europe) will post copies so you can study current pricing before you decide on a course of action. Also recommended is the newsletter *Travel Unlimited* (PO Box 1058, Allston, MA 02134) which publishes details of the cheapest airfares and courier possibilities for destinations all over the world from the USA.

In general, November and December are the dearest and most congested months to travel, while the northern summer, corresponding to the Samoan winter, is the cheapest and easiest time to get a booking – and is fortunately also the driest and most comfortable season to visit the equatorial Samoas.

Non-Discounted Tickets Due to excessive competition between carriers and a lot of governmental red tape in determining fare structures, flights originating in the USA are subject to numerous restrictions and regulations. This is especially true of bargain tickets; anything cheaper than the standard tourist or economy fare must be purchased at least 14 days, and sometimes as much as 30 days, prior to departure.

In addition, you'll have to book departure and return dates in advance and these tickets will be subject to minimum and maximum stay requirements: usually seven days and six months, respectively. It's often cheaper to purchase a return ticket and trash the return portion than to pay the one-way fare. From the USA, open tickets which allow an open return date within a 12-month period are generally not available, and penalties of up to 50% are imposed if you make changes to the return booking.

From the US mainland, the major carrier gateway city to the Pacific is Los Angeles but there are also direct flights to Honolulu from nearly every other major city in the country, including Seattle, Denver, Houston, New York and others. Economy fares must often be purchased two weeks in advance, with a requirement of a minimum stay of two weeks and a maximum stay of three months.

Polynesian Airlines flies direct from Los Angeles to Apia for US$668 return and Air New Zealand flies via Honolulu three times weekly for US$898 return. If you just want to get within striking distance, there are good package deals to Fiji beginning at US$899 for a one-week visit, including airfare and accommodation; from Nadi and Suva, Air Pacific flies to Apia three times weekly.

To/From Canada

As with US-based travellers, Canadians will find the best deals travelling to the Pacific

Ocean region via Los Angeles and/or Honolulu.

Air New Zealand now flies direct from Vancouver to New Zealand, via Honolulu. Alternatively, Canadians can fly Qantas or Air Pacific direct to Nadi from Vancouver, with an intermediate stop in Honolulu. The Air Pacific Vancouver to Nadi flight leaves on Thursday and Saturday. After a 24-hour stopover in Nadi, you can continue to Apia, having had enough time to spend a wonderful day at one of the Nadi area's beautiful offshore islands during your wait!

Travel CUTS has offices in all major Canadian cities. The *Toronto Globe & Mail* carries travel agents' ads. Travellers interested in booking flights with Canadian courier companies should obtain a copy of the *Travel Unlimited* newsletter mentioned in the To/From the USA section.

To/From Europe

There is no straightforward way to get from Europe to the South Pacific. Europeans will have to get themselves to the North American west coast, Sydney or Auckland and work out a route from there. Considering the location of the South Pacific relative to Europe, a round-the-world ticket may be the most economical way to go (see the discussion of RTW tickets earlier in this section).

Currently, the best fares to the South Pacific are with Air New Zealand from London. The Air New Zealand fares work out cheaper if you fly from Europe to the Pacific islands, with Australia or New Zealand as your final destination. It allows a total of two free stopovers between London and Australasia, which may include Los Angeles, Hawaii, Western Samoa, Fiji, Tonga, the Cook Islands or New Zealand. It's also possible to break your journey in Los Angeles, overland to Vancouver, and continue from there for no extra charge.

These tickets may be used in combination with another carrier as part of an RTW routing. Currently, Air New Zealand fares to New Zealand average around UK£800 from mid-April to mid-June and from UK£910 to UK£1180, with two free stopovers and an extra UK£40 for each additional stopover. If your final destination is Australia, the fares are a bit cheaper (UK£700 mid-April to mid-June and UK£870 to UK£1144 for other times) but they still allow the two free stopovers. On the other hand, if you opt not to continue on to Australia or New Zealand, flights directly to Tonga or Western Samoa (with free stops at Los Angeles and Honolulu) will cost from UK£920 to UK£1070.

Finding Discounted Tickets There are bucket shops by the dozen in London, Paris, Amsterdam, Brussels, Frankfurt and a few other places. In London, several magazines with lots of bucket-shop ads can put you on to the current deals. In these magazines, you'll often find discounted fares to the US west coast, Honolulu, New Zealand or Australia, some of which will allow stopovers or inexpensive connections to the Pacific islands.

A word of warning, however: don't take the advertised fares as gospel truth. To comply with advertising laws in the UK, companies must be able to offer *some* tickets at their cheapest quoted price, but they may only have one or two of them per week. If you're not one of the lucky ones, you'll be looking at higher priced tickets. The best thing to do is begin looking for deals well in advance of your intended departure so you can get a fair idea of what's available. Look for travel agents' ads in the Sunday papers and travel magazines. Following is a list of publications and organisations which have travel information for budget travellers:

Trailfinder
  This magazine is put out quarterly by Trailfinders (☎ (071) 938-3939/3366) from 9 am to 6 pm Monday to Friday UK time or fax (071) 938-3305 anytime), 42-48 Earls Court Rd, London W8 6EJ, UK. It's free if you pick it up in London but if you want it mailed, it costs UK£6 for four issues in the UK or Ireland and UK£10 or the equivalent for four issues in Europe or elsewhere (airmail). Trailfinders can fix you up with all your ticketing requirements as well. They've been in business for years, their staff are friendly and are highly recommended.

Time Out
Tower House, Southampton St, London WC2E 7HD (☎ (071) 836-4411). This is London's weekly entertainment guide and contains travel information and advertising. It's available at bookshops, newsagents and newsstands. Subscription enquiries should be addressed to Time Out Subs, Unit 8, Grove Ash, Bletchley, Milton Keynes MK1 1BZ, UK.

TNT Magazine
52 Earls Court Rd, London W8, UK (☎ (071) 937-3985). This free magazine can be picked up at most London Underground stations and on street corners around Earls Court and Kensington. It caters to Aussies and Kiwis working in the UK and is therefore full of travel advertising.

Globe
Globe is a newsletter published for members of the Globetrotters' Club (BCM Roving, London WC1N 3XX). It covers obscure destinations and can be handy to help find travelling companions.

To initiate your price comparisons, try contacting travel agents such as Trailfinders (☎ (071) 938-3939)/3366); STA Travel (☎ (071) 937-9971); and Bridge the World (☎ (071) 911-0900) all in London; or the exceptionally helpful and highly recommended Travel Bug (☎ (061) 721-4000) in Manchester. For courier flight details, contact Polo Express (☎ (081) 759-5383) or Courier Travel Service (☎ (071) 351-0300).

On the continent, the newsletter *Farang* (La Rue 8 á 4261, Braives, Belgium) deals with exotic destinations, as does the magazine *Aventure au Bout du Monde* (116 rue de Javel, 75015 Paris).

To/From Australasia

Travelling to the Samoas from Australia or New Zealand will be straightforward, but not necessarily inexpensive. In addition to the student travel agencies listed earlier in this chapter, you may want to check with the Pacific Island Travel Centre (☎ (02) 262-6011 in Sydney; (☎ (03) 663-3649 in Melbourne; fax (02) 262-6318) which specialises in Pacific travel and may be able to quote a good fare. Another possibility is Pacific Unlimited Holidays which has offices in Sydney (☎ (02) 390-2266; fax (02) 2902419) and in Melbourne (☎ (03) 650-2387; fax (03) 654-6994). If you are interested in surfing in Samoa, Surf Travel in Sydney (☎ (02) 527-4722; fax (02) 527-4522) can organise a package deal.

Air New Zealand, Polynesian and Air Pacific all have return service from Sydney to Apia for around A$1000. Polynesian Airlines, which offers twice weekly nonstop service to Apia, entails the least hassle. Air New Zealand flies from Sydney twice weekly, with a stop in Auckland. Air Pacific does the run to from Sydney to Apia three times weekly with a change in Nadi. Air New Zealand flies between Auckland and Apia twice weekly and Polynesian flies three times weekly for about NZ$1800.

To/From Other Pacific Islands

Within the Pacific region, island-hopping isn't that difficult or expensive, but some routes will present scheduling problems. Between Pago Pago and Nuku'alofa, Tonga, Samoa Air flies four times weekly; to the Vava'u group, it flies twice weekly. To Nuku'alofa, the return fare is US$300; to Vava'u, it's US$280 for the weekend flight and US$200 if you travel during the week – perhaps a bit steep for flights of just over an hour! From Nadi and Suva to Apia there are three flights weekly by Air Pacific, while Polynesian does the run nearly every day. Polynesian also connects Apia and Pago Pago with Hawaii, Los Angeles, Nuku'alofa (Tonga), Auckland and Sydney. From the Cook Islands, you'll have to fly via New Zealand, Fiji or Hawaii, and the same goes for French Polynesia.

You'll get far better deals by applying through a travel agency specialising in independent travel rather than through package tour brochure jockeys or directly through the airlines. For some suggestions, see under To/From the USA, Canada, Europe and Australasia earlier in this chapter.

Airline Offices

The following airlines, most of which have offices in several countries, offer service to the Samoas.

Air New Zealand

Australia
5 Elizabeth St, Sydney 2000, NSW, Australia (☎ 223-4111)

Canada
Suite 1250, 888 Dunsmuir St, Vancouver, BC, Canada (☎ (604) 689-3331)

New Zealand
Parkroyal Hotel Bldg, cnr Queen Elizabeth II Square & Customs St, Private Bag 92007, Auckland 1, New Zealand (☎ 357-3000)

Tonga
Tungi Arcade, Taufa'ahau Rd, PO Box 4, Nuku'alofa, Tonga (☎ 21646; fax (676) 21645)

UK
Ground Floor, New Zealand House, Haymarket, London SW1, UK (☎ (081) 741-2299)

USA
1960 East Grand Avenue, Suite 1050, El Segundo, CA 90245, USA (☎ (800) 262-1234)

Western Samoa
Beach Rd, Apia, Western Samoa (☎ 20825)

Air Pacific

Fiji
Victoria Parade, Suva, Fiji (☎ 304388)

Western Samoa
Beach Rd, Apia, Western Samoa (☎ 22693; fax 20023)

Polynesian Airlines

America Samoa Tafuna International Airport, PO Box 487, Pago Pago, American Samoa (☎ 699-9126; fax (684) 699-2109)

Australia
50 King St, Sydney, NSW, Australia (☎ 268-1435; fax (61-2) 299-1119)

New Zealand
283 Karangahape Rd, PO Box 68-423, Auckland, New Zealand (☎ 309-5396; fax (64-9) 275-3890)

Tonga
PO Box 1175, Nuku'alofa, Tonga (☎ 21565; fax (676) 24225)

USA
6053 W Century Blvd, Suite 780, Los Angeles, CA 90045, USA (☎ (310) 646-2675; fax (310) 646-2668)
2828 Paa St, Suite 3185, Honolulu, HI 96819, USA (☎ (808) 836-7659; fax (808) 836-8010)

Western Samoa
NPF Bldg, Beach Rd, PO Box 599, Apia, Western Samoa (☎ 22737, after hours 23097; fax (685) 20023)

Samoa Air

America Samoa
Main Office: Tafuna International Airport, PO Box 280, Pago Pago, American Samoa 96799 (☎ 699-9106; fax 699-9571).
Local Information/Reservations: Ofu, American Samoa (☎ 655-1103); Ta'u, American Samoa (☎ 677-3569)

Niue
Alofi, Niue (☎ 4317; fax (683) 4010)

Tonga
Vava'u, Tonga (☎ 70477; fax (676) 70221)

Western Samoa
Apia, Western Samoa (☎ 22901; fax (685) 23851); Faleolo Airport, Western Samoa (☎ 22606)

Departure Tax

There is a departure tax of WS$20 for every person flying out of Western Samoa, payable at the airport at the time of check-in. You only need to pay the tax once during a 30-day period, so if you'll be returning and leaving again, hang onto your receipt. The American Samoa departure tax is US$3 but it's included in the price of airline tickets.

SEA

Cargo Ship

Many travellers come to the South Pacific with grandiose dreams of island hopping aboard cargo ships, but few actually do. The truth is that the days of working or bumming your way around the world on cargo ships are just about over. All sorts of insurance and freight company restrictions have made such travel difficult.

Those who are serious about trying to take this route should approach the captain while the ship is in port. On some freight lines the captain has the option of deciding who goes and who doesn't. The newspapers in Pago

Pago, Apia, Nuku'alofa, Suva and Honolulu (the most difficult of all) list sailing schedules and routes of the various lines up to three months in advance.

The one exception to this rule applies to those travelling between the Tokelau Islands and Western Samoa. There is a once-monthly cargo ship that sails to and from Apia, providing the only passenger link that Tokelau has with the rest of the world. For sailing dates and fares, contact the Office of Tokelau Affairs (☎ 20822) in Apia, Western Samoa.

Shipping Offices

Following are the addresses and telephone numbers of shipping offices in the area:

Blue Star Line, PO Box 129, Pago Pago 96799 (☎ 633-2767)

Polynesia Shipping Services, PO Box 1478, Pago Pago 96799 (☎ 633-1211)

Kneubuhl Maritime, Hawaii-Pacific Lines, Pago Pago 96799 (☎ 633-5121)

Matai Maritime Agency, South Seas Steamships, Lumana'i Bldg, Pago Pago 96799 (☎ 633-4210)

Yacht

Between the months of May and October the harbours of the South Pacific swarm with cruising yachts from all over the world. Almost invariably, they'll be following the favourable winds west from the Americas.

Routes from the US west coast take in Hawaii and Palmyra before following the traditional path through the Samoas, Tonga, Fiji and New Zealand. From the Atlantic and Caribbean, yachties will access this area via Venezuela, Panama, the Galápagos Islands, the Marquesas, the Society Islands and Tuamotus, possibly making stops at Suwarrow in the northern Cook Islands, Rarotonga or Niue en route. Thanks to the cyclone season, which begins in late November, most yachties will want to stay clear of Fiji or Tonga and be on their way to New Zealand by the early part of that month, (Cyclone Val struck on 6 December, 1991).

Access to the Samoas is almost always from the northern Cook Islands or directly from French Polynesia. Often, yachts will anchor in Pago Pago Harbor to stock up on provisions at one of the local supermarkets because American Samoa has the lowest grocery prices between Venezuela and South-East Asia. From there, most of them stop at Apia and a few cruise around Savai'i before moving on to the Tongan groups.

The significance of all this is that the yachting community is very friendly, especially toward those who display an interest in yachts and other things nautical. Often they are looking for crew, and for those who'd like a bit of low-key adventure, this is the way to go. Most of the time, crew members will only be asked to take a turn on watch – that is, scan the horizon for cargo ships, stray containers and the odd reef – and possibly to cook or to clean up the ship. In port, they may be required to dive and scrape the bottom, paint or make repairs. In most cases, sailing experience is not necessary and crew members have the option to learn as they go. Most yachties will charge crew US$10 to US$15 per day for food and supplies.

The best places to secure a passage on a cruising yacht are, naturally, east of the Samoas. The west coast of the USA is a prime hunting ground – San Francisco, Newport Beach, San Diego and Honolulu are all good. Likewise, it shouldn't be too difficult to crew on in Papeete or Rarotonga.

The best way to make known your availability is to post a notice on the bulletin board of the yacht club in the port (both Apia and Pago Pago have yacht clubs). It would also be helpful to visit the wharfs or wait at the dinghy dock and ask people if they know anyone setting off on a cruise around the time you'd like to go who might be looking for crew members.

It may be a matter of interest that the most successful passage-seekers tend to be young women who are willing to crew on with male 'single-handers' – those who sail alone. Naturally, the bounds of the relationship should be fairly well defined before you set out.

For sanity's sake, bear in mind that not everyone is compatible with everyone else. Under the conditions of an ocean voyage rivalries and petty distress are magnified

Top: Samoan children (GC)
Middle Left: Savai'i man (GC)
Middle Centre: Samoan children, Aunu'u (DS)
Middle Right: Samoan boy, Aleipata, 'Upolu (GC)
Bottom: Young girl & plantation workers eating cacao (DS)

Various flowers (DS)

many times, so only set out on a long passage with someone you can feel relatively comfortable with. Remember that, once aboard, the skipper's judgement is law.

If you'd like to enjoy some relative freedom of movement on a yacht, it's a good idea to try to find one that has wind-vane steering. Nobody likes to spend all day and all night at the wheel staring at a compass, and such a job would go to the crew members of the lowest status more often than not. Comfort is also greatly increased on yachts that have a furling jib, a dodger to keep out the weather, a toilet (head) and a shower. Those that are rigged for racing are generally more manageable than simple live-aboards. As a general rule, four metres of length for each person aboard affords relatively uncrowded conditions.

For those not interested in cruising, yachties have a mind-boggling store of knowledge about world weather patterns, navigation and maritime geography and are a good source of information regarding such things.

Arriving by Yacht

Apia Harbour Yachts arriving in Apia Harbour should pull up alongside inside the basin rather than outside where they may block large freighters.

Entry for yachts is fairly straightforward. Customs will want you to pull up alongside the wharf at Apia Harbour with the quarantine flag raised. Port quarantine officials will come aboard first and will probably check for yellow fever vaccination certificates, although they aren't officially required unless you're coming directly from Africa or South America.

When the yellow flag is lowered, customs officials will board and check documentation. Crew members must be guaranteed onward passage with the yacht or have an air or ferry ticket away from Western Samoa. (An air ticket out of Pago Pago will normally also suffice.)

Pago Pago Harbor The anchorage at Pago Pago Harbor is free for seven days. After that, you are charged about US$15 per month, more or less, depending on the length of your yacht. Those arriving by yacht from Hawaii must present a US customs clearance document from Honolulu.

Yacht people have mixed feelings about the anchorage in Pago Pago Harbor but most agree it's the most unpleasant in the South Pacific. There's a noisy generator that runs all night, the harbour bottom is lined with rubbish, mostly slippery discarded plastic bags, and the tuna canneries belch out a foul nose-wrenching cloud five or six times a day. In addition, boats leave the 'fertile' harbour covered with a worm-like tubular scum that grows to unbelievable thicknesses in a matter of days and fouls depth sounders, anchor chains, through-the-hull fittings and propellers after only a short visit.

Having said all that, Pago Pago is the safest anchorage in the South Pacific, although when a stiff wind howls up and funnels in from the sea, you'll begin to wonder.

Getting Around

This chapter contains information relevant to both Samoas. There are separate Getting Around sections at the end of the chapters dealing with the individual islands of Western and American Samoa.

AIR

The main inter-island transport in the Samoas is provided by Samoa Air and Polynesian Airlines. The former flies between Pago Pago, Ofu, Ta'u and Apia and the latter, between Pago Pago, Apia and Savai'i. Inter-island transport is all on small planes, mainly De Havilland Otters.

Samoa Air has two morning and two afternoon flights between Pago Pago and Apia. Monday to Thursday, the fare is US$60 one way and on weekends (Friday to Sun) it's US$78. Polynesian Airlines also flies daily between Apia and Pago Pago, but the fare is slightly higher. Polynesian flies four times daily between Apia's Fagali'i Airport and Ma'ota Airport on Savai'i for WS$30/57 one way/return.

BUS

Buses are a common method of getting around either Samoa. Travelling by public bus in Western Samoa is an experience that should not be missed by anyone. The buses are vibrantly coloured, wooden-seated vehicles that blast reggae music at volumes that, depending upon your opinion of reggae music, inspire you to either get up and dance or become ill with a throbbing headache.

The biggest problem with bus travel in Western Samoa is that bus services operate at the whims of the drivers. That is, if your driver feels like knocking off at 1 pm, he does, and passengers counting on bus service are left stranded. Never, under any circumstances, rely on catching a bus after about 2 pm.

In American Samoa, the island of Tutuila is served by small aiga buses (pick-up trucks with a bus frame attached at the back).

Although the buses run until early evening – normally around 7 pm – the only buses running on Sundays are those taking people to church. It is also difficult to find transport after about 2 pm on Saturday. In Western Samoa, buses are scarce on Saturday afternoons and Sundays.

Paying the fares will go more smoothly if you have as near to the exact change as possible. The buses make so many stops and starts that the going is slow anyway, but a driver's having to dig for $19.50 in change will hold things up considerably.

To stop a bus in either Samoa, wave your hand and arm, palm down, as the bus approaches. To signal that you'd like to get off the bus, either knock on the ceiling or clap loudly. Pay the fare to the driver or leave the money on the dash as you leave.

Although most visitors don't notice it at first, there is a seating hierarchy on Samoan buses, and a great deal of amusement can be derived from observing the manner in which Samoans seat and stack themselves.

Unmarried women normally sit together. Foreigners and older people must have a seat and sit near the front of the bus. Don't worry about arranging this yourself – the Samoans will see to it that everything is sorted out. When all the seats are full (or a young woman boards and there is no other woman to sit with), people begin stacking up. Women sit on laps of women, men on men (although some mixed stacking now goes on occasionally) and I've seen them stacked up to four high.

When this resource is exhausted, people sit on kero tins and sacks in the aisle. If someone in the rear of the bus is blocked by those seated, everyone systematically files off the bus, lets them off, and reboards without a word. You get the feeling they've been doing this for a long time.

Details about specific routes and fares are provided in the Getting Around sections of the chapters dealing with individual islands.

CAR & MOTORBIKE

In either of the Samoas, hiring a car or motorbike will give you the opportunity to see the sights around the main islands very quickly but will also rob you of some of the unique cultural experiences that can be gained on public transport and without the liability of a vehicle. In addition, the villagers tend to look with a bit of disdain upon those who zip around in rented cars ogling their families and villages while cut off from the reality of it all by air-conditioned luxury. If you're in a hurry, however, it will probably be the most convenient option.

In either country, car rental can also be arranged with locals but they do know how much the rental agencies charge and they will demand at least as much – more if a driver is provided.

Getting around 'Upolu in Western Samoa or Tutuila in American Samoa by car or motorbike is quite straightforward and won't require a daring demeanour or any special skills. You'll normally get by using your driving licence from home but occasionally, visitors to Western Samoa will be required to pick up a local driving licence from the Ministry of Transport (near Magrey Ta's Beer Garden in Apia). You'll need two passport-sized photos and WS$10.

Rental in Western Samoa

You must be at least 21 years of age to hire a car in Western Samoa and tariffs on hire cars are regulated by the government. For a rundown of rental agencies and their daily rates, see under Getting Around in the 'Upolu chapter. There are no rental agencies on Savai'i, but several Apia car-hire agencies allow clients to take their vehicles to Savai'i on the car ferry. Many people take the cars over anyway but doing so invalidates the CDW insurance and can be risky.

When hiring a vehicle, check for any damage or scratches before you get into the car and note everything on the rental agreement, lest you be liable for the damage when the car is returned. Furthermore, fend off requests to leave your passport or a cash deposits against possible damages.

In all cases, renters will be required to pay for the fuel they use. This can be tricky because fuel is only readily available in Western Samoa when the tanker has come in recently. Although petrol is quite cheap – about 60 *sene* (cents) per litre – shortages and/or rationing are not uncommon. On 'Upolu, petrol is available only in Apia, at Faleula (10 km west), Vailele (five km east) and at Nofoali'i, about five km east of Faleolo Airport.

Western Samoa drives on the right. The speed limit within the Apia area and through villages is 40 km/h; outside populated areas, it's 55 km/h. While you're out exploring the island, never leave a car unattended in a village or it's quite possible that some sort of mischief will befall it. If you hit a domestic animal on the road, keep driving; if you stop, you'll suffer the wrath of the offended village which, according to my sources, could mean the risk of personal injury, or possibly the destruction of your vehicle. Instead, note the name of the village and arrange to make fair restitution through the police in Apia.

Rental in American Samoa

In American Samoa, hiring a car will be the best way to reach the more remote parts of Tutuila if you don't have an unlimited amount of time. While the aiga buses frequently ply the main roads, very few traverse the passes over to the north coast of the island where some of the most interesting villages and nicest beaches are found.

There are a couple of car-rental agencies in the Pago Pago area, but you'll pay standard US mainland prices. Few tourists spend more than a stopover here, and it doesn't pay for rental firms to offer discounts and specials on hire cars.

BOAT
Ferry

Ferries and launches connect all the main Samoan islands except Manu'a. The largest car ferry, the *Queen Salamasina* owned by the Western Samoa Shipping Corporation, runs between Pago Pago Harbor and Apia twice weekly. It leaves Apia for Pago Pago on Tuesday and Thursday at 10 pm and returns on Wednesday and Friday at 4 pm but schedule changes are common and during the summer, the frequency often drops to one sailing per week in each direction. The trip takes about eight hours each way.

The fare from Apia to Pago Pago is WS$30 but it's US$25 in the opposite direction (about twice as much) so if you're making a return trip, it's better to purchase a return ticket from Apia and a one-way ticket from Pago Pago. In Apia, buy tickets from the Western Samoa Shipping Corporation (☎ 20935), which is housed in the Ministry of Transport in the government building across Beach Rd from the wharf. In Pago Pago, tickets must be purchased at least one day in advance from Polynesia Shipping (☎ 633-5728), which is on the dock in Fagatogo.

Samoans are usually not very good sailors (neither are a lot of travellers) and the ship isn't all that clean to begin with. The sight of people puking and the general smell and trashy nature of the ship may have effects even on those not usually prone to seasickness. You'd be advised to drop a Dramamine three hours or so before the voyage or pop on a scopolamine patch 12 hours before sailing if you want to avoid the worst of it. The toilets on board the *Queen Salamasina* aren't very exciting either.

Travellers on overnight ferries should carry a ground cover and sleeping bag if they plan to do any sleeping on the boat. If it's

windy or rainy, you may wind up sleeping under the tables in the stuffy lounge, but if the weather is fair, stake out a space on the upper deck and hope that a squall doesn't blow up in the middle of the night. Food and drinks are not usually available on board so bring some goodies, too, if you think you'll be able to eat.

For information on travelling by ferry between 'Upolu and Savai'i, see Getting There & Away at the end of the Savai'i chapter.

Yacht

The yachtie route through Samoa begins in Pago Pago and runs west to Apia Harbour and to the three anchorages on Savai'i. August, September and October are the best months to go yacht hitchhiking around the Samoas. Details about crewing on to a yacht are outlined in the earlier Getting There & Away chapter.

Private yacht owners who intend to cruise around Savai'i should apply for a cruising permit at the government immigration office in Apia. The permit will be issued in one or two days. If you're sailing out of Western Samoa from Savai'i, check out of the country in Apia before leaving the harbour or you'll have to sail back against prevailing winds to do so.

HITCHING

This is fairly easy throughout the Samoas but rides won't generally be very long, perhaps only from one village to the next, and it could take you a good while to go a longer distance. Still, given the abysmal state of the bus service on Savai'i, hitching is the best way to see that island, and it will give you an out if you're caught in the nether lands of 'Upolu or Tutuila after the buses have stopped running for the night.

You might be expected to pay a small fee for a ride so offer what you think the ride is worth – never more than about WS$1 or WS$2 per person – although offers of payment will normally be refused.

Women hitching alone shouldn't have any problems but it might be a good idea to only

Samoan canoe

accept rides when there are women and/or children in the car.

WALKING

Rural roads in Western Samoa are quite pleasant for walking, although you may have to run the gauntlet with the children when passing through villages. For more information, see Hiking under Activities in the Western Samoa Facts for the Visitor chapter.

TOURS

While they provide a quick and effortless way to do the sights in minimal time, organised tours aren't for everyone. They can, however, be an interesting 'cultural' experience, if you don't mind encountering the odd traveller who has touched down in six island nations in two weeks (and is complaining that they're all the same). In Western Samoa, the average cost of a day tour is about WS$50 per person – less if you book as a larger group. Half-day tours to local beaches are run on Sundays, providing something to do if you don't want to read a book, sleep all day, wander around in a daze or go to church.

The following agencies operate tours around the islands:

Annie's Tours – PO Box 4183, Mata'utu, Apia, Western Samoa – offers full and half-day tours around 'Upolu Island (☎ 21550; fax 20886).

Coconuts Beach Club Tours, PO Box 3684, Apia, Western Samoa – puts together unique custom tours based upon individual interests. Excursions around 'Upolu cost WS$15 per person per hour, including 4WD vehicle rental, driver, English-speaking guide, petrol and admission fees (☎ 24849; fax 20071).

Jane's Tours & Travel Ltd – PO Box 70, Apia, Western Samoa – sightseeing tours around 'Upolu Island (☎ 20218; fax 22680).

Oceania Travel & Tours – PO Box 1572, Apia, Western Samoa – is a recommended agency which offers tours around Western Samoa as well as efficient travel services and airline ticketing. It also offers quickie packages to Savai'i (one day, including flights, transfers and accommodation, for WS$225) and Pago Pago (two days, with flights, car hire and accommodation for WS$340). However, when you work out the prices of the individual components, Oceania is not such a good deal (☎ 24443; fax 22255).

Moana Tours – c/o Seb & Rene Kohlhase Sports, Moto'otua, Apia, Western Samoa – is a Lalomanu-based organisation operated by an enthusiastic Swiss expat and his three sons. Tours are mostly confined to the Aleipata area and the main emphasis is on watersports.

Snorkelling trips to Nu'utele Island cost WS$25 per person, including equipment rental; if you include a sail around Nu'utele Island, the trip costs WS$35. Trips around the Aleipata Islands visiting beaches and searching for sea turtles and sea bird colonies cost WS$30 per person for one to 1½ hours. Moana also offers boat charters (WS$80 for the first hour and WS$60 for each subsequent hour), deep-sea fishing trips and sailboard and catamaran rental. Other possibilities include camping on the Aleipata Islands, surfing, spear fishing, Samoan feasts and Samoan language lessons from local people (☎ 22790; fax 22480).

P & F Schuster Tours – PO Box 312, Moto'otua, Apia, Western Samoa – is a small agency which organises tours around 'Upolu Island and transfers between Faleolo Airport and the big Apia hotels: Aggie's and the Kitano Tusitala. You can also make arrangements to be dropped at other accommodation. The transfers meet all international flights (except those from American Samoa) and cost WS$6 per person (☎ 23014; fax 23636).

Retzlaff's Tours – PO Box 1863, Saleufi, Apia, Western Samoa – offers sightseeing tours around 'Upolu Island (☎ 21724).

Safua Tourist Travel – PO Box 5002, Salelologa, Savai'i, Western Samoa – offers excellent cultural and scenic tours including tapa making, kava ceremonies and sightseeing around Savai'i Island. Also, airport transfers and Savai'i day tours from Apia (☎ 24262).

Samoa Scenic Tours – PO Box 669, Apia, Western Samoa – offers full and half-day tours around Apia, 'Upolu, and to Manono Island (☎ 22880; fax 23626).

Samoa Tours & Travel – PO Box 727, Pago Pago, American Samoa 96799 – offers tours around Tutuila Island, village visits and island feasts (☎ 633-4545).

Vaisala Hotel Tours – PO Box 570, Vaisala, Savai'i, Western Samoa – offers airport transfers between Salelologa and Vaisala and day tours around Savai'i Island (☎ 58016; fax 58017).

Western Samoa

Introduction

Western Samoa is Polynesia at its purest and most traditional. There is no other place in the Pacific that has so well maintained its identity in the face of so many outside influences. Even so, the overwhelming and confusing impression visitors get after they've spent a bit of time here is that nothing is as it seems.

The islands are larger and younger than those of American Samoa. They lack the tortured nature of Tutuila and Manu'a, offering, instead, a gentler and warmer aspect. Though the mountains appear less dramatic, the largest island, Savai'i, has recently experienced the forces of vulcanism in near-apocalyptic proportions. Much of the northern slope of that island is covered in lava flows that destroyed property and buried villages as recently as during this century.

Apia, the place first settled by Europeans, is now the capital of independent Western Samoa. Many South Pacific travellers believe it to be the most enchanting of all tropical ports. Beneath its rambling island ambience, though, are the scars of an embattled period of foreign occupation and the subsequent courting of outside support on the part of warring chiefs. As a result, Western Samoa seems more reluctant than other Pacific nations to open up, heart and soul, to foreign interests, but it is still obvious that changes are coming.

The human face is as friendly and fascinating as the land is intriguing and beautiful, but here too, casual observation tends to belie the real character of the place.

It is tempting to have a quick look around and determine that 'contentment reigns supreme': the people who resist the economic temptations of increased industrialisation do turn a healthy and happy face upon the rest of the world. Friendly and welcoming, they enchant every outsider who washes up on their shores. Most visitors imagine they have stumbled across a long-sought idyll and enviously extol the virtues of the Samoans' apparently easy lot.

The poet Rupert Brooke made an observation that is quoted in nearly all discussions of Samoa and Samoans: '...the loveliest people in the world, moving and dancing like gods and goddesses, very quietly and mysteriously, and utterly content. It is sheer beauty, so pure that it's difficult to breathe it in.' In consensus was Robert Louis Stevenson, one of Western Samoa's most famous adopted residents, who wrote: 'They are easy, merry, and leisure-loving... Song is almost ceaseless.'

It's a proud country and a clean one. The rural villages of Western Samoa emanate a friendly and inviting yet well-scrubbed atmosphere. There's hardly a space in any village not deliberately decorated with shells, white coral rock, black pebbles or flowers. There is no rubbish on the ground, no filth, and while few are wealthy, there is no poverty.

Every village has a malae (green) where people, laughing and carefree, gather to play kirikiti or volleyball every day when chores are finished. They sing and play music all week then go to church on Sunday and sing some more.

It would seem on the surface that all is well in paradise, but there is a hidden reef just below. The fact is that the social system of Western Samoa produces as much pressure and mental agony as it does well-being. Beneath the veneer of lightheartedness is a strict and demanding code of behaviour and expectations that stifle individuality, ingenuity and creativity and can produce as much insecurity and psychosis as materialism does elsewhere. Add to this the rapid modernisation currently taking place in the Pacific, and you have a formula for disaster.

While some people accept this situation as normal and learn to deal with it (or even break away from it, causing a whole new set of problems for themselves), others feel restrained and become frustrated. Unable to reconcile their natural inclinations with the prevailing system, they feel somehow inferior. Many are inwardly unhappy and some, especially young men, feel that they can't measure up to societal expectations and become violent or suicidal.

The coming years should provide an interesting lesson and a poignant warning to both Samoan traditionalists and pervasive outside interests that seem as if they would like to homogenise the world. Hopefully Western Samoa will be able to cope.

Despite all the paradoxes (or because of them), it is a rare traveller who doesn't like Western Samoa. There are plenty of sights to see and things to do, and although it is pos-sible to frantically visit most of the high points of one major island or the other in a week, to really appreciate what the country has to offer will require more time.

Slide down a waterfall into a tropical pool, climb over lava flows to a gaping volcanic crater, hike to an ancient jungle-covered pyramid, visit the gateway to the Polynesian underworld, spend a lazy day on the beach or exploring the underwater realm, or just stroll down a country road on a Sunday morning and see the smoke of cooking fires wafting up through the trees. But above all, allow Western Samoa plenty of time and absorb as much as you can of this fascinating place.

Facts about Western Samoa

HISTORY

For the discussion of Western Samoan history prior to partition in 1900, see the Facts about the Region chapter at the beginning of the book.

Early Colonial Period

In February 1900, after the bitter colonial power struggle between the US, Britain and Germany left Germany in control of Western Samoa, Dr Wilhelm Solf was appointed governor and the new caretakers of the colony settled in to rule. The DHPG (see History in the Facts about the Region chapter), the corporate overlord of the country, began to import foreign labour to further its cause in Western Samoa. At least 7000 Melanesians were brought from German claims in New Guinea and the Solomons to work on the plantations; and they soon began bringing in Chinese as well.

As would be expected in such a situation, health and working conditions were deplorable, but of the two groups, the Chinese seemed to fare better because they were actually paid a wage, however minimal, for their labour. In 1908, a Chinese consul was appointed to oversee their affairs in Samoa and the Chinese were given the official and legal status of Europeans. They were also given the freedom to work for whomever they chose, while the Melanesians were restricted to employment with the DHPG.

Although the Germans had agreed at annexation to rule 'according to Samoan custom', they hardly kept their word. Upon assuming the governorship, Solf deposed the king of the time, Tupu Samoa, and determined that the highest power to be in charge of local affairs would be an ali'i (paramount chief). His next official act was to disarm the people, and at the end of his first year of rule, all the gift rifles distributed during the dispute between the three powers were confiscated.

In 1903, Solf established a Lands & Titles Commission, ostensibly to determine land ownership and settle conflicts. What it actually determined, however, was that 35% of arable Samoan land had already been sold to Europeans.

Early 20th Century

Although the first decade of the 20th century was more peaceful than the previous decades had been, Solf continued to ignore Samoan tradition in favour of personal and European interests, causing a breakdown in communications between the Samoans and their colonial rulers. In matters of dispute, the governor assumed the role of dictator.

By 1908 many Samoans had decided they could take it no longer. An official resistance force, the *Mau a Pule* (Mau Movement), was organised on Savai'i by Namulau'ulu Lauaki Mamoe, the talking chief of Fa'asalele'aga district. Its members tried by all peaceful means available to persuade the Germans to see things from a Samoan viewpoint, but Solf was unmoving. Fearing violence, Germany sent warships, and in January 1909 Namulau'ulu and company were exiled to the Micronesian island of Saipan in the Mariana Islands (at the time a German colony).

While all this was going on, nature was wreaking havoc on Savai'i. In 1905 Mt Matavanu exploded and the entire island heard and felt the eruption that devastated the north coast, destroying crops and polluting the water supply. Fortunately, there was enough warning to evacuate the area before it disappeared under the river of boiling lava that surged down from the mountain and no one was killed. The Mormon and Catholic churches in the area were flattened but the flow 'miraculously' separated to spare the Methodist church; it goes without saying that some Catholics and Mormons may have had second thoughts about their religious affiliations.

Eruptions continued until 1910, and the

German administration acquired land on 'Upolu on which to resettle the displaced and famine-stricken Savai'i people.

When Archduke Francis Ferdinand was assassinated in Sarajevo in 1914 and Austria-Hungary declared war on Serbia, Germany was involved in a rush to colonise as many countries as possible before the entire world was swallowed up by other powers. German imperialism, however, was thwarted by Germany's alliances with Austria. When Russia allied itself with Serbia, Germany declared war on Russia. Britain, France and the USA joined Russia and WW I ensued.

At the outbreak of war, Britain persuaded nearby New Zealand to seize German Samoa. Preoccupation with affairs on the home front prevented Germany from resisting. New Zealand occupation continued peacefully under the military leadership of Colonel Logan until 30 April 1920.

Interestingly, when the Mau Movement leaders in Saipan heard of the New Zealand takeover, they decided it would be necessary to learn English if they wanted to deal with the new administration at home. The leader at the time, I'iga, built an outrigger canoe on Saipan and escaped to the American colony on Guam, arriving after only two days at sea. In honour of this crossing, the strait between Saipan and Guam is now known as I'iga Pisa. I'iga finally was allowed to return home and was invited by Colonel Logan to serve as the Secretary of the Office of Samoan Affairs, a position that he held until 1954.

It was during Logan's rule that the ship *Talune* was carelessly permitted to dock in Apia Harbour. Shortly thereafter, 8500 Western Samoans, 22% of the population, died of Spanish influenza. During the crisis, the New Zealand administration refused offers of medical assistance from American Samoa.

Although the Mau Movement's leaders had been exiled, the organisation continued at home, and by the 1920s tolerance for the New Zealand rule was growing thin. It remained a peaceful organisation and many European residents of the Samoas also joined. The administration became tense about its popularity and had several of its European affiliates were banished.

The growing hostility between the factions came to violence on 28 December 1929. One of the exiles, a Mr Smyth, was enthusiastically greeted in Apia by the Mau upon his return after three years away. Armed police took the opportunity to nab some Mau members who were wanted, and a fight resulted. The authorities fired a machine gun into the crowd of unarmed people and 11 were killed, including the movement leader, Tupua Tamasese Lealofi III.

The Mau were officially disbanded and a New Zealand warship was sent to enforce the policy of the increasingly paranoid administration. When a Labour government came into power in New Zealand in 1935, the conflict cooled down and relations between Samoans and the government improved.

Independence

During WW II, US marines stationed on 'Upolu were involved primarily in public works that might have been useful in the case of attack. When they left, the Kiwi grip on Samoa was relaxed and the islands acquired the status of a United Nations Trustee under the administration of New Zealand.

In 1947, the Council of State was established to serve as the executive body of local government, although it was still subservient to the United Nations Executive Council. It consisted of the New Zealand High Commissioner, who was president of the group, and two Samoan chiefs, who were advisers. A legislative assembly was established simultaneously.

Seven years later a constitutional convention met, and in 1957 the entire government of Western Samoa was reorganised, obviously in preparation for the independence of the country. In September 1959 a prime minister, Fiame Mata'afa, was appointed, and the following year a formal constitution was adopted.

A proposal of independence was put before the United Nations in January 1961.

This resulted in a referendum that asked all Western Samoans whether or not they approved of the constitution. It also asked whether or not they wanted independence on 1 January 1962. Of course, the overwhelming response was in favour of freedom from foreign rule. This was the first and last time that the Western Samoan commoner was allowed a say in government matters until 1990, when universal suffrage was adopted. Until that time, only matais were permitted to vote in elections.

The two high chiefs who had served with the New Zealand High Commissioner on the Council of State, Tupua Tamasese and Malietoa Tanumafili II, became joint heads of state. The death of the former, on 5 April 1963, left the latter as the sole head of the newly independent state of Western Samoa.

The official economic plan was to proceed slowly from a subsistence economy towards a cash economy, but by 1965, the vision of imminent prosperity had faded. Labour disputes and a devastating cyclone in 1966 did nothing to improve the situation. Numerous Samoans emigrated to New Zealand, and many more made plans to do so.

Modern Trends

Western Samoa became increasingly dependent on foreign economic aid during the '60s and '70s, and the idea of promoting foreign investment and tourism began to take hold. Roads were sealed, the airport was improved, and the Tusitala Hotel (it has since been taken over by Japanese interests and is now known as the Kitano Tusitala Hotel) was opened to accommodate business visitors and holiday makers. Although they didn't exactly receive the hordes they were expecting, tourism is today one of the country's economic mainstays and is expanding rapidly.

In recent years, rural development programs have been implemented, but forward-thinking individuals have also taken note of the fact that the country's resources are not unlimited and have promoted birth control, education and environmental conservation. Rising prices, recession, one of the world's highest suicide rates (for an independent nation) and discontent among youth, however, threaten to negate any progress, and the difficulties of a young and struggling nation promise to characterise Western Samoa for many years to come.

'Ofa & Val

Serious storms seem to occur on an average of every 10 to 15 years, but in the early 1990s, the Samoas were slammed with two of the strongest and most destructive storms on record. Cyclone 'Ofa, struck Western Samoa in February 1990, bringing winds of up to 250 km/h, killing 16 people and levelling much of the island of Savai'i.

Then on 6 December 1991, just 22 months later, the clean-up was interrupted by Cyclone Val, widely reported to be the planet's 'worst storm in living memory'. Val pummelled the islands for five days with winds of up to 260 km/hour and waves of up to 25 metres in height. Although the property destruction amounted to nearly three times that of its predecessor, the death toll was exactly the same. Again, Savai'i was the hardest hit.

GOVERNMENT

The national government of Western Samoa operates under a British-based parliamentary system which has been revised to accommodate local custom.

Although the constitution of Western Samoa provides for a head of state to be elected by the fono (the parliament or legislature) every five years, the current holder of that position, Malietoa Tanumafili II, was one of the two initial heads of state designated to hold that title for life when the country gained its independence. However, that provision will not take effect until he retires from office.

The position of head of state, known as *O le Ao O le Malo*, is titular only, but its holder does have the power to appoint or remove the prime minister and grant pardons. All official acts, however, are subject to the approval of the fono. Future heads of state will be chosen from a body known as the *Tama'a'aiga* (four royal families).

The 49-seat fono is comprised of 47 members of parliament, headed by a speaker. The remaining two seats in the fono are held by members elected by a small body of naturalised Samoans and in theory represent the interests of ethnic Europeans and Chinese who are citizens of Western Samoa but are not members of any aiga. The beehive-shaped fale fono (the fono building), opened in June 1972, is on the Mulinu'u Peninsula near Apia.

Until recently, voting rights were restricted to the country's 20,000 official matais but unfortunately, their selections were often influenced more by cronyism, obligation or family ties than by professed beliefs, policies or ability. Universal suffrage by all citizens 21 years or age or over was adopted by referendum in 1990, but only matais have the right to stand for election.

There are currently three political parties represented in the fono: The ruling Human Rights Protection Party under Prime Minister Tofilau Eti Alesana (30 seats), the Samoan National Development Party (16 seats) and the Samoa Democracy Le Fa'amatai Party (one seat).

The prime minister, who serves a three-year term, in turn selects a cabinet or 12 ministers from the fono. The constitution also provides for a Council of Deputies to serve as a resource for 'backup' heads of state to act in an official capacity in the absence of the title-holder. Up to the present, however, only one of the three positions has been filled – the one belonging to Tupua Tamasese Lealofi IV, the son of the Mau leader murdered by New Zealand police in 1929.

The judicial branch of government is comprised of four courts – the supreme court, the magistrate's court, the lands & titles court and the court of appeals. Although court proceedings are held in English, they are always simultaneously interpreted into Samoan. Although the system is based on the British, Samoan tradition is also considered in cases where it becomes an issue.

Local governments include administrative districts that oversee the operation of educational and medical facilities, agricultural offices and police. Villages are still governed by the matai system.

Lands held in trust for aiga by respective matais comprise 80% of Western Samoa. They are called customary lands and can be leased to, but never purchased by, other aiga. Although there are still alienated lands within the country, the Berlin Act of 1889 disallowed any land claims based upon trade with Europeans for alcohol or firearms. Mission lands and those currently held by outside corporations and individuals occupy only about 8% of the territory. The remainder is held by the state.

For information on local government, see the discussion of the Matai System under Culture in the earlier Facts about the Region chapter.

ECONOMY

Considerably more than that of American Samoa, the economy of Western Samoa is based on subsistence fishing and agriculture. Diversification is forthcoming, however, and large plantations of commercial products are being developed on both main islands under the direction of the United Nations.

In fact, a great deal of Western Samoa's foreign exchange is provided by the United Nations Development Fund, the Asian Development Bank and the European Community. It also depends heavily on foreign aid from the USA, Europe, Japan, and Australasia and from family support payments from Samoans working overseas.

Emigration to Australasia and North America remains common, but with it comes the stress of living in a fast-paced world, an element to which Samoan emigrants often find it difficult to adjust. The families of many Western Samoans who were born in New Zealand – and are technically New Zealand citizens – manage to collect income support and other social payments from the New Zealand government, although they physically remain in Western Samoa.

Despite all this, more than 65% of Western Samoa's work force is employed by the government, which suffers from high levels of corruption. Furthermore, wages are pathetically low relative to local living costs: the minimum legal wage for employees of private companies is just over WS$1 per hour. It's understandable then that many Western Samoan workers find it difficult to resist trading their professional jobs in Western Samoa for drudgery work at the tuna canneries in American Samoa or an unsettling life in the fast lanes of New Zealand, Australia or the USA.

Agriculture

Coffee, bananas and copra have historically been the most important export crops, and for awhile, cacao was the star on Western Samoa's economic horizon. In 1980, US$5 million worth of cacao was produced and through the 1980s, the export amount increased steadily every year. Although the 1990s have seen waning enthusiasm for this crop, large plantations still cover parts of northern 'Upolu and south-west Savai'i.

Western Samoa's banana export business, which was decimated in the late 1950s by disease, cyclone damage, mismanagement and competition from Latin America, was revived somewhat in mid-1993 when the 12-hectare plantation of the Agricultural Store Corporations began exporting four container loads of bananas to New Zealand each month.

The largest coconut plantation in the southern hemisphere is at Mulifanua, 40 km west of Apia, and in order to get the most out of the land, cattle, which are used primarily for domestic consumption, graze between the trees there. It was first owned by the German government and then by the New Zealand administration. Now it is maintained by the Western Samoan government. There is also a small commercial fishery that provides for the domestic market.

The American corporation Potlatch Forests, Inc, began acquiring Savai'i timber leases in 1968 but abandoned the project shortly thereafter. Japanese companies are

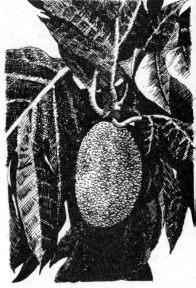

Breadfruit

now becoming interested in the country's timber potential and an Australian firm has already begun cooperating with the Western Samoan government to harvest and export tropical hardwoods, much to the dismay of environmentalists. It's estimated that at the present rate of logging, Western Samoa's forests will have disappeared within 20 years. See also under National Parks in the Facts about the Region chapter.

Western Samoa has traditionally been one of the world's largest producers of *taro niue* (a tasty and easily stored strain of taro), exporting WS$6.9 million worth of the root crop annually, mainly to expatriate populations in New Zealand, Australia and the USA. In July 1993, however, a virulent fungal blight, *Phytophthora colocasiae*, was discovered in the Samoas. (This infestation is a close cousin of the infamous potato blight which killed almost a third of Ireland's population in the 1840s.) By the end of 1993, it had already spread throughout 'Upolu and affected 60% of the crop on Savai'i, causing failure of 40% of the crop. Projections predict 100% failure in 1994.

What taro Samoans do require must now be imported. In order to remedy the problem, the preferred plan is to halt the taro crop for an entire year and sanitise the fields, thereby eradicating the fungus. Unfortunately, it would also play havoc with the Samoan export economy. Fiji is now scrambling to take up the slack in production of taro niue while researchers are pursuing temporary substitute crops such as giant taro (which Samoans don't really prefer), sweet potato and cassava.

Manufacturing & Foreign Investment

Western Samoa's manufacturing concerns are tiny on an international scale but still account for at least 80% of the country's export income. Its best known product, Vailima beer, has been turning up not only in American Samoa, but also in Hawaii and further afield. A Japanese joint venture, Yazaki Samoa, Inc, is now manufacturing automobile components near Apia and has plans for further expansion.

In order to make itself more appealing to foreign investment and joint ventures, Western Samoa has introduced tax breaks for foreign manufacturers who export at least 95% of their production. So far, the keenest takers have been Japanese and Korean firms. The country is also setting itself up as an offshore banking centre, providing a tax haven situation for Asian, European and North American businesses. For information on investment in Western Samoa, contact the Secretary, Department of Trade, Commerce & Industry (☎ (685) 28471; fax (685) 21646), PO Box 862, Apia.

Tourism

Tourism is on the increase and is rapidly becoming one of the country's major earners. Most foreign visitors come from American Samoa, New Zealand and Australia, but Germany, the USA, Canada and Japan are also discovering the islands as a viable and pleasant destination.

Facts for the Visitor

VISAS & EMBASSIES

Visitors entering Western Samoa will require a valid passport and an onward ticket. You'll also be required to provide a contact address within the country, so have the name of a hotel ready upon arrival. Stays of up to 30 days are initially granted but they may be extended by several weeks at a time by the immigration office (☎ 21291) in Apia. Take along WS$10 and two passport-sized photos and don't make any other plans for the rest of the day. You may also need to have proof of hotel accommodation, onward transport and sufficient funds for your requested period of stay.

Permanent immigration to Western Samoa is quite difficult – even for spouses of citizens – but teachers and people with medical and other expertise are always in demand for temporary contract jobs. Foreign investors and those willing to form joint ventures are also welcome on a limited basis.

Specific details are available through British and New Zealand consulates abroad.

For those arriving by yacht, see the introductory Getting There & Away chapter for information on entry requirements. If you intend to cruise between 'Upolu and Savai'i, see under Yacht in the introductory Getting Around chapter for information about cruising permits.

High Commissions & Consulates

The following is a list of the country's foreign diplomatic and trade representatives. In other countries, Western Samoa is represented by New Zealand and British diplomatic missions.

Note that the US embassy in Apia does not issue visas to visit the USA. If you're headed for Hawaii and beyond, pick up your visa beforehand.

Australia
  Western Samoa High Commission, PO Box 3274, 33 Murray Crescent, Manuka, ACT 2603 (☎ (06) 239-6996; fax (06) 239-6252)
Belgium
  Embassy of Western Samoa, 95 Avenue Franklin Roosevelt, 1050 Brussels (☎ (2) 660-8454; fax (2) 675-0336)
Germany
  Western Samoa Honorary Consulate, Spaldingstrasse 70, D-2000 Hamburg 1 (☎ (40) 233818)
Japan
  Western Samoa Honorary Consulate General, Marunouchi Bldg, 4-1 Marunouchi 2-chome, Chiyoda-ku, Tokyo 100 (☎ (813) 211-7604; fax (813) 214-7036)
  Western Samoa Representative Trade Office, Commission to East Asia, GPO Box 354, Tokyo 100-91 (☎ (813) 3280-6666; fax (813) 3344-47449)
New Zealand
  Western Samoa High Commission, PO Box 1430, 1A Wesley Rd, Karori, Wellington (☎ (4) 720-953; fax (4) 712-479)
  Western Samoa Consulate General, PO Box 68147, Auckland (☎ (9) 303-1012; fax (9) 302-1168)

USA
    Embassy of Western Samoa, 11/55th St NW,
    Suite 510, Washington, DC 20005 (☎ (202) 833-
    1743; fax (202) 833-1746)
    Western Samoa United Nations Mission, 820 2nd
    Avenue, Suite 800, New York, NY 10017
    (☎ (212) 682-1482; fax (212) 972-3978)
    Western Samoa Honorary Consulate General,
    Prince Kuhio Federal Bldg, Suite 4315 A, 300
    Ala Moana Rd, Honolulu, HI 96813

Foreign Consulates in Western Samoa

There are a few foreign representatives in
Western Samoa. All of the major diplomatic
offices are strung out along Beach Rd in
Apia, except that of the People's Republic of
China, which is on Tiavi Rd, near Vailima.
Correspondence may be addressed to the
consulate name, Apia, Western Samoa.
Some useful office include:

Australian High Commission
    Tamaligi, Apia (☎ 23411)
British Consul
    B Barlow, NPF Bldg, 2nd Floor, Apia (☎ 21895)
Chinese Embassy
    Vailima (☎ 22474)
French Consul
    NS Paul, Gold Star Bldg, 2nd Floor (☎ 22711)
German Consul
    William Keil, NPF Bdg (☎ 22695)
Korean Consul
    G Carruthers, Carruthers Bldg (☎ 21414; fax
    21416)
Netherlands Consul
    Terence Bethem (☎ 24337)
New Zealand High Commission
    Tamaligi, Apia (☎ 21404)
Swedish Consul
    Herman Retzlaff, Matautu opposite Harbour
    Light (☎ 20345)
USA Embassy
    John Williams Bldg (☎ 21631)

Consuls of other countries are resident either
in Suva, Fiji, or Wellington, New Zealand.

If you're heading to New Zealand from
the Samoas, the New Zealand High Commission will process visa applications in
three days. The Australian High Commission offers similarly rapid service. Yachties
en route to either of those destinations can
pick up a variety of useful fliers detailing
types and amounts of supplies and provisions that may be brought into those countries

CUSTOMS

Tourists can bring in one bottle of alcohol
and up to 200 cigarettes but all sexually
explicit publications or other material the
officials consider objectionable will be confiscated.

As usual, it's illegal to import live animals.
Plant material, vegetables or meat may not
be imported without a permit from the Quarantine Section of the Department of
Agriculture.

MONEY

The two main banks in Western Samoa and
those that change travellers' cheques and
foreign currency are the Bank of Western
Samoa and the Pacific Commercial Bank,
both of which have their main branches on
Beach Rd in Apia. They also have subsidiary
offices in Salelologa on Savai'i. They're
open weekdays from 9 am to 3 pm. There are
also currency-exchange branches at Faleolo
Airport, which are open for incoming and
outgoing flights.

Each morning the banks receive the daily
exchange rates by fax, and changing money
is a straightforward process. They'll
exchange just about any 'solid' currency, but
most preferable are US, New Zealand and
Australian dollars, and pounds sterling.
Travellers' cheques will generally fetch
about 4% more than cash. No one will try to
get the best of you here and there are no black
market-related hassles to contend with.

When you're leaving Western Samoa,
excess tala may be re-exchanged for foreign
currency (normally limited to US, New
Zealand and Australian dollars) in the banks
or at the exchange branches at Faleolo
Airport.

In a pinch or on weekends, cash and
travellers' cheques can be exchanged at
Aggie's, the Tusitala and the Vaisala for only
a pittance less than the official rate. Some
travel agencies will exchange cash US
dollars.

Currency

The Western Samoan *tala* (dollar), which is
divided into 100 *sene* (cents), is the unit of

currency in use. Bank notes currently in circulation come in denominations of WS$2 (note the new plastic banknotes!), 5, 10, 20, 50 and 100. Coins come in 1, 2, 5, 10, 20 and 50 sene and WS$1.

Thanks to Western Samoa's proximity to American Samoa, the most acceptable foreign currency is US dollars, which are normally negotiable in shops, restaurants and hotels (indeed, some hotels quote their rates in US dollars so they don't sound so expensive!). A set of mint coins is available for WS$20 from the Treasury near the Maketi Fou.

Exchange Rates

US$1	=	WS$2.57
A$1	=	WS$1.83
C$	=	WS$1.86
FF 1	=	WS$0.45
DM 1	=	WS$1.54
UK£1	=	WS$3.84
NZ$1	=	WS$1.49

Credit Cards

As usual in developing countries, credit cards – Visa, MasterCard and American Express – are accepted by tour companies, airlines and up-market tourist shops, hotels and restaurants. Those on a budget should only bring a credit card to use in emergencies, or to make cash advances.

To make a credit card cash advance or report a lost or stolen card, Visa holders should contact the Bank of Western Samoa; MasterCard patrons should go to the Pacific Commercial Bank. The American Express representative is Beehive Travel (☎ 21815; fax 24987) in the Wendt Complex at Saleufi, Apia.

Costs

After Fiji, Western Samoa is the cheapest place to travel in the South Pacific, which places it in a particularly good position to attract budget travellers. In Apia, which most people use as a base while exploring the main island of 'Upolu, you can find basic accommodation for as little as WS$15, pleasant budget accommodation for WS$30 and a

filling meal for WS$1.50 to WS$3. On the big island of Savai'i, food and lodging cost a bit more.

If you're prepared to use public transport, you can travel anywhere on 'Upolu for less than around WS$2 and can get to Savai'i for WS$4. The fare from the Salelologa ferry landing to anywhere on Savai'i will be less than WS$3. Therefore, the maximum cost of getting from anywhere in the country to anywhere else in the country (except Apolima) on public transport will be less than WS$10, a bargain by any standard and you'll gain the cultural experiences to be had travelling as the locals do.

If you prefer to use taxis, fly between the islands and hire a car or travel on tour buses, Western Samoa is still relatively inexpensive, but it will be impossible on a bare-bones budget.

Western Samoa also charges foreigners an airport departure tax of WS$20 per person per month, so be sure to reserve this amount when re-converting tala to foreign currency before you leave. If you'll be departing the country more than once in the same 30 days (eg for a quick trip over to Pago Pago), keep your departure tax receipt so you won't be obligated to pay twice.

Consumer Taxes

There is a hotel tax of WS$1 per person per night, but it is normally included in the quoted price of the room. There's also a 10% GST on goods and services which is normally included in marked prices.

Tipping

Tipping in Western Samoa is a no-no, although the current increase in American tourists, who are accustomed to throwing 15% to 20% on the table as a matter of course, may bring about some changes in the higher priced establishments.

TOURIST OFFICES

The newish Western Samoa Visitors' Bureau (☎ /fax 20886), PO Box 2272, Apia, is housed in a modern fale on the reclaimed area. Bureau staff are quite helpful and can provide you with up-to-date information on hotels and happenings around the country. The office is open from 8 am to 4.30 pm Monday to Friday and on Saturday from 8 am to noon.

The bureau publishes a free monthly newspaper, The *Visitor*, which contains advertising by most of Western Samoa's tourist-related businesses as well as some interesting background articles on the country and the society. They're happy to post them out so write if you'd like to get hold of a copy before your trip or make advance inquiries.

POST & TELECOMMUNICATIONS
The main post office is on Beach Rd, Apia, one block east of the clock tower. It was consolidated with the communications office (International Telephone Bureau, or just ITB) after the old post office was destroyed in a suspicious fire in 1986. Postal services, philatelic information and first-day covers (souvenir envelopes with first-issue stamps) are available at the counter between 9 am and 4.30 pm.

Postal Rates
Postal rates are determined by weight so there's no difference between rates for letters, postcards and parcels up to two kg. To post an item to anywhere in the Pacific islands, including Australia and New Zealand, the rate is 60 sene for up to 10 g, 90 sene for up to 20 g and WS$1.80 for 50 g. To North America or Asia, it's 75 sene for 10 g, WS$1.15 for 20 g and WS$2.35 for 50 g. To Europe, Latin America and the Caribbean, you'll pay 85 sene for 10 g, WS$1.35 for 20 g and WS$2.85 for 50 g. Finally, postage to Africa and the Middle East is WS$1 for 10 g, WS$1.60 for 20 g and WS$3.40 for 50 g.

A parcel weighing one kg will cost WS$30.30 to the Pacific islands and Australasia; WS$40.35 to North America or Asia; WS$50.35 to Europe or Latin America; and WS$60.40 to Africa.

Poste Restante
Poste restante is located in a separate office just down Post Office St behind the main lobby. If you're to receive mail in Apia, have it addressed to you (include the name of your yacht, if applicable), Poste Restante, Chief Post Office, Apia, Western Samoa. Ask those writing to you capitalise or underline your surname for filing purposes so there will be no ambiguity.

Telephone
The ITB is open for telex, telegraph and international calls from 8 am to 10.30 pm daily. There's a pay phone in the office which charges 20 sene for a three-minute local call, but it isn't always functioning. If that's the case, you may be able to convince the staff to let you make a local call there for 50 sene or so; however, it's not standard practice. For international calls, prepare for waits of up to an hour, although things are becoming more efficient all the time and it probably won't take that long. Fax services are available upstairs.

The country code for Western Samoa is 685.

ELECTRICITY
The area around Apia is served by hydro and diesel-generated power that emerges at 240 volts, 50 cycles (hz) AC. Outlets accept the three-pronged plugs used on New Zealand and Australian appliances. Use of American appliances would require a fair bit of mutilation of the plug (or an adapter) as well as a voltage converter.

As recently as the late 1980s, rural Western Samoa was still without electricity services. Outside of Apia, especially on Savai'i, everything shut down at dusk, except on nights of a bright moon, when villagers stayed out late socialising by moonlight! Now, villages are being systematically electrified at a rapid pace, and during my last visit, only a couple of Savai'i villages were still waiting for electricty.

Regarding the power supply, the following advice comes from a reader:

Power fluctuations can damage a computer and make your clock run faster/slower. If you are planning on staying for awhile, bring a decent surge protector for anything electronic. I know of a company which has replaced the motherboard in their computer three times!

Stephen How Lum, Australia

LAUNDRY

In Western Samoan laundries there are usually attendants who will wash, dry and iron your clothes, but prices are quite high relative to other costs within the country. For specifics, see under Apia in the 'Upolu chapter.

MEDIA

Western Samoa now has its own TV broadcasts which are operated under contract by Television New Zealand (which supplies equipment, programming, service and staff training) but the system is still in its nascent stages. Limited US network programming is available on station KVZK Pago Pago, due to the proximity of American Samoa. Cable programming is also available in the big hotels.

The Voice of Western Samoa, 2AP, offers a range of radio programming in both Samoan and English. WVUV comes in from American Samoa, as do shortwave broadcasts of the BBC and Voice of America.

Several small weekly newspapers provide minimal coverage of international news and rather more comprehensive treatment of local politics and sports. The *Samoa Observer* (☎ 21099; fax 21195), PO Box 1572, Apia, comes out on Wednesday, Friday and Sunday; the *Samoa Weekly* (☎ 20872), PO Box 1462, Apia, on Thursday; and the *Samoa Times* (☎ 20945), PO Box 2028, Apia, probably the best of the three, on weekdays.

For foreign newspapers, the best source is the gift shop at the Hotel Kitano Tusitala in Apia. It normally has the *Sydney Morning Herald*, the Melbourne *Age* and *New Zealand Morning Herald* just a day or two after publication.

HEALTH

The National Hospital in Apia is inland, on Leifi'ifi St in the village of Leufisa. Health treatment is free to Western Samoan citizens and legal residents but foreigners must pay an obligatory WS$15 for a visit. Before you settle in for that long wait to see the doctor, be sure to visit the 'booking' window and check in so they'll know you're there. Then proceed to the clinic waiting room, but don't forget to bring a book to read while you wait.

If you can't spend a day waiting to see the hospital doctor – especially if you need a tetanus vaccination after a dog bite (a common problem in Apia) – you'd do well to shell out a bit more money and visit a private practice. For recommendations, see under Apia in the 'Upolu chapter.

Prescription medicines are available at the hospital dispensary for a nominal fee. Keep in mind, though, that some pharmaceutical companies ship expired supplies to places such as Western Samoa and the drugs you receive there may not retain their full potency, especially if they're more than one or two years out of date. Check the dates before buying. There is also a chemist opposite the public library on Beach Rd, but supplies seem to be very limited.

Although the staff at the National Hospital are fairly well-equipped to handle tropical diseases, infections and minor injuries, the health-care budget of Western Samoa is minimal and just doesn't stretch to include the equipment and expertise you can expect in Europe, North America or Australasia. If you come down with a serious ailment and can't get home easily, your best bet would be to fly to New Zealand or Hawaii for diagnosis and treatment. The latter, however, can be extremely expensive.

Water

The water that emerges from taps is only certified safe in Apia, and can appear murky at times, especially after heavy rains. Carry some sort of purification tablets or filters if you're concerned about such things.

ACTIVITIES
Hiking

Although Western Samoa isn't especially

known for its walking opportunities, there are still plenty of possibilities for keen hikers and trekkers on all the islands – plantation tracks, sandy beaches, reefs, rainforests and volcanoes all invite exploration on foot.

Even on short hikes, however, the sun and the almost perpetually hot, humid conditions can take their toll. Be sure to carry sufficient water and salty snacks to replenish body elements lost to heavy sweating and always protect yourself from the sun with a hat and an effective sunblock cream. Be sensitive when collecting fruit or coconuts – every tree belongs to someone and visitors should ask permission before collecting indiscriminately.

Some of the most popular routes on 'Upolu include the walks to Pe'ape'a Cave or to the south coast in 'O Le Pupu-Pu'e National Park; the short stroll to the summit of Mt Vailima to see the graves of Robert Louis and Fanny Stevenson; the muddy route to Lake Lanoto'o in the central highlands; and along the coastal route from Falefa Falls to Fagaloa Bay.

On Savai'i, there's even more scope. For short hikes, there's the stroll to Olemoe Falls and Pulemelei Mound or the blowholes south of Salelologa. Longer day hikes might include exploration of the Mt Matavanu area, the Tafua Peninsula Rainforest Reserve or the Falealupo Peninsula. For more of an expedition, you can hire a guide and scale 1850-metre Mt Silisili, the highest point in the Samoas. Due to heavy going through dense vegetation, plan on at least three days for this trip.

Watersports

Snorkelling The best and easiest place to catch a glimpse of the underwater scene in Western Samoa is at Palolo Deep near Apia, but you will also find countless other opportunities all over the country. Although just about any stretch of reef with more than a metre of water over it will qualify as a snorkelling site, the best areas for inexperienced snorkellers are along the Aleipata coast on the far eastern end of 'Upolu and around the islands of Manono and Apolima

on the far western end. Just off the south coast, near Poutasi, is Nu'usafe'e Islet, which offers some of the most diverse corals and fish around 'Upolu.

Strong swimmers and snorkellers can also tackle the turbulent waters en route to the excellent snorkelling around Nu'utele and Nu'ulua islands and between Malaela village and Namu'a Island, all in the Aleipata district. Just be extremely wary of the pounding surf and the sometimes overpowering current that ploughs through this area! On Savai'i, the snorkelling is best at Vaisala and Tuasivi.

Snorkelling gear may be hired at Palolo Deep (Apia), Coconuts Beach Club & Resort (Maninoa), Samoan Village Resort (Apolima-uta) and Moana Tours (Lalomanu), all on 'Upolu.

Diving & Deep-Sea Fishing Although diving in Western Samoa isn't as good as in some other Pacific countries, it's still very good and there are several fishing and diving charters.

A well-established option is Samoa Marine (☎ 22721; fax 20087), PO Box 4700, Apia, with its main office on the roundabout near the clock tower. The proprietor, Peter Meredith, charges around WS$80 for one-tank dives and WS$100 for two. Bring your own regulator and buoyancy compensator. Snorkellers are welcome to come along if there's space, but naturally, only certified divers have access to the diving equipment.

A typical four-hour trip is to the main reef off Faleula, 30 minutes by boat from Apia. Charters to Aleipata and Apolima can also be arranged for negotiable rates; the price will depend largely on the season and the number of divers interested.

Peter normally likes to take at least four people, but during the slow season, he'll accept fewer. In addition to diving gear, he hires out beefy underwater cameras for use on dives.

Samoa Marine also operates pricey fishing charters on a no-fish-no-pay scheme. Moana Tours at Lalomanu village in the Aleipata district of 'Upolu also run deep-sea fish charters using Samoan fishing methods. Half-day/full day fishing trips for skipjack, yellowfin tuna, dolphinfish, red snapper and barracuda cost WS$220/400 for up to three people.

A new but highly recommended option is available at Coconuts Watersports at Maninoa on the south coast of 'Upolu. Diving trips along the south coast reefs with a qualified diver cost WS$112 per person, including all equipment. If you have your own equipment, they're WS$100 per person. If you're not a certified diver but are interested in learning, one-day resort courses, including instruction, equipment and one dive, are available for WS$225 per person. For those who are content with the view from the surface, snorkelling trips cost WS$40, including equipment rental.

If you have your own diving gear but need transport, ask about yacht charters at the yacht club on Friday nights or Sunday afternoons. Quite a few skippers of yachts are, of necessity, also certified divers, and those with credentials to teach and certify others will normally be happy to do so – ask around the harbour if you're interested (but bear in mind that making such informal arrangements could invoke the wrath of established local diving schools). During my last visit, the going rate for scuba certification was US$200 and required a minimum of eight days of instruction. Many skippers will also give classes in celestial navigation or sailing for a reasonable fee.

Surfing & Windsurfing Due to tricky coral and surf conditions, surfing anywhere in Samoa should probably be left to the very experienced. According to those who know, the best surfing and windsurfing in the country is at Fagamalo, on the north coast of Savai'i, followed by Solosolo Beach 10 km east of Apia. Keen surfers may want to speak with Simon Schauble at Samoa Surf Tours (☎ 685-26377; PO Box 225) beside the Office of Tokelau Affairs in Apia, Western Samoa. He can take surfers out on his boat to the good surfing spots around the island.

For a more sedate experience, on Sunday, you can hire sailboards at Apia Yacht Club for use on the harbour. Sailboards may also be hired from Coconuts Watersports at Coconuts Beach Club Resort for WS$20 per hour. With Moana Tours at Lalomanu village in Aleipata, catamarans can be rented for WS$20 per hour or WS$50 for four hours; sailboards cost WS$15 per hour and WS$40 for four hours.

THINGS TO BUY

Aggie's Gift Shop and Kava & Kavings both sell locally produced handicraft items and artwork but their prices will generally be higher than those of the Handicraft Cooperative, which is on Beach Rd between the other two shops, or of the little kiosks at the back of the Maketi Fou.

Kava & Kavings probably sells the largest variety of kava bowls, and if you have the time they'll custom make one in just about any shape you'd like.

On the pavement in front of the Chan Mow supermarket (the former Burns Philp store) on Beach Rd, women sit on the pavement selling necklaces, combs, kirikiti balls and other novelties and inexpensive souvenirs. The Morris Hedstrom store near the corner of Fugalei St and Beach road also has a selection of handicrafts for quite acceptable prices. If you're just interested in poking around and seeing what you can find, have a look in the new flea market along Saleufi St between Beach Rd and Convent St.

The Office of Tokelau Affairs on Fugalei St sells handicrafts from that island group, including stamps and indigenous arts quite different from traditional Samoan work. Look for such interesting (if kitsch) items as coconut flasks, coconut shell handbags, model Tokelauan canoes and piggy banks made of woven coconut frond. In addition, more conventional artwork is available; it's reasonably priced and very well executed.

Island Styles, a sweat shop of sorts, has its factory and principal outlet on Tiavi Rd, not far above Vailima. It sells a variety of locally made fruit wines, souvenir T-shirts, hand-printed clothing, colourful lavalavas and, inevitably, kitsch handicrafts. The most popular items are New Zealand wool jumpers, which sell for WS$25 or so – a third to half of what you'd pay in New Zealand. Island Styles also has an outlet in Wesley Arcade in the town centre. At Coconuts Beach Resort on the south coast of 'Upolu, you can buy brilliant hand-painted T-shirts.

For some other ideas, a reader has the following suggestions:

A souvenir bottle of Robert Louis Stevenson coconut liqueur comes wrapped in a Hessian-like material and looks great. It is available in groceries and gift shops for around WS$30 (less at Island Styles). If possible, look for a fresh bottle. The one I brought back to Australia had lumpy bits.

Local ground coffee appears to be available in all grocery shops and gift shops. Not everyone stocks the whole coffee beans although I did see some at the Hotel Tusitala gift shop. Or why not try a different gift – locally made toilet paper. At around WS$1.40 a roll, it's something authentically made in Western Samoa. And for lovers of good food, locally made chili sauce can be found in most grocery shops. Coconut soap also makes a good gift for the folks back home and is found in most shops around town for WS$2 (WS$4 gift-wrapped). Chan Mow and souvenir shops sell many designs of hand-woven place mats made from coconut leaves.

Stephen How Lum, Australia

'Upolu Island

With a land area of 1115 sq km, cigar-shaped 'Upolu is the second-largest island of Western Samoa, yet it has, by far, the largest population – over 115,000. Despite its relatively small size, 'Upolu feels much larger than most other Pacific islands, with relatively gentle, sloping mountains and large upland areas. Although the bulk of development is along the coast, it isn't confined to a strip a few metres wide as it is in American Samoa, and there are several villages and settlements scattered around the central highlands.

The island stretches 72 km from east to west and up to 24 km from north to south. Apia, the national capital and hub of activity, is situated roughly in the centre of the north coast. This combined with a fairly good system of roads provides easy accessibility from Apia to all parts of the island.

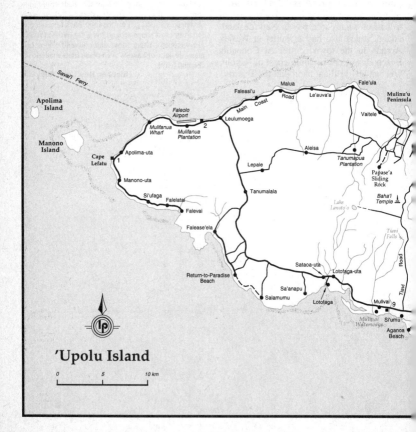

'Upolu Island

In general the climate of the north coast – the leeward side – is drier and more comfortable than that of the windward south coast. Overall, the sunniest and coolest time to visit is between May and October.

What's more, since Apia offers some of the least expensive accommodation in all Polynesia, it may be a good spot for budget travellers to take a break and savour the scene. Especially if you're coming from Tahiti, American Samoa or Melanesia, it will give your budget a chance to recover from the strain it probably experienced in those places.

History

As usual, there are a number of ancient stories about the origin of the name 'Upolu. The most interesting one tells of the marriage of an earthly chief called Beginning and Timuateatea, a daughter of Tagaloa. They had a son they named Polu who, like many young boys, grew bored and lazy during his teenage years. Being a typical father, Beginning thought his son ought to get a job and looked around for something for the boy to do. When he looked over towards nearby Savai'i, he realised that it might be a good idea to send Polu over there to check out the

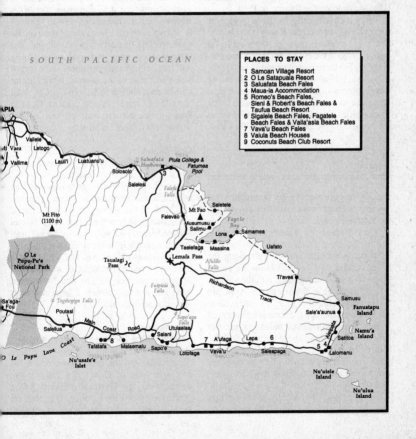

PLACES TO STAY

1 Samoan Village Resort
2 O Le Satapuala Resort
3 Saluafata Beach Fales
4 Maua-ia Accommodation
5 Romeo's Beach Fales,
   Sieni & Robert's Beach Fales &
   Taufua Beach Resort
6 Sigalele Beach Fales, Fagatele
   Beach Fales & Vaila'asia Beach Fales
7 Vava'u Beach Fales
8 Vaiula Beach Houses
9 Coconuts Beach Club Resort

island and ascertain whether it had any inhabitants.

He called Polu and instructed him to pay a visit to his heavenly grandfather, who would provide him with carpenters to help him build a canoe for the journey. Polu refused initially, but Beginning insisted and the boy finally agreed to do the job. Up in heaven, the god Tagaloa noted that Polu in turn had to urge the uninterested and lazy carpenters to help him build his canoe.

When his grandfather asked the boy the name of his home island, Polu replied that it had none. In honour of the boy's coercion of the carpenters, Tagaloa named the island 'Upolu, meaning the 'urging of Polu'.

There is considerable evidence to support the currently accepted theory that before European contact, most of the people on 'Upolu lived in the cool highlands. On north-west 'Upolu there is archaeological evidence of dense inland settlement and there are many more ancient sites in the interior than there are on the coast. It is assumed that missionaries and trading opportunities eventually brought the people down to the coast.

Apia

Apia is the only place in Western Samoa that could conceivably be called a city, but it would be more accurately described as an agglomeration of urbanised villages. Although its population remains around 35,000, its suburbs spread west along the level coastal area and climb up the gentle slopes towards the hills and into the valleys.

Although few buildings in Apia are extremely old, the primary attractions around town include the numerous historical monuments and colonial buildings, most of which are strung out along the waterfront on Beach Rd and on the Mulinu'u Peninsula. In addition to being a good place to shop, eat and relax, Apia also lends itself to casual wandering.

In my opinion, the shabby, rambling, lazy and romantic charm of Apia is unmatched by

any other Pacific capital except perhaps Port Vila in Vanuatu. This is Michener's *Tales of the South Pacific*, Maugham's *MacIntosh* and *The Pool* and everything else that is the legacy bequeathed to Western Samoa by early European missionaries, trading companies and rogues. It is lovely but it is not Polynesia – not unless that term can be extended to include late arrivals to the region – but even so, Polynesia is only 10 minutes away by slow bus.

Having said all that, the modern world is coming to Western Samoa, bringing with it changes that will erode the South Seas ambience that sets Apia apart. Modernisation is forging ahead at a staggering pace (for Apia, anyway) and the number of private vehicles is skyrocketing (in 1993, the city received its first two sets of traffic lights!). Unless the town planners employ discretion in issuing building permits and implement some sort of historical preservation scheme, Apia's future will be as a showcase for the likes of such mutant structures as the Samoa Central Bank, Fesili Motels and the new seven-storey government building.

Orientation

Apia is the service centre of Western Samoa, and it is here and only here that you'll find shops, supermarkets, communications offices, tourist information, travel agencies, etc. Most of the activity in Apia is centred along Beach Rd between Aggie Grey's Hotel and the Maketi Fou, with the business district spreading south from the clock tower into the area known as Chinatown. The wharf lies at the eastern end of the harbour, which is full of yachts between August and November, and there is nearly always a large container ship alongside the docks.

Information

Tourist Office The Western Samoa Visitors' Bureau (☎ /fax 20886) is housed in a large Samoan fale on the reclaimed area on the northern side of Beach Rd (above the remains of the German warship *Adler*, destroyed in the 1889 typhoon). The staff are quite friendly and if you're not in a hurry,

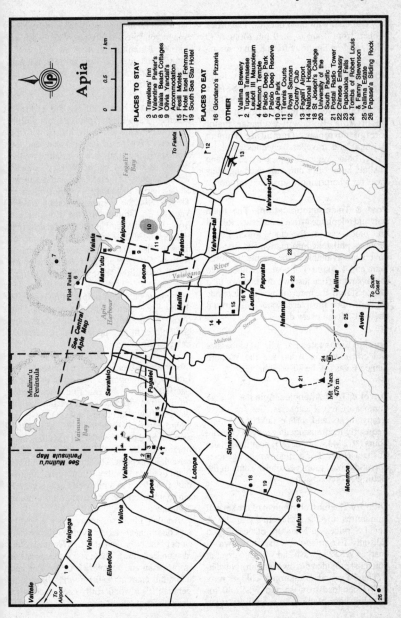

Apia

0   0.5   1 km

PLACES TO STAY

3   Travelers' Inn
5   Valentine Parker's
8   Vaiala Beach Cottages
9   Olivia Yandall's
    Accommodation
15 Fesili Motels
17 Hotel Insel Fehmarn
19 South Sea Star Hotel

PLACES TO EAT

16 Giordano's Pizzeria

OTHER

1   Vailima Brewery
2   Tupua Tamasese
    Leulofi III Mausoleum
4   Mormon Temple
6   Palolo Deep Park
7   Palolo Deep Reserve
10 Apia Park
11 Tennis Courts
12 Royal Samoan
    Country Club
13 Fagali'i Airport
14 National Hospital
18 St Joseph's College
20 University of the
    South Pacific
21 Postal Radio Tower
22 Chinese Embassy
23 Papaloaloa Falls
24 Tombs of Robert Louis
    & Fanny Stevenson
25 Vailima Estate
26 Papase'a Sliding Rock

they can help with most queries. The office is open from 8 am to 4.30 pm Monday to Friday and on Saturday from 8 am to noon.

Money Both of Western Samoa's main banks, the Bank of Western Samoa (☎ 22422) and Pacific Commercial Bank (☎ 20000) have their main offices on Beach Rd in Apia. Both will exchange major foreign currencies (including Tongan pa'anga) and travellers' cheques. Alternatively, both Aggie Grey's and the Kitano Tusitala hotel offer currency-exchange services for a surprisingly small commission.

Post & Telecommunications The main post and telephone office is on Beach Rd just one block east of the clock tower. Postal services, philatelic information and first-day covers are available at the counter between 9 am and 4.30 pm. For poste restante, go to the separate office just two doors down Post Office St from the main lobby. The telephone office is open for international calls from 8 am to 10.30 pm every day.

Foreign Embassies For a list of embassies and consulates in Apia, see the Western Samoa Facts for the Visitor chapter.

Travel & Tour Agencies Apia has a large number of travel agencies, but for travel arrangements and airline tickets the most frequently recommended agency is Oceania Tours (☎ 24443; fax 22255) near the Kitano Tusitala Hotel. For a rundown of agencies operating local tours, see under Tours in the Getting Around chapter.

Laundry The most convenient of the several laundrettes in Apia is Sapolu's Laundry & Legal Services on Mata'utu St near Beach Rd, only five minutes' walk from town. It charges WS$2 to wash and WS$3 to dry, but you must provide your own washing powder.

The 3-Corners Laundromat charges only WS$2 per load to wash and WS$2.40 for bringing your clothing to a semi-dry state,

but it is a rather long walk from the centre. Again, you must supply your own washing powder. Alternatively, there are Faupepa's Laundromat near the National Hospital and another laundry service opposite the Mormon temple.

Bookshops Compared to the literary deserts of Pago Pago, Apia is a bibliophile's paradise. New books, many dealing with the subjects of Polynesia, Pacific issues and the Samoas in general, are available at the Wesley Bookshop in the Wesley Arcade, with branches in Salelologa and Asau on Savai'i and in Pago Pago, American Samoa. There's also the Wendt Bookshop on Mt Vaea St in Chinatown, the Educational Bookshop and the 'Three Corners' area (Mt Vaea St and Vaitele St). A limited number of titles is also available at tourist prices at Aggie's Gift Shop, Kava & Kavings on Beach Rd and the Western Samoa Visitors' Bureau.

If you're only after pulp reading material, the two CCK Family Shopper stores in Apia (look for the brightly coloured flags) are good places to pick up inexpensive second-hand paperbacks.

Libraries On Beach Rd is the Nelson Public Library, in my opinion the best in the South Pacific, where you can find background information on any conceivable Pacific theme. They guard their books jealously, as well they should – most of the Pacific titles are very hard to come by – but travellers may borrow books for WS$5 plus a WS$15 refundable deposit. The library is open from 9 am to 5 pm Monday, Tuesday and Thursday; from 9 am to 8 pm Wednesday; from 8 am to 4 pm Friday; and from 9 am to noon Saturday.

Another library of interest is the lovely air-conditioned waiting room on the ground floor of the New Zealand High Commission, also on Beach Rd. There is a vast amount of information and literature on New Zealand and a fair amount dealing with Polynesia in general. It's a wonderfully cool place to sit through a hot afternoon.

Medical Services The following private medical and dental clinics have been recommended by the Western Samoa Visitors' Bureau. All of the following are in the Apia area:

Apia Medical Clinic (☎ 20942)
Alama Medical Surgery (☎ 24120)
Faletoese Clinic (☎ 23344)
Leavai Dental Surgery (☎ 20172)
LTP Surgery (☎ 21652)
Saleufi Medical Clinic (☎ 21084)
So'onaleole Dental Surgery (☎ 21145)

Emergency Services For emergencies requiring immediate attention, phone the fire (☎ 20404), police (☎ 22222) or ambulance (☎ 21212) services. The all-purpose emergency number is (☎ 999), which will connect you with an operator who will dispatch the specific service you need.

Churches

Christianity plays a major role in Samoan life and the churches of Apia reflect the fact that there's also a certain financial responsibility associated with church-going. Clean and well kept, they dominate the Apia skyline nearly as much as they do in small villages.

The landmark of the city's waterfront is the sparkling white Catholic cathedral on Beach Rd; before the new government building and the Samoa Central Bank were constructed in front of it, the cathedral could be distinguished up to 20 km out to sea. Construction on the cathedral was begun in 1885 and completed 20 years later. The Wesleyan church nearby is also an imposing structure.

A lovely and unassuming building is the Anglican church, the only one in Western Samoa, which is on Leifi'ifi St not far from the National Hospital. Although it's not an old building, it has some beautiful stained-glass work in the windows. The cornerstone inscription states that it was laid on '3 December 1944. The 50th anniversary of the falling asleep of Tusitala'.

When the Reverend John Williams of the London Missionary Society was killed on 20 November 1839, on Erromanga in Vanuatu, he was subjected to the cannibalistic traditions of the Melanesians of the day. His bones were recovered, however, and buried on the site where the Congregational church – Taimane o le Vasa Loaloa or 'Diamond of the Wide Ocean Church' – now stands. Of all Apia's churches, its old-style wooden architecture is the simplest and most pleasant. It is also one of the best places to hear Samoan voices practising hymns and choral presentations. Samoans also like to point out that it was in this church that Aggie and Charlie Grey were married in 1926.

Across the street is the monument to Williams and his 'martyrdom'. It was erected in 1930, commemorating 'the first hundred years of Christianity in Samoa'.

For interest only, you may want to take a look at the large bible monument beside the Apia Protestant church, not far from Aggie's Hotel.

Clock Tower

The clock tower in the centre is a landmark for anyone who's ever tried to give directions around Apia. It was originally constructed in memory of those Western Samoans who fought and were killed in WW I.

It was built on the site of an old bandstand where sailors on incoming warships were serenaded by their compatriots. Its clock and chimes were a gift to the city from one of Western Samoa's most successful early businesspeople, Mr Olaf Frederick Nelson, whose father had come from Sweden in 1868 and opened a chain of trading companies around the country. It was donated in memory of his only son, Ta'isi, who died in the influenza epidemic introduced to the islands by the New Zealand ship SS *Talune* in 1918.

Just to the south-east, on the harbour side of Beach Rd, is another monument – this one 'In memory of our sons who served overseas in the World War of 1939-1945', of which there are more than 60 listed. It was donated by the Mothers Club of Western Samoa, whose membership is listed opposite the names of the soldiers.

Market Area

The Maketi Fou is the centre of activity in Apia and has the biggest and best selection as well as the lowest prices in the South Pacific. It hums 24 hours a day, and to have a stall there is so prestigious that family members take turns staying the night so as not to lose their privileged spots.

The busy, crowded atmosphere is enlivening at just about any time. Every kind of meat and produce available in Western Samoa is sold in this vibrant and colourful place. Here matais gather to chat and drink 'ava and the general public comes to socialise. On the harbour side is the fish market and nearby are kiosks where you can have a very nice main course of fish or chicken and trimmings for less than WS$2. Other kiosks sell ready-made palusami, fa'ausi pudding and Coke bottles full of sea slug innards. At the back of the main market are shops selling tinned foods, bread and handicrafts.

Just west of the market is the central bus terminal serving the entire island of 'Upolu, where colourfully painted wooden buses blast reggae music and compete for passengers on their seemingly endless cycles around the market square.

Also just west of the market is the Hotel Kitano Tusitala, which was built on the site of the boarding house for the employees of the Deutsche Handels und Plantagen Gesellschaft der Sudsee Inseln zu Hamburg (called just DHPG when they were in a hurry).

The main office of DHPG, which grew out of the ruins of Johann Cesar Godeffroy's trade empire, is housed in the building that is now the Western Samoa Trust Estate Corporation on Beach Rd. On the front lawn of the hotel is a pile of stones, once a cairn, constructed in honour of what would have been Godeffroy's 100th birthday.

Late on Friday nights, opposite the market, street preachers emotionally exhort sinners to penitence backed by a swaying and singing choir. It's like a good old US bible-belt salvation show, Polynesian style.

Government Buildings

The most imposing addition to the Apia skyline is the new government office building, a product of Chinese benevolence, which towers above the reclaimed area behind the Western Samoa Visitors' Bureau. Its universally unpopular design was only slightly improved by the addition of the Samoan fale – a last minute concession to fa'a Samoa – which forms its top floor. It won't be long before all the scattered government agencies in Apia relocate to this building, so by the time you read this, the other buildings described in this section may have different functions.

The immigration office on the corner of Leifi'ifi St and Beach Rd was built during the German occupation. On the opposite side of Leifi'ifi St is the Department of the Prime Minister and the supreme court, another two-storey colonial building. It was on the street here that the bloody clash between the heretofore peaceful Mau (Samoa for Samoans) Movement and the New Zealand police brought about the deaths of 11 Samoans, including the Mau leader, Tupua Tamasese Lealofi III, on 28 December 1929.

At 7.50 am every weekday, the Police Band of Western Samoa marches and performs in front of the prime minister's office. Vehicle and pedestrian traffic is stopped and the national anthem is played while the flag is raised. It's a great way to start the day, especially in the 'winter', when the sun is low and the long rays cast a serene morning glow over the harbour.

Samoa Central Bank

Western Samoa's answer to offshore banking, the new Samoa Central Bank also lies on the reclaimed area, not far from the new government office building. According to the architect, this rather appalling structure is intended as a modern representation of a Samoan fale – or more accurately, half a fale. It probably looked a lot better on paper than it does sinking into the reclaimed muck and blocking Apia's harbour view.

Aggie's Hotel

When Aggie Grey died in June 1988, one of the South Pacific's landmark buildings was destroyed to make way for progress. Anyone who knew Aggie's old building will probably be sorry to see what's happened to it, but I suppose the tourists of the future will welcome the comfort to be found in the pseudo-South Seas structure that's there now.

In fact, this addition is just the most recent in a long line of hotel extensions. The original operation expanded in 1954, 1960 and 1965. The immense hand-tied traditional fale that serves as a dining room, lounge and entertainment area was added in 1968, while a pool was installed the following year. Even more rooms were added in 1972, 1973 and 1978. The most recent construction accommodates more than 100 additional guests, which means that the capacity has risen from 20 to more than 300 since the operation began.

Palolo Deep National Marine Reserve

Past the wharf on Beach Rd, near the palagi enclaves of Mata'utu and Vaiala, is the Palolo Deep National Marine Reserve. There is excellent snorkelling in Palolo Deep, and a friendly Samoan named Siaki provides shady and comfortable fales for picnicking and relaxing on a bit of reclaimed land he's dredged out there. Siaki is so committed to his project that he's even named his young daughter Palolo. He's also planning a campground on the site, so if you'd like to camp in a quiet and secluded spot, check on the progress of the project.

If you're going out on the reef or to the viewing platforms at low tide, you'll need some sort of foot protection against the rough coral. At high tide you can just snorkel out. The real attraction at Palolo Deep is the sudden drop from the shallow reef into a deep blue hole flanked by walls of coral and densely populated by colourful species of fish. After one afternoon there, you'll want to return again and again.

The reserve is open between 6 am and 6.15 pm daily. Admission is WS$1 per person. The rental fee for snorkel gear also includes admission. A snorkel, mask and fins cost WS$6 per day. Just the mask and snorkel cost WS$4 and a mask alone costs WS$3. There's a snack bar that sells chips, beer and soft drinks.

Apia Park

Apia Park – 16 hectares of freehold land originally called Solf Field – was purchased in 1908 by Mr Hansen, the general manager of the DHPG, for the purpose of horse racing. It had been agreed that the Apia Sports Club would develop the field and repay him for the land in instalments.

The first race was held in honour of the Kaiser's birthday on 22 October 1910, and meets were held regularly thereafter. The New Zealand administration that took over Samoa at the start of WW I determined after the war that the field was still the property of Mr Hansen, a German, and therefore in enemy hands. They took over the title and decided that it would henceforth be used for recreation.

Apia Park is still used for sporting events – primarily rugby – and in 1983 it was the venue for the South Pacific Games. Annual rugby and football tournaments also take place here and are well attended. If you hope to visit at such times, try to book accommodation in advance. Rugby is played between March and June, followed in turn by football (soccer), field hockey and rugby league. Volleyball and basketball are played in the gymnasium (another product of Chinese benevolence) and tennis courts are open to the public daily. For more information on sport, see under Entertainment later in this chapter.

Mulinu'u Peninsula

The Mulinu'u Peninsula, a prominent spit of land extending from the western end of Apia, seems to serve more than anything else as a repository for political monuments – German, British, American and even Samoan.

German & US/British Memorial Walking along the Mulinu'u Peninsula from the Kitano Tusitala Hotel, the first monuments you'll see (on your left) are naval memorials, one erected by Germany and the other jointly

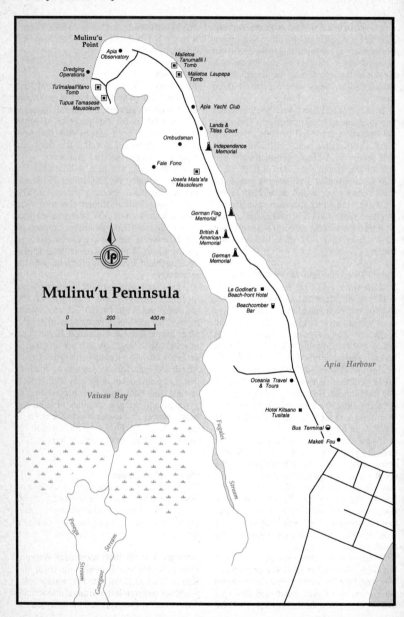

Mulinu'u
Point

Apia
Observatory

Malietoa
Tanumafili I
Tomb

Malietoa Laupepa
Tomb

Dredging
Operations

Tu'imaleali'ifano
Tomb

Tupua Tamasese
Mausoleum

Apia Yacht Club

Lands &
Titles Court

Ombudsman

Independence
Memorial

Fale Fono

Josefa Mata'afa
Mausoleum

German Flag
Memorial

British &
American
Memorial

German
Memorial

Le Godinet's
Beach-front Hotel

Beachcomber
Bar

Mulinu'u Peninsula

0   200   400 m

Apia Harbour

Oceania Travel
& Tours

Vaiusu Bay

Hotel Kitsano
Tusitala

Bus Terminal

Maketi Fou

Fugalei
Stream

Pesega
Stream

Gasegase
Stream

by Britain and the USA. The latter was constructed in memory of those European personnel killed in the civil strife at the close of the 19th century. The German monument is a memorial to those aboard the *Olga* killed in the naval battle on 18 December 1888.

German Flag Memorial This memorial, erected in 1913 just one year before the New Zealand takeover of Western Samoa, commemorates the raising of the German flag over Western Samoa on 1 March 1900.

Josefa Mata'afa Mausoleum Josefa Mata'afa was the puppet paramount chief supported by the Germans after they annexed Western Samoa in 1899. The *loa*, the mausoleum of the Mata'afa family, sits on the lawn in front of the fono. It is not of Samoan design and it seems that the Germans constructed it hoping to undermine the pride the locals had in their leaders by altering their age-old burial customs. The Tupua Tamasese dynasty mausoleum, also on the peninsula, is similar.

Fale Fono Nearly every visitor who sees this building compares its shape to that of a beehive. It was opened on 31 May 1972 to serve as the new fono building. It's a curious construction for Samoa but is architecturally sound, apart from a recent glitch involving asbestos in the roofing, which necessitated temporary closure while the problem was corrected.

Typhoon Monument This is the monument to the 145 German and American personnel killed in the 1889 typhoon.

Independence Memorial This relatively elaborate monument commemorates the independence of Western Samoa granted on 1 January 1962.

Lands & Titles Court The Lands & Titles Court, located in the old fono building, is the entity that settles land rights cases in the event of the death of a traditional owner or a dispute over unverified ownership of land.

Until recently in Western Samoa, land titles were not recorded on paper and land rights were handed down by oral tradition. This method of determining ownership, however, has understandably become rather subjective of late. This is chiefly because Samoan landowners hold great advantage among the Samoan population, automatically inheriting the office of matai and becoming eligible to stand for election to public office.

Apia Yacht Club If you expect a yacht club to exude elegance, this casual little place is considerably less exclusive than its name would imply. It is housed in a shed near the end of the peninsula and welcomes Samoans, expats, palagi yachties and their visitors and anyone interested in the nautical chat that invariably dominates the conversation there. On Friday nights, people gather to drink, socialise and enjoy the WS$4 meals that are served up there. On Sunday afternoon there are barbecues, and sailboard and fautasi races.

Apia Observatory This old German weather station was built at Mulinu'u Point in 1902. On fine days, the surrounding green lawns offer opportunities for picnics or just lazing and reading a book.

Chiefly Tombs On the eastern side of the peninsula, near the observatory on Mulinu'u Point, are the tombs of Malietoa Tanumafili I and Malietoa Laupepa, the father and grandfather, respectively, of the present ceremonial head of state. Gardens are planted around the tombs as a mark of respect.

At the very end of the peninsula are two more tombs, the mausoleum of Tupua Tamasese and the magnificent seven-tiered tomb of the Tu'imaleali'ifano dynasty.

Shelling Forget the romantic image of searching for seashells on white sand beaches beneath the swaying palms. Short of reef diving, the best shelling available on 'Upolu seems to be in the sludge piles left by

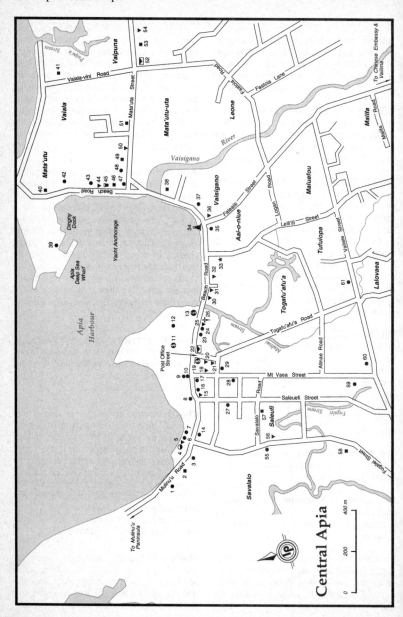

Central Apia

PLACES TO STAY

2 Hotel Kitano Tusitala
38 Aggie Grey's Hotel
40 Harbour Light
41 Vaiala Beach Cottages
46 Seaside Inn
49 Betty Moors Guest House
51 Manusina Lodge
53 Olivia Yandall's Accomodation
57 Ah Kam's Motel
58 Valentine Parker's

PLACES TO EAT

5 Sunrise Restaurant
15 Skippy's
18 RJ's Coffee Shop
20 Isa's Ice Cream & Treats
21 Gourmet Seafood
25 Pelrose Mini-Market
30 Don't Drink the Water
31 Love Boat
32 Otto's Reef/Wong Kee's
36 Apia Inn & Daphne's Coffee Shop
44 Waterfront Restaurant
50 Canton Restaurant
54 Maxine's Quality Cakes & Pies
56 Treasure Garden Restaurant

OTHER

1 Oceania Travel & Tours
3 CCK Family Shopper
4 Bus Station
6 Maketi Fou (Central Market)

7 Fish Market
8 RSL Club
9 Clock Tower
10 WWII Memorial
11 Samoa Central Bank
12 New Government Building
13 Western Samoa Visitors' Bureau
14 Air New Zealand/Morris Hedstrom
16 Flea Market
17 Polynesian Airlines
19 Bank of Western Samoa
22 Post & Telephone Office
23 Wesley Bookshop
24 S V Mackenzie & Co
26 Catholic Cathedral
27 Tivoli Cinema
28 Samoa Air
29 Downtown CCK
30 Kava & Kavings
33 Police Station
34 John Williams Memorial
35 New Zealand High Commission
37 Australian High Commission
39 Harbour Master & Ferry Landing
42 Apia Squash Courts
43 Western Samoa Shipping Corporation
45 Magrey Ta's Beer Garden
47 Taxi Stand
48 Sapolu's Laundry
52 Matu'uta-uta Post Office & Bank of
   Western Samoa
55 Office of Tokelau Affairs
59 Educational Bookshop
60 3-Corners Laundromat
61 Mt Vaea Club

the massive dredging going on at the end of the Mulinu'u Peninsula. There you can find a good selection of cowries, cones, helmets and a variety of more exotic specimens. Having said that, once you've had a look at the shells – if they're not in imminent danger from the dredging operation – please leave them in place for the next person that happens to come along.

Places to Stay

Except where stated that tax is included, all prices in this section are subject to the addition of 10% GST.

Places to Stay – bottom end

In Apia, several budget establishments offer the lowest-priced accommodation available. They are all nice and none really stands out

above the others on all counts. One of the cleanest, *Valentine Parker's* (☎ 22158; fax 20886), PO Box 395, Apia, is also the furthest from the city centre. Even so, quite a few travellers swear by it. Valentine charges WS$25 per person for a double room with shower and toilet. Single/double rooms cost WS$20/30 with access to communal toilets and cold-water showers but no cooking facilities.

Another popular place is *Betty Moors Guest House* (☎ 21085; fax 20886), PO Box 18, Apia, which is good if you just want a cheap place to drop yourself after a day of sightseeing. Its primary advantage over Valentine's is that the route back from the restaurants and bars is short and well lit and that Betty herself is a very friendly and interesting person. Betty charges WS$20 per person for a cubicle-like room; try to get one with a window.

There are, however, a few disadvantages, the biggest ones being the lack of fans to stir the normally stifling stagnant air and the noise problem caused by the cubicle layout. Every whisper can be heard throughout the building, so you're obliged not to make noise. Another quirk is the light switches, which are all in the hallway – people are frequently being awakened at night by other guests' incorrect identification of light switches! Doors don't lock very well, either, but Betty will keep an eye on things while you're out and will also watch your luggage while you're travelling around Savai'i.

Don't plan on settling in for too long, however. Victims in the early stages of Polynesian paralysis report that Betty has evicted them in hopes of curing the condition before it becomes too serious!

The third alternative is the odd blue and pink striped *Olivia Yandall's Accommodation* (☎ /fax 23465), PO Box 4089, Apia, in a garden setting near Apia Park in Mata'utu. It's friendly but isn't as clean or well-kept as it could be and several readers reported having to ask for clean sheets when they checked in. Six-bed dormitory style fales cost WS$15 per person with shared bathroom and toilet facilities. Showers are cold, but you'll find that a blessing in this near equatorial climate. Individual fales with kitchen and private facilities cost WS$44 single or double occupancy.

The most popular inexpensive hotel, which is especially viable for two sharing a room, is the *Seaside Inn* (☎ 22578; fax 22918), PO Box 325, Apia, between Aggie's and the wharf. It's very convenient – only a five-minute walk from town – and the friendly owners seem to know exactly the sort of place travellers are seeking. Nice clean rooms with bath and toilet cost just WS$33/44/55 a single/double/triple, including breakfast and room tax. Rooms without facilities are WS$31/42, also including breakfast. Outside, there's a comfortable sitting area and guests have access to cooking and laundry facilities, and discounts

are available during slow periods (which are rare!). Advance bookings are advised; otherwise, you may have to wait a couple of days for a space.

Another highly recommended option is the friendly *South Sea Star Hotel* (☎ /fax 21667), PO Box 800, Apia, in Alafua village. It occupies a leafy setting just a two-minute walk from the University of the South Pacific campus. Clean and comfortable rooms with shared facilities cost only WS$30/40. A continental breakfast costs an additional WS$7 and an English breakfast is WS$10. Other meals are available in the attached Cappuccino Club restaurant for WS$15 for lunch and WS$25 for dinner. To get there, take a taxi (WS$4) or the Alafua bus (40 sene) from the Maketi Fou.

Places to Stay – middle

In Apia, most middle-range hotels accept credit cards.

When the Seaside Inn is full, some people stay at the nearby *Harbour Light* (☎ 21103; fax 20110), PO Box 5214, Apia, while awaiting a room. Units are self-contained, with air-conditioning and private facilities, but they're a bit expensive at WS$62/75 a single/double.

Equally central but a step down in quality is the newly renovated *Ah Kam's Motel* (☎ 20782; fax 20886), PO Box 1299, Apia. Single/double rooms with fan and private facilities cost WS$75/100, including tax. A suite costs WS$125/150 for singles/doubles, WS$200 for triples.

Another handy place is the new *Manusina Lodge* (☎ 20909; fax 20886), in Mata'utu-uta, also known as the 'Rugby Club' due to its proximity to Apia Park and its popularity with rugby players and patrons. On one wall are the autographs of the entire Manu Samoa Rugby team which played in the 1991 World Cup match and, typical of a rugby club, it also has a well-patronised bar. Air-conditioned rooms with private toilet and shower cost WS$75/100. The owner will sometimes allow guests to use the kitchen facilities to prepare their own meals.

Out on the quiet Mulinu'u Peninsula is *Le*

Godinet Beachfront Hotel (☎ 25437; fax 25436), PO Box 9490, Apia, the only Apia hotel which is right on the water (in spite of the name, it's not much of a beach). Air-conditioned rooms with private facilities cost WS$100/125 a single/double. Le Godinet is actually better known for being one of Apia's finest restaurants, serving unforgettable lobster and seafood dishes and a super Polynesian buffet on Friday nights.

As evidence of excessive tolerance by the Apia Planning Commission, take a look at the new *Fesili Motels* (☎ 26476; fax 22517) opposite the National Hospital. This monstrosity comes complete with a supermarket, convenience store, snack bar, bank, rooftop disco, Chinese lanterns, a double-decker bus and assorted hearses. Although it professes to be 'ideal for groups or families', accommodation seems to take a back seat to everything else – the arch over the entry reads 'Fesili Investments' – and the primary interest seems to come from the youth of Apia. If for some reason you do want to stay here, single/double rooms with private facilities, TV, fridge and air-conditioning cost WS$100/125.

If you arrive in the height of summer, you may want to consider staying at *Le Tiara Village* (☎ 22400), PO Box 446, Apia, which lies in the cooler highlands four km up the hill from the centre of Apia. It's a bit isolated but the lush, quiet surroundings are pleasant and the management is exceptionally friendly. The fully self-contained fales accommodate one or two people and cost WS$138. There's a great view toward the sea and as a bonus, you could play chess on the striking linoleum floors.

The *Travellers' Inn* (☎ 26055; fax 20110), opposite the Mormon temple, is a 20-minute walk or five minutes by bus from town. It's primarily used by visiting church dignitaries but provides a quiet alternative to in-town accommodation. Rooms with fan and communal facilities cost WS$50/63. Add air-conditioning, a fridge, toilet and shower and it jumps to WS$63/75. All room prices include tax and breakfast. Credit cards are not accepted.

Places to Stay – top end

The main up-market places to stay in Apia, *Aggie Grey's* (normally known as just Aggie's) and the *Kitano Tusitala*, lie at opposite ends of Beach Rd. Room standards at either hotel compare to upper middle range anywhere, but those at Aggie's are a bit more interesting, especially the fales named after movie stars who stayed there while filming in Samoa. (During my last visit, a German film company was continuing the tradition by filming the mini-series *Flugt ins Paradis* – Escape to Paradise – and using tourists as extras.) Bus transport is available between the airport and either hotel for WS$6.

Aggie Grey's Hotel (☎ 22880), PO Box 67, Apia, is loaded down with Australians, Americans, Germans and New Zealanders on package tours while the staff are all carefully selected Samoans who attempt to graciously cater to the mostly Western clientele. However, it can seem a bit stilted at times.

A standard single room costs WS$188, doubles are WS$212 and triples cost WS$238, with discounts for children under 16. For fale accommodation, add WS$50 per night to the above prices. Rooms in the new wing at the front (no children under 16 permitted) cost WS$275/300/325. To all these rates, add 10% GST.

Meal plans cost an additional WS$88 per person per day (but it would be a shame to be confined to eating at the hotel and miss out on Apia's other offerings). For guests, complementary afternoon tea, including hot drinks, cakes and sandwiches, is served from 3 to 4 pm.

The pleasant and worthwhile fale bar, which is open from 9 am to 11 pm daily, offers nightly Polynesian musical entertainment. On Wednesday, don't miss the famous fiafia with dancing, singing and music by Aggie's relatives and the hotel employees. If you watch from the bar, you won't be required to buy dinner, and the entertainment value is certainly worth the price of drinks. For a slightly more elegant bar scene, go to Le Kionasina at the front of the hotel, which is open from 3 to 11 pm Monday to Saturday.

Aggie Grey

The daughter of William Swann, a Lincolnshire chemist who'd migrated to Samoa in 1889, and Pele, a Samoan girl from Toamua village, Agnes Genevieve Swann was one of the Pacific's most famous personages and did more for Western Samoan tourism than any other individual.

In 1917 she married Gordon Hay-Mackenzie, the recently arrived manager of the Union Steamship Company. They had four children before Gordon died eight years later. Soon afterwards she married Charlie Grey, who was, unfortunately, a compulsive gambler. Charlie succeeded in losing everything they had and Aggie had to look for some means of supporting the family.

While Western Samoa was going through some tumultuous times with New Zealand rule, Robert Easthope, known as 'Obliging Bob', operated the International Hotel in western Apia which was dismantled upon his death in 1932 and rebuilt in the eastern end of town near the Vaisigano River. In 1942, the American soldiers arrived in Apia (carrying 'unimaginable wealth' in their long-awaited palagi ships of Samoan myth), and Aggie saw an opportunity to earn a little money. With a US$180 loan, Aggie bought the building and began selling hamburgers and coffee to US servicemen for 25 cents each.

Response to the business was overwhelming, and although supplies were difficult to come by during WW II, Aggie managed and built up an institution which became famous Pacific-wide as a social gathering place for war-weary soldiers. She even succeeded in getting through the New Zealand-imposed prohibition of alcoholic beverages, securing them for her customers by unofficial methods.

When James Michener published his enormously successful *Tales of the South Pacific*, Aggie Grey was so well known throughout that realm that it was widely assumed that she was the prototype for the character of the Tonkinese madam, Bloody Mary. Michener admits to visiting Aggie's whenever he could to get away from 'unutterably dull and militarily stuffy' Pago Pago, where he was frequently stationed, but he denies that anything but the good bits of Bloody Mary were inspired by Aggie Grey. In an interview with Aggie's biographer, Nelson Eustis, Michener said that when he returned to New York to edit the manuscript of his first book and needed to know what Bloody Mary would do or say, he used Aggie as a reference.

Over the next few decades, the snack bar expanded into a hotel and numerous celebrities stayed there while filming or travelling in the area. (Many of the fale rooms are named after famous people who stayed there.) Aggie wanted it to be a place visitors to Western Samoa could feel was their home. It's a safe bet to say that the price of 'calling it home' will preclude most long-term travellers from doing so, but nearly all visitors will find themselves there time and again for drinks at the pleasant bar, Wednesday night at the fiafia, delicious Samoan coffee, and wonderful 'splurge' buffet meals.

Aggie Grey

When Aggie died in June 1988, at the age of 91, the hotel was undergoing another expansion. Unfortunately, the rambling old style of the place is being abandoned for a more modernistic high-rise approach, apparently because multi-storey was the only way to accommodate the growing number of tourists descending on the place. Hopefully this destruction of historic character won't be too often repeated throughout Apia or the town will certainly lose much of the charm that is today its greatest appeal.

If you'd like to read more about Aggie Grey and her establishment, pick up a copy of her biography, *Aggie Grey of Samoa*, by Nelson Eustis, which is available for a reasonable price at her hotel gift shop and at several shops around Apia. ∎

The other big hotel, *Hotel Kitano Tusitala* (☎ 21122; fax 23652), PO Box 101, Apia is a bit less of a tourist venue and more of a business traveller's hotel. More elegant in its atmosphere, it is also quieter, but the staff aren't as carefully selected as those at Aggie's and there have been communication problems of sorts. Standard, air-conditioned single/double/triple rooms cost WS$150/200/225. 'Deluxe' rooms with TV cost WS$200/250/300. Children can stay for free. The swimming pool and tennis courts figure prominently in the overall theme. The Tusitala's fiafia is on Thursday nights and costs WS$35 per person with the meal.

A third up-market option, which actually straddles the middle and upper price ranges, is *Vaiala Beach Cottages* (☎ 22202; fax 22713), PO Box 2025, Apia, not far from Vaiala Beach east of Apia. Self-contained cottages, complete with cooking facilities, cost WS$163/188 a single/double, plus WS$25 per additional person up to four people. The location is extremely quiet and the ambience friendly but be warned that it's a dark walk back from town at night and there are quite a few canine sentries along the way.

Finally, there's the three-storey *Hotel Insel Fehmarn* (☎ 23301; fax 22204), PO Box 3272, Apia, at Moto'otua on Falealili St (further up the hill, this becomes Tiavi Rd or the Cross-Island road). It's named after the German Baltic Sea island where the grandfather of the present owner was cast adrift on a roof beam during a storm on 13 November, 1872; after 27 hours at sea, the 12-year-old was rescued by a French brig.

With large air-conditioned rooms, balconies, TV and private facilities, it's a quiet but rather stark alternative to the hotels nearer the shore. Single/double rooms cost WS$163/188; the 3rd-floor rooms are the nicest, affording views across Apia and out to sea. The hotel also has a swimming pool, laundromat and restaurant but they see little activity.

Places to Stay – out of town

An increasing number of places to stay are springing up around 'Upolu Island, including a mushroom crop of bare bones beach fales and several fully-fledged resorts.

Beach Fales Travellers will find a concentration of basic beach fales around the eastern end of 'Upolu, mainly in the Aleipata area. Locals have seen a money-spinning opportunity in these basic and easily-constructed shelters – they consist of little more than a raised wooden floor sheltered by a roof – so expect many more such places to spring up in the near future.

While this sort of grass roots tourism has brought money to villages which lack a strong economic base, the down side is that the competition has also created bitter feelings and envy between once cooperative Samoans – some of whom belong to the same family – and at times, you may sense the tension. Opportunistic theft is also becoming a problem in previously tranquil areas, so the fales are for sleeping only. Luggage and valuables may be stored in the homes of fale owners.

Just 25 minutes east of Apia is *Saluafata Beach Fales* (☎ 40216), PO Box 820, Apia, down by the shore at the village of Saluafata. The eight beach fales and four rooms in the family house (which is not on the beach) cost WS$10 per person. Day access to the beach, which offers good snorkelling around the offshore islet, costs WS$1 per person. Bookings for accommodation or meals at the associated restaurant (WS$5 per meal) should be made between 6 am and 5 pm Monday to Saturday. Book into the fales at the restaurant on the main north coast road.

The greatest density of beach fales is at Lalomanu village in the Aleipata district. In one cluster, which is strung out along the finest beach in Western Samoa, are the recommended *Romeo's Beach Fales* (☎ 20878; fax 20886), *Sieni & Robert's Beach Fales* (☎ 20878; fax 20886) and *Taufua Beach Resort*. All of these places charge WS$25 per person and WS$15 for meals (the meals at Sieni's should be avoided!), which is perhaps a bit high for what amounts to camping on the beach. In all cases, sleeping mats and mosquito nets are supplied.

Further west, near the villages of Saleapaga and Lepa, are several more bunches of fales. Granted, they're situated on a lesser beach, but the accommodation is identical to those at Lalomanu. *Sigalele Beach Fales* charges WS$15 per person and an additional WS$5 for meals. Just beside them are the *Fagatele Beach Fales* (☎ 20886; fax 20878), which cost WS$20/30 for a single/double and WS$5 for meals, and *Vaila'asia Beach Fales*, which cost WS$15 per person plus WS$5 for meals.

Visitors to this area should be aware that beer is not permitted in this village (although the rule is relaxed for foreigners). Non-compliance is punished with a fine of five pigs. Anyone who can't pay the fine is banished from the village for life without possibility of appeal so think twice before you offer someone a beer!

For a slightly different angle, there's the *Maua-ia Accommodation* (☎ 22790; fax 22480), which is run by Urs, a Swiss expatriate, and his three sons. It consists of a caravan opposite Aleipata Beach which contains a fridge and stove and sleeps up to three people for WS$40/50 a single/double, WS$60 a triple. There have been thefts reported here, so keep your valuables away from the windows or store them in the owner's home.

For bicycle hire, Urs charges WS$12 per day for a Chinese one-speed bike or WS$18 per day for a multi-geared mountain bike. The owner also operates a variety of boat charters and tours under the name of Moana Tours. For specifics, see under Tours in the Getting Around chapter and under Watersports in the Western Samoa Facts for the Visitor chapter.

Resorts – bottom end On a decent beach at Tafatafa on the south coast are the *Vaiula Beach Houses* (☎ 22808; fax 20886), PO Box 6600, Apia, owned by the Peterson family. The complex includes two four-room homes which cost WS$15 per room and several open fales for WS$10 each. Camping

in your own tent, including use of the resort facilities, costs WS$5 per tent and picnickers are charged WS$5 per car. If you just want to swim or lie on the beach, you'll pay WS$2 per car. There are no restaurants or shops nearby but guests may use the communal cooking facilities, so bring food from elsewhere. Mosquito nets are also available.

Resorts – middle Near the village of Vavau on the south coast, the *Vavau Beach Fales* (☎ 20954; fax 22680) were developed by the Pacific Regional Tourism Development Programme with financial aid from the EC and are managed by Vavau village. For a poorly maintained self-contained unit, without any other facilities, they charge WS$160/184 single/double. This is far too much for what's on offer and provides evidence that someone is out of touch with reality.

The beach is beautiful, however, so if you want to be alone, you won't have trouble getting a booking and with some persistence, more reasonable prices may be negotiated. There's no restaurant or shop, so all food must be brought from elsewhere. Currently, access is only from the village of Vavau; the signposted route down from the main road was damaged in 1993 and ends at the lip of a gaping ravine.

More affordable and convenient is *O Le Satapuala Beach Resort* (☎ 42212; fax 42386), which lies just one km east of Faleolo Airport and likes to refer to itself as 'the airport hotel'. Enclosed beach fales with fans, kitchens and private facilities cost WS$59/79 for single/double occupancy. Basic open-sided fales *(faleo'o)* are WS$20 per person for a private fale or WS$10 for dormitory-style shelter, either option including use of sleeping mats and mosquito nets. Camping on the site costs WS$5 per person and a meal plan is available for WS$50 per person per day. If you'd prefer a cultural experience, home stays may be arranged for WS$50 per person, including bed, transport and meals.

Another program, which is a bit slow getting off the ground, is a two-night Samoan survival training programme on Apolima

Island. For WS$300 per person, participants are taken to Apolima and taught how to live off the land, Samoan style.

The attached bar and restaurant are quite popular with locals and expats, especially on Thursday, Friday and Saturday nights, when there's live music and no cover charge. Request octopus in coconut milk! On Fridays, there's a WS$5 barbecue and on Sundays, they stage a well-attended Samoan umu lunch for WS$20 per person.

Resorts – top end On the south coast at Maninoa village is *Coconuts Beach Club & Resort* (☎ 24849; fax 20071), PO Box 3684, Apia, an up-market resort. It's run by Barry and Jenny (Afa and Sieni) Rose, a couple of escaped Los Angeles lawyers who did a computer search for paradise and came up with Western Samoa. The result is Coconuts, a refreshingly unpretentious resort constructed of native materials in a design which seems remarkably sympathetic to its setting.

The main complex, which is buried in the forest, is reminiscent of a jungle treehouse. The magical upper level rooms, all with large private balconies, air-conditioning and double bathtubs, cost WS$340/375 a single/double while rooms on the lower floor are WS$275/310. If you prefer the sand at your front door, individual beach-front fales cost WS$390/438 for singles/doubles. Away from the beach, standard air-conditioned bungalows are WS$210/235. For the more budget-minded, there are three airy fan-cooled bungalows with private facilities for WS$138 a double. In addition, home stays in Maninoa village may be arranged for WS$10 to WS$20. Due to Coconuts' increasing popularity, advance bookings are strongly advised.

Even if Coconuts is beyond your accommodation budget, it's worth visiting Sieni's 3-Stool beach bar and Mika's American Bistro restaurant, where you'll find a variety of typically American and European dishes, including the best lobster you'll ever taste (I promise). The best night to go is Saturday when the staff and friends from five local villages enthusiastically stage a fiafia, which

is attended by local people as well as hotel guests.

In addition, Coconuts has its own diving and snorkelling shop and tour company, operated by Roger and Gayle. Their unusual jungle boat cruise is certainly one of the highlights of Western Samoa – a cruise aboard the *African Queen* through the beautiful and mysterious mangrove-lined waterways around the village of Mulivai. Car hire is also available. For further information on their offerings, see under Watersports in the earlier Western Samoa Facts for the Visitor chapter; Tours in the Getting Around chapter; and under Getting Around later in this chapter.

At Cape Fatuosofia on the western tip of 'Upolu is the other up-market option, the new German-run *Samoan Village Resort* (☎ 20749; fax 22468). It occupies a beautiful setting but unfortunately, the beach is rather poor. The standard double rate is WS$200 for self-contained bungalows for a single night or WS$140 per night for multiple nights. Deluxe fales in the garden cost WS$250 and on the shore, WS$375. For each additional person, up to four people per bungalow, the charge is WS$15. At the time of writing, seven units were open but there are plans for 32. There's no restaurant yet but supplies are available in the village shop at Apolima-uta. Bicycles, snorkelling gear and small canoes may be used by guests free of charge. For an airport transfer, the charge is WS$25.

Places to Eat

Breakfast The cheapest and one of the best places for breakfast is the *Maketi Fou*, and every visitor should eat there at least once for the cultural value if nothing else. Don't miss fresh koko Samoa (WS$1) and Samoan pancakes (10 sene each). If you're really hungry, try fish or chicken for WS$1.50 and wash it down with coffee, tea or koko Samoa.

The best coffee in town is the locally grown variety, which to my knowledge is served only at *Aggie Grey's Hotel*, but it costs WS$4 per cup! In the fale restaurant at Aggie's, a buffet continental breakfast of

Samoan pancakes, fruit, cereal, toast and hot drinks will cost WS$12 while a full English or American breakfast is WS$20. (Or for a real treat, go to the hotel gift shop where you can pick up a slice of toast bedecked with cold tinned spaghetti – yum yum!). Similar fare is available at the *Kitano Tusitala Hotel* where a continental breakfast costs WS$12, a full English or American breakfast is WS$18, a full stack of pancakes costs WS$10 and a bottomless cup of coffee is WS$3.

If your budget doesn't stretch to that, another place for a good Western-style breakfast is *Daphne's Coffee Shop*, on the ground floor of the Ioane Viliumu building. It has cakes and doughnuts as well as eggs on toast, ham and bacon, but the coffee is not very good. A similar place (but with better coffee) is *Josie's Coffee Lounge* in the NPF (National Provident Fund) building near Polynesian Airlines. At lunch time, both of these places also serve snacks and sandwiches.

Lunch & Snacks Again, the *Maketi Fou* has the least expensive (but probably the healthiest) lunches in town, including chicken, beef, Chinese and curry dishes for as little as WS$1.50. Another good cheap option is the cafeteria at the Pelrose Mini-Market beside the Catholic cathedral. For WS$2, you can choose between hearty portions of noodles, beef or chicken curry, fried chicken and other dishes. They're also good for breakfast.

Apia is full of cheap and greasy snack places that cater primarily for young Samoans, but those on a strict budget will appreciate the option of eating junk food – hamburgers, hot dogs, fried chicken or fish & chips and washing it down with a chocolate shake – for around WS$5.

One of the best and most popular of these fast-food joints is *Skippy's* upstairs in an arcade, just behind Bettino's Barbecue on Beach Rd. It's owned by an Australian and a Samoan who are successfully bringing Australian cuisine, such as it is, to Western Samoa. For fish & chips with salad, you'll pay WS$3.50. Chicken and chips is

WS$4.50. Also highly recommended is *Terry's Burger* diagonally opposite the Mormon temple, where you'll find a genuine US-style burger and chips for WS$3.50. For dessert, try the lemon cake with guava or the bundt cake with passion fruit glaze.

A similar place is *Isa's Ice Cream & Treats* on Post Office St one block back from Beach Rd. In addition to the standard greasy fried fare and sugary soft drinks, they have gooey banana splits, shakes and sundae-like concoctions. A double scoop of ice cream costs WS$1 and thick shakes are WS$2.50.

The *Love Boat* on Beach Rd specialises in pizza, hamburgers and beer but standards are slipping and its popularity is waning a bit. Their burgers aren't as good as those at some other places (such as Gourmet Seafood), but they've recently added a new Chinese menu which includes chicken or beef with noodles, curries and various vegetables dishes, all with rice, for WS$4 to WS$8.

Also recommended for lunch is Aggie's Hamburger Deluxe which is available at lunch time (11.30 am to 2 pm) in the fale bar at Aggie Grey's Hotel for WS$8.50.

A bit more sophisticated – and more expensive – is the well-patronised *Giordano's Pizzeria* opposite the Insel Fehmarn Hotel. For a very good pizza large enough for two people, you'll pay WS$12. In a slightly higher price range is *Apia Inn* which serves continental-style lunches in the WS$15 range from noon to 2 pm, Monday to Friday.

For good ice cream, try the kiosks in the Maketi Fou or go to *Carruther's* on Beach Rd in the centre. You can't miss it. Since custom discourages eating it in the street, you'll see plenty of folks packed into the small area and spilling out the door munching ice cream. It's not comfortable but it's a good way to beat the heat (as long as the heat doesn't beat you to the ice cream). Another place for ice cream, as well as other snack meals or coffee, is *RJ's Coffee Shop* on Mt Vaea St near the clock tower. They also serve delicious fresh pies or bread.

Dinner Almost anyone who's stumbled across it will agree that the grimy little *Wong Kee's*

in the alley behind Otto's Reef is among the best Chinese restaurants in Western Samoa; it is also one of the cheapest. It isn't certain what sort of addictive substances are put in the food but once you try it, you'll be hooked, if you can ignore the 'wildlife' that runs about and the decor, which features Asian calendar photos of fully-clothed bimbos. Try the delicious and unique spring rolls and onion rolls. They serve soft drinks and fresh drinking coconuts but if you want alcohol, you can BYO from Otto's Reef next door.

The *Canton*, next door to Betty Moors Guest House, is owned by Wong Kee's brother. It's cleaner and more expensive but the food isn't quite as good. On the plus side, it's open on Sundays.

Another Chinese Restaurant of note is the *Treasure Garden*, which is comparable in both price and quality to the Canton and seems to be a favourite among expats. The average price of a meal is WS$12; about double that for prawn dishes. It's open nightly except Sunday until 9.30 pm.

Yet another option for Chinese food is the *Sunrise Restaurant* by the sea just north-west of Maketi Fou. The slightly higher than average prices are offset by the typically huge portions. One reader wrote 'They also serve Samoan takeaway meals complete with paper napkin and plastic fork all wrapped up in newspaper for WS$5 to WS$7. My meal cost WS$6.20 and I couldn't eat the lot!'

One of Apia's favourite restaurants is the recently refurbished *Gourmet Seafood* at the corner of Convent St and Post Office St. It has daily lunch specials, including Samoan specialities like oka and other fish dishes for less than WS$5 and fish & chips for WS$5.50. It also offers a range of omelettes and burgers. For dinner, there's a great seafood platter with salad for WS$8.50.

On Friday nights, try the *Apia Yacht Club* for basic WS$4 dinners; guests are welcome. *Love Boat* is open late for pizza, burgers and drinks (small and pathetic though they are).

Continental cuisine and rich desserts are available at the German-owned *Apia Inn*

(☎ 21010), upstairs in the Ioane Viliumu building. It is quite up-market but is good for a bit of self-indulgence. Their fortés include French, Italian and central European fare, especially steak, fish and lobster dishes. Similar is the elegant *Le Godinet's* (☎ 23690) on the Mulinu'u Peninsula. They're best known for their seafood and their Friday night Polynesian buffet. For lobster with deliciously prepared vegetables, you'll pay WS$22; lobster thermidor is WS$29; a seafood crêpe costs WS$9.50; and a New Zealand sirloin steak costs WS$22 (or WS$32 for steak and lobster). Both these places require advance bookings; if possible, phone in the early afternoon.

Another favourite is *The Waterfront* (☎ 20977) opposite the wharf but although the quality is high, portions tend to be a bit small. It's open nightly except Tuesday for steak, seafood, pasta dishes and curries and Sunday is Mexican night, with tacos, burritos and a live jazz/blues band. Chocolate fiends will appreciate the 'Mud Pie' available on the dessert menu.

On Wednesdays, the fale restaurant at Aggie Grey's Hotel offers a dinner buffet and on Saturday, a buffet 'Mongolian barbecue'. If you want to treat yourself, this is the way to go, but you'll shell out WS$40 per person (plus drinks) for the privilege of heaping it on and pigging out to your heart's content. At other times, Aggie's fale restaurant is only marginal and is quite expensive by Samoan standards. Better value is to be found in Le Tamarina restaurant near the hotel entrance, where you'll get a buffet lunch for WS$32 and well-prepared á la carte dinners for WS$29 to 40. It's open Monday to Saturday. On Wednesday night there is fiafia entertainment at 7 pm to go with your meal. The *Tusitala* has a similar but less elaborate daily spread with a Polynesian buffet on Saturday night, a poolside barbecue on Sunday and a fiafia on Thursday nights.

Self-Catering Both *Burns Philp* and *Mackenzie's* have outlets in Apia and stock imported tinned and packaged foods, but prices are extremely high. Smaller shops are a bit better, but the kiosks and stalls around the *Maketi Fou* are the best value; the best prices for produce, fish and meat are at the market. Oddly, the fish market has the greatest bustle just before dawn on Sunday morning; it's worth a stop before you set off to see the wafting smoke of the Sunday morning umu fires in the hinterlands. You'll also find great European-style sausages at the German butcher inside the Samoa Commercial Bank building.

Freshly baked dark bread, rolls and whole-wheat bread are available three times daily from the unassuming kiosk next door to Daphne's Coffee Shop.

If you're interested in buying wine, a reader has written with the following recommendation:

I have discovered a place to buy inexpensive wine...We picked up bottles of French wine for WS$13 each. For one of the best selections of imported (Australian, New Zealand, French, etc), try Netzler's Store on Salenesa Rd in Moto'otua, just south of Malifa and just around the corner from the undertaker's shop. Netzler's is also famous among palagis for their selection of fresh meat and vegetables and 'the best pies in Apia'.
Stephen How Lum, Australia

Entertainment
Bars & Nightclubs The 'in' bar at the moment is *Magrey Ta's Beer Garden* beside the Seaside Inn, which stages an excellent and well-attended disco. On Friday nights from 9.30 to 10.30 pm they stage a fiafia with live music, including dancing from all the around Polynesia. The cover charge is WS$3.

Another popular place, especially with Peace Corps volunteers, is *Don't Drink the Water* on Beach Rd, which is air-conditioned and specialises in Margaritas, yellowfin tuna sashimi and youthful chat. It draws quite a few local young people, especially those who've spent time working or going to school overseas. It's closed on Sundays.

The *Lalaga Bar*, near Valentine Parker's, is a good option if you like live bands, drinking and dancing but unaccompanied women may feel uncomfortable so go alone at your own risk! On the other hand, the seedy *Tijuana Club* isn't recommended for anyone.

The unquestionable favourite among locals – the place where Samoans let their hair down and dance 'til they drop – is the *Mt Vaea Club* on Vaitele St, several blocks back from the waterfront. Although the crowd is overwhelmingly local, foreigners are welcome and if you're in search of alcohol, heavily amplified music and excessive body heat – this is the place to be.

Admission is WS$3 per person and you'll want to bring enough money for drinks – with all the action, this place is a lot like a sauna and you'll sweat buckets. Beer is more economical when you buy the litre bottles, which cost WS$3.50. The music is normally disco-style, but occasionally you'll catch a live band. If you're thinking of acting up, note that the bouncers are huge even by Samoan standards!

Otto's Reef on Beach Rd is a tame sort of pub catering mainly for expats, business people and sports fans. There's a TV that picks up American Samoan programming, CNN News and the cable Sports channel for those who want to catch up on what's happening outside paradise.

The fale bar at *Aggie Grey's Hotel* has live Polynesian-style music nightly and a pleasant, if slightly artificial, atmosphere. It's a good spot to meet well-heeled locals. Slightly more refined is Aggie's Le Kionasina bar in the new wing at the front of the hotel; it's open 3 to 11 pm Monday to Saturday.

The *Hotel Kitano Tusitala* stages live music and dancing until midnight nightly, Monday to Saturday; most of the interest lies with local teenagers.

Fiafias Of all the fiafias in Samoa, the best attended is the Wednesday night production staged by the staff of Aggie Grey's Hotel. Admission is free if you buy a meal or drinks at the bar. The Kitano Tusitala version is presented on Thursday nights.

The elaborate fiafias at the big hotels are not the only ones around. The Beachcomber, a pub on the Mulinu'u Peninsula, stages one on Saturday nights at 10 pm and includes dancing and music from all over the Pacific. Some claim it's the best show in Samoa. There's a WS$3 cover charge, but once you're in, drinks are sold at standard prices. On Friday nights, free sausage and biscuit hors d'oeuvres are available. It's a good deal.

In my opinion, however, Samoa's finest fiafia is the Saturday night presentation at Coconuts Beach Club Resort on the southern shore of 'Upolu. It's more a gathering than a tourist show; the participants seem to enjoy themselves immensely and people from the surrounding villages also attend. The rough edges on the program only serve to enhance the friendly atmosphere. In the finale, a series of fire-knife dancers – some as young as 10 years old – use their imaginations and come up with some impressive performances.

Sport For information on upcoming sporting events, just ask any Samoan male; they all seem to be incredibly well-informed on the subject! Otherwise, try the Ministry of Youth, Sports & Culture in the government building on Beach Rd (as with all ministries, this will soon be shifted to the new government building on the reclaimed area).

Typically well-attended amateur rugby matches are held at Apia Park on Saturday afternoons from April to June and sporadically at other times of year. Rugby League evening matches are held in the same venue from July to November. The soccer season runs from late June to August and field hockey is played between August and December.

With the new Japanese ownership of the Hotel Kitano Tusitala, golf has also arrived in Western Samoa. The 18-hole Royal Samoa Country Club (☎ 20120), which is operated by the hotel, lies just seaward of Fagali'i Airport near Apia. Green fees are a very reasonable WS$10 per player, and hotel guests, visitors and locals are welcome to play. Golf clubs may be hired at the office. On Saturday, the course is open to men only; on Tuesday, only women may play.

Individuals wishing to play squash should book a court at Apia Squash Courts (☎ 23780) near the Seaside Inn or Heem's Squash Courts (☎ 20183) out of town. If you prefer tennis, the public courts at Apia Park are open from 8 am to 6 pm seven days a week. Court rental is WS$1 per player per half hour of play.

Around the Island

Venturing into Apia's hinterland will reveal 'Upolu as the archetypal tropical island, with beaches, reefs, rainforests, mountains and quiet villages. Those who've always dreamed of sliding down a jungle waterfall into a crystalline pool will not be disappointed, either, and unlike those constructed at tourist resorts in Hawaii, it's all natural!

Vailima

In December 1889, Robert Louis Stevenson arrived in Samoa for the first time and loved the place so much that he bought 1¼ sq km in the hills above Apia – a bargain at only UK£200 the lot. Sickly with tuberculosis, he decided to return to Samoa from Australia for health reasons in February 1890, and set about constructing what would be the largest and most elaborate house in the country.

At an altitude of about 200 metres, it lay in a cooler and more comfortable zone than the capital, and here the Tusitala felt that he could write in peace and comfort. He made a point of including a European-style fireplace to give the house a warm and homely appearance and ward off the cool of the highlands during the winter months. He planted lawns, gardens and fruit trees and imported fine furniture from Scotland.

When Stevenson died, in 1894, the property was purchased by a wealthy German retiree and philanthropist, Gustav Kunst, who added extensions to each end of the house. During the New Zealand administration, it was occupied by the government administrator. It now serves as the official residence of Malietoa Tanumafili II, the head

Robert Louis Stevenson

In December 1889 the already famous Scottish author and poet, Robert Louis Balfour Stevenson, and his wife Fanny Osborne, arrived in Apia aboard the schooner *Equator*. He'd left Europe in search of some relief from worsening tuberculosis and the distressing general sickliness that had plagued him all his life.

Enchanted by Samoa, in 1890 he purchased 1¼ sq km of land in the hills above Apia for UK£200 from the American trader Harry Jay Moors.

Stevenson's health improved, and with his family he set sail for Australia. Upon arrival in Sydney, however, he again became ill, and it was decided that the climate of Samoa was what he needed above all. The Stevenson family returned to Apia in September 1890 and constructed Vailima. For their home, they imported furniture from Stevenson's native Scotland and dressed their Samoan employees in lavalava with patterns of the Stuart tartan.

In the late 1800s, during the period of strife between Britain, the USA and Germany, Stevenson became an activist for Samoan rights, maintaining that the people should be left to govern themselves and determine their own destiny in accordance with their customs. Most of the Europeans would have liked to see him deported at the time but to do so would have been very unpopular indeed.

Stevenson came to be loved by the Samoans for his friendliness towards them and his ability to entertain with stories. They respectfully and affectionately referred to him as Tusitala (teller of tales).

Stevenson's time in Samoa was short however. He spent nearly every waking hour working, apparently in a race with what he realised was rapidly failing health. On 3 December 1894, after just over four years in Samoa, he died of a stroke at Vailima.

The Samoan chief Tu'imaleali'ifano, while paying his respects, uttered the words that echoed the sentiments of many Samoans: 'Talofa e i lo matou Tusitala. Ua tagi le fatu ma le 'ele'ele.' This means: 'Our beloved Tusitala. The stones and the earth weep'.

Stevenson had stipulated that he wished to be buried atop Mt Vaea, part of the Vailima estate. Just two months before his death, in gratitude for his kindness to them, a delegation of Samoan chiefs had arranged for a hand-dug road to be made between Apia and Vailima, which they called *Alo Loto Alofa* , the Way of Loving Hearts.

Realising that Stevenson must be buried as quickly as possible before the tropical heat created problems, these same chiefs worked through the night clearing sections of bush up the mountain to make a path for the funeral procession. The burial service was Christian, but afterwards the European coffin was laid atop a base of coral and volcanic pebbles and the grave lined with black stones, a practice normally reserved for Samoan royalty.

No discussion of Stevenson in Samoa would be complete without citing his requiem, two of the most beautifully poignant verses he ever composed.

Under the wide and starry sky,
Dig the grave and let me lie.
Glad did I live and gladly die,
And I laid me down with a will.

This be the verse you grave for me:
Here he lies where he longed to be;
Home is the sailor, home from the sea,
And the hunter home from the hill.

Fanny, who was known as 'Aolele by the Samoans, stayed on for a while in Samoa but died in California in 1914. In her will, however, she requested that her ashes be taken also to Mt Vaea and buried beside her husband's. Her requiem, which was also composed by Stevenson, reads:

Teacher, tender comrade, wife,
A fellow farer, true through life,
Heart whole and sould free,
The August Father gave to me. ∎

Robert Louis Stevenson

of state, although he doesn't actually live there.

The distinctive home (it had a red roof when Robert Louis Stevenson lived there) is six km inland from Beach Rd and is flanked by the Mt Vaea National Reserve. Visitors are welcome to have a look at the grounds and wander along trails through the lush and colourful botanical gardens that have been developed there.

To commemorate the centennial of Stevenson's death in 1894, the directors of the RLS Museum/Preservation Foundation in the USA set about looking for funds to restore the home, estate and nearby grave site (on Mt Vaea) to its former state – including the red roof. They will also create a Robert Louis Stevenson museum on the upper floor of the house.

On my most recent visit, the restoration was underway – the old house had been reduced to a ruin in hopes of having it ready for the grand opening and commemorative celebration in December, 1994. The anticipated cost will be between US$1 million and US$5 million. For information on the RLS Museum Preservation Foundation, contact them at PO Box 29041, Phoenix, AZ 83058, USA (☎ (602) 968-3999) or PO Box 850, Apia, Western Samoa.

Getting There & Away To get to Vailima, take the Avele, Mulivai or Lotofaga bus from the Maketi Fou or wave it down on Falealili St around the Insel Fehmarn motel. The entrance to Vailima is between two stately rows of shady trees. The drive leads to the house (once the renovation is completed, you may be denied entry by the guards) and the track which begins just to the north goes to the botanical gardens. If you keep following that track, you'll cross Mulivai Stream and enter the Mt Vaea Forest Reserve.

Mt Vaea

Although participants in group tours stop-

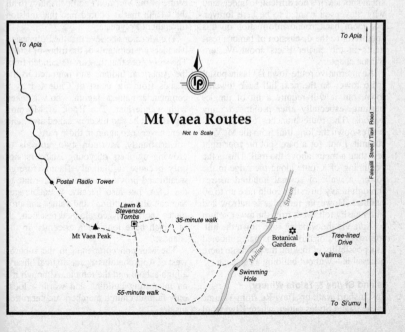

ping at Vailima may snicker at the very idea of such physical exertion, the climb to the top of Mt Vaea to the tombs of Robert Louis and Fanny Stevenson is worthwhile and not at all difficult. To get started, go to the Vailima entrance and follow the obvious track across Mulivai Stream. From there, take the sharp left turn and in five minutes you'll reach a fork where a sign announces that the short trail to the top will take 35 minutes and the left fork, the long route, will require 55 minutes.

I'd recommend walking up via the long route, a leisurely stroll through cool but sticky rainforest which shouldn't take more than about 30 or 40 minutes even for casual hikers. You can then return by the easy 10 to 15-minute short trail, which starts its descent just east of the tomb.

The summit affords a magnificent view of Apia and the surrounding mountains. Take water and a lunch for a pleasant picnic on the lawn beside the graves. It's a tranquil and silent spot and it's not difficult to understand why Stevenson wanted to be here forever. For more background information on this spot, refer to the discussion of famous residents in the earlier Facts about Western Samoa chapter.

An alternative route down is via the postal radio tower on the next hill back towards town, but it will require a bit of jungle-bashing, especially after prolonged rainy periods. The route branches off about 20 metres down the long trail from the Mt Vaea summit. Look for a bare spot on your right less than a metre above the trail. This is the beginning of a route along the ridge to the tower, a walk of several hundred metres through heavy bush that could take up to 30 minutes. However, the ridge is narrow and fairly easily followed; from the tower, return to Apia via the winding road down the hill. Improvement of this route is being mooted as a possibility of making the gravesite more accessible – without building a cable car.

Island Styles & Talofa Winery
Just a short walk up Tiavi Rd from Vailima is the Island Styles outlet, where Kiwi wool jumpers and Samoan clothing are made. It's more or less an obligatory stop for all the passing tour groups but surprisingly, prices are not that high. The unique hand-printed clothing is very well designed and executed.

They also accommodate tastes for more kitschy items; if you want a coconut shell ashtray or a deck of playing cards bearing photos of Vailima, this is the place to find it.

You can also purchase the nice and inexpensive Talofa fruit wines which are produced here. They're brewed from local fruit products and taste cool and refreshing in the tropical heat. Some favourites include passionfruit, pineapple, ginger and guava. A new product is coconut liqueur which, when drunk over ice, is vaguely reminiscent of Bailey's Irish Cream.

Mormon Temple
Beneath the heralding figure of the angel Moroni (of Book of Mormon fame), the white temple that establishes Apia as the centre of the Mormon Pacific displays to all the wealth that is poured into that mission throughout Polynesia.

The Mormons believe that the Polynesian islanders are remnants of the tribes of Israel. The story goes that they are descended from the American Indians and migrated to the islands from the coast of Chile led by a commander named Hagoth, who was taken with wanderlust. The Book of Mormon reports that he and his crew sailed away and were never seen again in those parts.

Christianity, Mormon-style, appeals to growing numbers of young islanders, not only because it blatantly flaunts foreign wealth and provides an emigration route to the USA, but also because it encourages Samoan arts, traditions and values and promotes sports and genealogical research, all of which have long been esteemed in the islands.

The Mormon compound in the suburbs west of Apia contains a genealogical library, a high school and the temple. Although it's an interesting building and worth a look, only faithful church members are permitted inside.

Top: Aleipata, 'Upolu with Nu'utele in the background (DS)
Middle: Aleipata, 'Upolu (DS)
Bottom: Beach at Olosega, falls at Gataivai &
Return-to-Paradise Beach (DS)

Top: Beach Road, Apia, 'Upolu (DS)
Middle: Samoan fale & laundry line, Manono (DS)
Bottom Left: Aggie Grey's Hotel, Apia, 'Upolu (GC)
Bottom Right: Anti-drug campaign sign, Tutuila (DS)

Top: Octopus (GC)
Middle: Paopao (canoes), Asau Harbour, Savai'i (DS)
Bottom Left: Sea, a delicacy made from sea slugs (GC)
Bottom Right: Night spearfishing catch (GC)

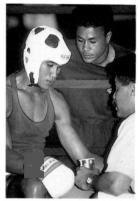

A	B
C	D	E
F	G

A (GC)   E (GC)
B (DS)   F (GC)
C (GC)   G (DS)
D (DS)

Samoans

Vailima Brewery & Bottling

The Western Samoa Breweries plant west of Apia produces soft drinks and the national beer, Vailima. It was opened in 1976 and has grown into Western Samoa's biggest industry, producing three million litres of beer annually. A German brewer was brought in to take charge of quality control, and he's apparently done a good job because the finished product is excellent, especially on a hot Samoan afternoon.

There are no formal tours of the brewery, but if you turn up with three or four people (no more, however) and display an interest, you'll probably be able to arrange a friendly, informal tour around the plant and, of course, a sampling of the product.

Tanumapua & Other Plantations

The Tanumapua Tropical Plantation, a few km inland from Vaitele, just west of Apia, makes for a pleasant rural outing from town. You can spend an afternoon strolling around the planted areas and tropical flower gardens, and seeing examples of such tropical crops as coffee, bananas, papaya, pineapples, kava and cacao. Other area plantations are also experimenting with temperate vegetables.

If you've always wanted to see a cacao pod, here's your opportunity. The whimsical trees are short and mouldy-looking affairs with cacao pods sprouting from the trunk and branches. If you can manage to find a ripe one (ask a plantation worker), open it and chew on the white cushioning material between the beans. It's delicious and the Samoans consider it quite a treat.

Originally cacao beans were grown as a cash crop on large, privately owned plantations, but a few years ago, Western Samoa Trust Estates Corporation (WSTEC) developed a hybrid strain, Lafi-7. It's currently the highest producing strain in the world but still requires the meticulous attention of smaller landholders. If you'd like to see cacao in action, visit WSTEC's Central Group Cacao Plantation which lies five km from Apia, near Tanumapua.

To reach Tanumapua, follow Alafa'alava Rd, which is the first left turning west of the Mormon temple. The plantation is on the right side about eight km up this road.

Papase'a Sliding Rock

A trip to the Papase'a Sliding Rock is obligatory for every visitor to Western Samoa, although once there, many can't seem to muster the nerve to enjoy the star attraction, a five-metre slide down a waterfall into a jungle pool. It's better than Disneyland. If the big one puts you off, though, there are three other smaller ones to choose from. Don't miss this place!

Take the Se'ese'e bus from the Maketi Fou and ask to be dropped off at the intersection for Papase'a. It's a good idea to remember the route the bus takes to get to this point because drivers divert from their standard route to drop visitors close to the park and you'll probably have to walk out to the paved road to catch a bus back to town.

Walk two km up the hill to the entrance. Admission to the park is WS$1, but pay only the women at the entrance and not the children who hound you as you approach. They have no authority to collect and you'll just have to pay again as you enter.

Mau Headquarters & Tamasese Tomb

Near the Mormon temple is the German bandstand that was used as the headquarters of the Mau Movement. Tupua Tamasese Lealofi III's tomb is not far from the bandstand and reflects the respect Samoans still hold for his chiefly titles and his many contributions to the cause of Samoan sovereignty.

Leulumoega Church

On the stretch of road between Apia and the Faleolo International Airport, there are more than 60 multicoloured churches representing numerous denominations. One of the most interesting of these is the Congregational Christian (London Missionary Society) church at Leulumoega, the design of which is unique on the island.

While you're in Leulumoega, visit the School of Fine Arts beside the Maloa Theological College, where you can appreciate some wonderful woodcarvings and other art work done by students.

Faleolo International Airport
Financed by the Asian Development Bank in 1972, Faleolo Airport makes Western Samoa accessible to the world. The terminal has a bank, souvenir shops and food shops but no restaurant. Several duty-free outlets operate in the international lounge.

Return-to-Paradise Beach
In the Lefaga district is the idyllic Return-to-Paradise Beach, made famous in the 1951 Gary Cooper film based on the James Michener novel *Return to Paradise*. The setting lives up to its name, but while the beach is picturesque, it is not ideal for swimming due to the shallow reefs, volcanic boulders and heavy surf pounding on it all.

You'll probably have to walk the 3½ km from the Main Coast Rd to the beach. Through the village of Mata'utu, where pedestrians pay a WS$1 custom fee (WS$3 per motorbike or WS$5 per car), turn left and follow the track the final km to the beach.

If you're not averse to tours, one way to escape the postmortem feeling of a Samoan Sunday is to take a tour to this beach. Aggie's offers one for WS$45, which is a bit steep, but since public buses don't run on Sundays, it's a good way to get out of town. Take a lunch for a pleasant beach picnic. There's always a volleyball game in progress, and it's a good sunny (most of the time, anyway) place to read or just lie out on the sand and contemplate how fortunate you are to be in Samoa!

Salamumu Beach
The next beach east of Return-to-Paradise, Salamumu, is just as pleasant, but less popular. Perhaps this has something to do with the custom fees, which are WS$2 per pedestrian, WS$5 per car and WS$6 per bus.

Nevertheless, with one of the nicest beaches on the island, remote Salamumu is a great place to relax. The village has been located on 'Upolu since 1909 when a volca-

nic eruption of Savai'i forced evacuation and relocation of Sale'aula village.

An Australian film company constructed an instant village on the site for the filming of a movie called *Coral Island*, and the fales there still offer a shady and comfortable spot to spend a day at the beach.

An even nicer, lesser-known and deserted beach can be found about one km to the west, but it is likely that the custom fee will still apply.

Baha'i Temple
From near the highest point of Tiavi Rd, the 28-metre Niue limestone dome of the Baha'i House of Worship points skyward. Designed by Iranian Husain Amanat and dedicated in 1984, this imposing and architecturally beautiful structure is one of seven Baha'i houses of worship in the world. According to church literature, it is a 'place of spiritual gathering and of the manifestation of divine mysteries'.

The nine sides of the building represent the nine major religions of the world and the nine primary points of the faith, which are inscribed above nine entrances. The doors on all sides represent welcome to mankind from all directions and absolute equality between races, sexes, nationalities and economic classes. Two of the inscriptions inside read 'Ye are all the fruits of one tree and the leaves of one branch' and 'The earth is but one country and mankind its citizens'.

There is an adjoining information centre, where attendants will happily answer your questions and pass out religious literature. It's not a high-pressure operation though, so it's worth a few minutes. Also, be sure to stroll around the surrounding well-groomed lawns and gardens. Worship services are held on Sundays at 10 am and visitors are welcome.

Lake Lanoto'o
Also known as Goldfish Lake, Lake Lanoto'o is an eerie, pea-green crater lake in the central highlands of 'Upolu. Anyone keen on the unusual should make a point of visiting this little-known spot that just

missed out becoming an easily accessible tourist attraction in 1919.

During the German occupation it had become quite a resort and the Germans built two huts and provided a rowboat for those who ventured in there. In 1919 local traders suggested that a road be built to the lake to allow easy access to holiday-makers, but proponents of 'controlled tourism' saw to it that the idea remained only a suggestion. Recently, however, rumours have surfaced regarding plans for a road to the crater and a tourist hotel to be built on the shore.

To get there, take Tiavi Rd beyond the Baha'i temple until you see a microwave relay tower on a low hill to your right. Ask the driver to drop you at the Lanoto'o Rd turn-off. Walk west on this road for about three km, at which point it will narrow into a track at a turn-off to the left. Don't turn, however.

Continue straight ahead for about another km to where the track makes a 90° turn to the left. Follow it until the array of radio towers and a satellite dish are visible on your left. At that point, look to the right and you should be able to make out a badly overgrown track leading away across a muddy bog-like area. This is the route.

After several hundred metres, the trail improves considerably, becoming slippery red clay. Follow it for about 30 minutes until it climbs a hill to a microwave reflector which could serve as a cool and breezy picnic spot. The murky green lake is in the volcanic crater to your left.

Lake Lanoto'o is full of wild goldfish that congregate around the shore. Locals used to collect them for pets until the government banned it. It's a great place for a swim too, but a little spooky due to alternating warm and cold currents and the fact that the bottom of the lake has never been found.

Very few visitors ever see this lovely and unusual spot. In order to avoid the multiple unpleasantries of ankle deep mud, thorn

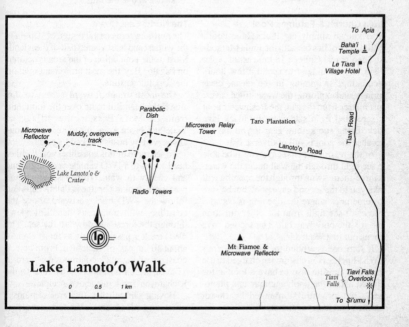

Lake Lanoto'o Walk

bushes, sleeping grass (which stings like nettle) and leeches, hikers should wear long pants and sturdy covered shoes. Don't forget to carry food and water.

Tiavi Falls

Heading south on Tiavi Rd, keep looking for a small parking area and track on your right. This is the overlook for the spectacular 100-metre Tiavi Falls (marked on the Hema Western Samoa map as Papapapai-tai Waterfall) far across a deep valley.

Pig Farm

Just down from the ridge on the southern slope of Tiavi Rd is the pork farm, home of 700 squealing pigs bound for Aggie's buffet. This non-attraction has for some reason become a source of amusement for travellers, so I suppose it rates a mention. It's run by an Aussie family who will be happy to show you around the place and discuss high-volume pig production.

Piula Church & Fatumea Pool

Also known simply as 'Piula Cave Pool', Fatumea Pool lies beneath the Piula Methodist Theological College 18 km east of Apia. It's a wonderful spot to spend a few hours picnicking, swimming in the clean, clear springs, and exploring the water-filled caves. Just metres from the sea, the freshwater pool is separated from salt water by black lava rock. Bring snorkelling gear if you have it because the pool is full of diverse fish.

At the rear of the first cave you'll be able to see light through the wall under the water. A three-metre swim through the opening will take you to the second cave pool, but be sure to remember where the opening is because you can't see light from the other direction and it's the only way out. The second cave opens out to a sea ledge.

If someone is around to collect it, there's a WS$1 per person custom fee charged to use the pool. Be sure also to have a look at the church above the pool, a unique and photogenic old structure surrounded by flower gardens and lush vegetation.

Piula church

Falefa Falls

Not far from Piula, near the village of Falefa, is the powerful Falefa Falls. The best vantage point for a photograph is on an old concrete platform just coastward from the overlook. It's also possible to scramble down onto the rocks just above the falls.

The North-East Coast

The north-eastern coastal region of 'Upolu is the wildest and least visited part of the island. Most of the population of the area is centred on Fagaloa Bay, the most prominent inlet on the 'Upolu coastline.

The most straightforward access to this area is the beautiful route over the mountain from Le Mafa Pass to the village of Taelefaga. From Apia, this route is occasionally served by buses marked Fagaloa.

To see more of this coastline, you'll either need access to a 4WD vehicle or enough time and energy to walk. Turn east across the precarious-looking bridge at Falefa Falls and follow the 4WD track eastward above the coastline, with numerous beautiful views through the forest and down to the sea. The 4WD track is passable only as far as Uafato, about 10 km east of Taelefaga. From here, a coastal walking track continues eastward to Ti'avea, which is connected by road to the Richardson Track just above Aleipata.

Having said all that, this area remains a quiet and aloof area. Visitors aren't as

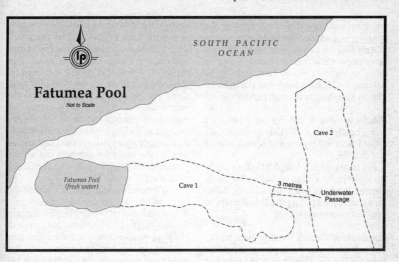

warmly received as they are elsewhere in Western Samoa, especially in the villages of Musumusu, Salimu, Taelefaga and Maasina. Travellers on foot will probably have a better reception than those arriving in a vehicle.

Fuipisia Falls

Heading south from Falefa Falls, cross 300-metre Lemafa Pass and descend toward the coast. Ask to be dropped at the start of the trail to Fuipisia Falls, a 55-metre plunge of the Mulivaifagatola River. From there, follow the track west for 300 metres to the lookout. You'll have to pay a WS$1 custom fee if there's anyone around to collect it.

Sopo'aga Falls

Three km along Le Mafa Pass road south of Fuipisia Falls and just south of the turn-off to the Main South Coast Rd, is a lovely garden, picnic site and overlook to the 50-metre-high Sopo'aga Falls and its immense gorge. To visit the site, there's a custom fee of WS$2 per person.

Just west of the falls lookout, along the road, an unassuming concrete bridge crosses the uppermost reaches of the Sopo'aga Falls gorge and the view down is quite impressive.

Aleipata District

The reefs in the Aleipata district at the easternmost end of the island are 50 metres or so offshore and the water is a remarkable chlorine blue making for the loveliest beaches and the best swimming available on 'Upolu and, possibly, in all Western Samoa. Snorkelling is supreme beyond the reef and there are lots of good shells around, but beware of the numerous cone shells found here. Some are mildly poisonous, but the most beautiful ones can be deadly.

The prominent offshore island of Nu'utele, which offers yet more glorious beaches, served as a leper colony from 1916 to 1918 when the lepers were relocated to Fiji. Ask either the local fisherfolk for access to the island or go with Moana Tours in Lalomanu. For a snorkelling excursion to Nu'utele, they charge WS$25 per person.

Around the village of Lalomanu are beach fales for picnicking and relaxing; the beach area in front of the bungalows may be used for a custom fee of WS$5 per vehicle (WS$10 if it's a bus, but with tourists, they'll often try to get the WS$10 even for cars) or WS$2 per person on foot. Around midday, tour groups stop off here for barbecues, so you may want to get there as early in the morning as possible. The first bus leaves the Maketi Fou for Lotofaga around 5 am, and from there it's a relatively easy matter to hitch or catch a south coast bus on to Lalomanu. Occasionally, buses run from the Maketi Fou straight through to Aleipata.

Places to Stay & Eat For information on hiring beach fales in the Aleipata district, see under Places to Stay – out of town, earlier in this chapter.

For meals, there's *Joseph's Coffee Shop* by the shore in the village of Satitoa. Sit on the ocean-view patio while the friendly ladies here can rustle up burgers, fish & chips or very tasty tuna sandwiches.

Lotofaga, A'ufaga & Sinalele Beaches

The custom fee to swim, picnic or sunbake at lovely Lotofaga Beach is WS$1 per adult. Further east are A'ufaga and Sinalele beaches, which cost WS$2 per adult and WS$1 per child.

Although it's unclear on some maps, there's no road connection between Salani and Utulaelae on the south coast, so if you're approaching from Saleilua along the Main Coast Rd, you'll have to detour via Sopo'aga Falls.

O Le Pupu-Pu'e National Park

O Le Pupu-Pu'e is one of the South Pacific islands' few fully fledged national parks. The name means 'from the coast to the mountain top', which is a fair description of its 29 sq km. The park was created in 1978 to protect a sample of the island's natural environment and the scientific, recreational and educational interests of its people.

The northern boundary is formed by a ridge between volcanic 840-metre Mt Lepu'e and 1100-metre Mt Fito. In the south is the rugged O Le Pupu Lava Coast. There was once an unstaffed open kiosk of exhibits loosely described as visitors' centre, but it was destroyed in the recent cyclones. The park entrance is near Togitogiga Scenic Reserve, which lies just outside the park to the east.

Hiking One of the most worthwhile walks is to the lava tube, Pe'ape'a Cave. The return walk will require a minimum of three hours and it's hot hiking so remember to carry plenty of water. Go to the car park at Togitogiga and take the left fork then walk about 1½ km through the plantation to the gate at the end. A nondescript route leads from there through the rainforest. Resign yourself to feeling hopelessly lost for more than an hour after you leave this point, as you look all the while for numbers and arrows painted on the trees and follow mashed down vegetation.

You'll come out at a dry lava riverbed and there will be a sign on the tree that says 'Cave' with an arrow pointing downstream. Several hundred metres down the riverbed, is a large pit-like cave – actually a lava tube – full of circling swallows, or *pe'ape'a*. It's possible to explore the cave with a torch, but be careful climbing down into the pit on the mossy, slippery rocks.

Once you've returned from the cave by the same route, you'll probably have to hitch back to Apia because the last bus will have already passed. Stop for a swim at Togitogiga Falls and then wish for luck in waving down a vehicle!

Another pleasant and easy four-km walking track leads south from the road at the far western boundary of the park to the magnificently rugged **O Le Pupu Lava Coast**.

About one km to the west near the village of Saaga-fou, outside the park boundary, a motorable track of the same length strikes southward to **Aganoa Black Sand Beach**. Although there are plenty of dark beaches on Savai'i, this is the only readily accessible one on 'Upolu. The custom fee to visit this beach is WS$1 per hiker, WS$2 per motorbike and WS$3 per car.

More adventurous walkers can make their way inland, up the mazes of riverbeds and through the rainforests to the summits of Mt Lepu'e and Mt Fito.

Togitogiga Falls The falls and reserve with the tongue-twisting name, Togitogiga, lie

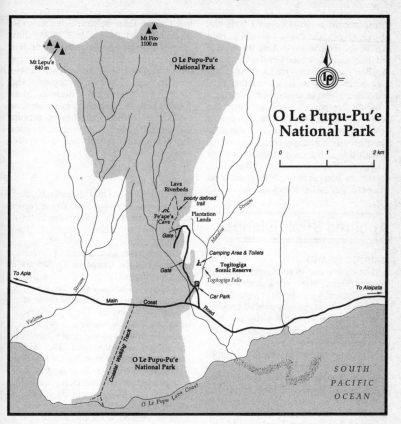

O Le Pupu-Pu'e National Park

just outside O Le Pupu-Pu'e National Park up a dirt track leaving from the park entrance. Several levels of falls are separated by pools, all great for swimming, and you can jump from the cliffs into the churning water below the largest one. The locals will be able to demonstrate the best spots; only the first time does the prospect of jumping seem formidable!

Mulivai Waterways

Around its mouth, the Tiavi Stream branches out into a beautiful maze of drowned forest and mangrove. This tidal estuary creates a wonderland for plant and bird life and a transition zone between freshwater and salt-water that sustains fish from both the sea and inland streams.

Quite simply, this is one of the most beautiful areas of Western Samoa and it's now readily accessible. From Coconuts Beach Club Resort, there's a short nature trail leading to the edge of the estuary. From there you can continue deeper into the maze by kayak, which may be hired from Coconuts Watersports for WS$15 per hour.

On the high tide, Roger and Gayle at Coconuts Watersports conduct a Jungle Boat

Cruise aboard a small covered boat, the *African Queen*. On the two-hour trip, they explore the waterways, looking for wildlife and listening to the exotic forest noises. (And they don't take seriously the North American tour organiser who suggested that they enhance the jungle atmosphere with electronically reproduced monkey chatter and parrot squawks!) There's even a chance of observing owls, which breed in this area. This trip costs WS$25 per person and is done at high tide in the early morning and late afternoon. For information or bookings, contact the hotel at the number given under Places to Stay earlier in this chapter.

Apolima Strait Islands

MANONO ISLAND

Although it's the third-largest island of Western Samoa, Manono has an area of only three sq km and a population of around 1500. You can walk all the way around it in 1½ hours. It can be visited as a day trip from 'Upolu, although it's both tempting and possible to stay longer.

According to Samoan legend, Manono isn't a Samoan island at all, but rather has been transplanted from Fiji. It is believed that it was originally the property of chief Lautala of Fiji, who came to conquer the Samoas on his island ship, *Manono*. He anchored first between Tutuila and Manu'a and attempted conquest but soon found the distance between those two island groups too great to manage. Next he tried simultaneous attack on Tutuila and 'Upolu, but again the distance was too great to assure victory on both fronts. Lastly, he sailed *Manono* around to the Apolima Strait between 'Upolu and Savai'i, anchored there, and decided the position was strategically sound. So many Samoans were killed by Lautala's imperialistic aspirations that the island, which has remained at its last anchorage to this day, was named *Manono*, meaning 'numerous'.

Manono today remains a quiet and tradi-

tional island. There are no vehicles, no roads, no noise and little evidence of the 20th century anywhere to be seen. People live almost exclusively in thatched fales – the main exception being the clergy, who always seem to have Western-style homes – and enjoy a semi-subsistence lifestyle. Most families make a trip to Apia every week or two to visit friends and relations, procure supplies and catch up on the news, but once they return home, they're back in old Polynesia.

Things to See

On 18 June 1835 the first Methodist missionary in Samoa, Reverend Peter Turner, landed on Manono. At Faleu village near Matasiva Point, there's a monument commemorating the 100th anniversary of the event.

The only other special point of interest on the island is the **Grave of 99 Stones** at Lepuia'i village, which dates back to the late 19th century. The story goes that the grave, which is that of a chief, contains one stone for each of his wives. The chief's descendants still live on Manono, however, and some believe that the story has been embellished over the years. They say he certainly was a busy man, but the legendary figure of 99 is probably an exaggeration.

While you're on Manono, have a look at the unique telephone box in the village and all the overwater toilets that represent the Samoan solution to the problem of sewage disposal. All around the island are nice beaches and excellent snorkelling opportunities.

Places to Stay & Eat

There is no formal accommodation on Manono and no place to buy food, so it's a good idea to bring supplies from Apia when you come. Your best bet as far as sleeping arrangements are concerned is to ask one of the pastors on the island if you can throw a sleeping mat on his floor. According to tradition, pastors open their homes to travellers and you are likely to be enthusiastically welcomed.

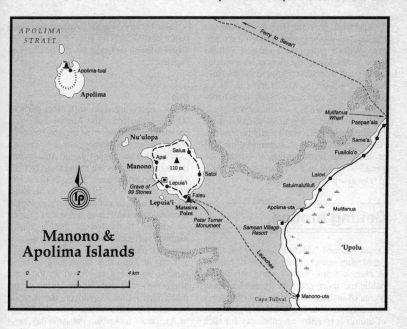

Manono & Apolima Islands

Getting There & Away

To visit Manono, take the Falelatai bus from Apia to Manono-uta on the western end of 'Upolu (WS$1.50). From there, small launches leave for Manono as often as there is passenger interest. You'll pay about WS$1 each way if there are more than several people waiting or a bit more if there are only a couple of passengers. If you miss the regular morning runs, special charters will cost as much as WS$20 for the entire boat.

APOLIMA ISLAND

Western Samoa's fourth island, Apolima, lies in the Apolima Strait, outside the reef that encircles 'Upolu and Manono. The remnant of a volcanic crater, it meets the sea in high, steep cliffs, and there's only a tiny and difficult entrance from the sea through to the single, hardly touched village of 150 people. The soil of the island is poor, and therefore fish and coconuts are the primary sustenance of the people.

The name of the island is said to be derived from *Apo i le Lima*, meaning 'poised in the hand', in reference to the spear used by one son of the Fijian king to kill his brother. The wound is the small and easily-defended entrance to the island's crater, which shelters the village and its harbour.

Visitors should make a point of climbing the concrete steps to the lighthouse for a good view. There are also sea-bird rookeries on the cliffs of the island.

Getting There & Away

Arranging a visit to Apolima Island will be tricky, but it can be done. The best possible situation would be to receive an invitation from a resident of the island, thereby assuring the islanders that your visit won't be too disruptive. If you're keen, seek out Mr Sa'u Samoa at the village of Apolima-uta on 'Upolu, who can arrange permission for you to visit. If you'd like, he can also arrange transport.

Otherwise, go to the shop at Apolima-uta and ask one of the launch pilots to take you over. With a group, your chances will be much better. Most boat owners are aware of the difficult manoeuvre through the pass into Apolima village, so you'll have to find a captain who's very game. They'll probably charge around WS$25 for the service.

Due to time constraints, a day trip to Apolima from Apia won't really be feasible. Although offers of accommodation will probably be forthcoming, to assume so would be unfair to the villagers, so it's best to take along food and a tent.

Getting Around

Getting around 'Upolu is an easy but time-consuming matter. There are lots of options to choose from, but if you're relying on public transport, don't try to visit too many points of interest in a single day. While it's normally possible to see more, a good rule of thumb is to allow an entire day for each excursion to a point of interest beyond the environs of Apia.

To/From the Airports
Airport buses, which are run by Schuster Tours, meet arriving and departing flights at Faleolo Airport. They charge WS$6 per person for the 45-minute trip between the airport terminal and the major hotels. Alternatively, you can flag down a public bus just outside the airport gate. As you face the highway, Apia-bound buses will be coming from your right (although some buses coming from your left will actually turn around at the airport gate and return to Apia). If you're going to the airport from Apia, take any bus marked Faleolo, Mulifanua or Falelatai.

Taxis between Apia and Faleolo Airport cost WS$30 each way, which is quite high by local standards. When you're going to the airport, don't let them get away with charging you the extra WS$1 for airport access; it's included in the taxi fare.

Taxis between Fagali'i Airport and Apia centre cost WS$5. By bus it's just 60 sene. To get to the airport, take any city bus marked Fagali'i.

Bus
Buses connecting Apia with other parts of 'Upolu leave from the Maketi Fou. Just because the bus has left the market, however, doesn't mean you're underway. It will return to the market after a spin around Apia (sometimes only as far as the roundabout in front of the market) as many times as the driver deems necessary to fill the bus to his satisfaction or until he realises that it's no longer economically feasible to waste fuel making the circuit. If he decides that he hasn't inspired sufficient interest in the trip, it is cancelled altogether.

Keep in mind that buses tend to begin running early and knock off in the early afternoon – and that 'Upolu by bus seems much larger than 'Upolu on the map! If you'd like to visit a remote spot – say Lefaga or Aleipata – and return the same day, be at the Maketi Fou in Apia by 6 or 7 am. Fares range from 40 sene to WS$3 and provide transport from Apia to just about any part of the island.

All buses prominently display the name of their destination in the front window. No tickets are necessary – just pay the driver at your destination.

If you are wandering far afield – say to Aleipata, Falelatai, Manono Island or the south coast – and plan to return to Apia in the evening, get an early start. If you depart later than 7 am, you'll be hard-pressed to see anything at your destination before you have to board the last bus back to town.

Any bus with the sign 'Pasi o le Va'a' in the window will be passing the airport and going on to Mulifanua Wharf, from where the Savai'i ferry departs. If it also says 'Falelatai' or 'Manono-uta', it will be going beyond to the Manono ferry dock or to the south-western end of the island. Catch the Mulifanua bus at least an hour before you plan to catch the Savai'i ferry. Manono-bound launches leave whenever people are waiting to go.

To reach the Aleipata district and the eastern end, catch the Lotofaga bus and change there to one eastbound along the south coast. Heading east along the north coast (to Piula, for instance), take the Falefa, Lufilufi, Faleapuna or Fagaloa bus. From Falefa you can get another bus through to Lotofaga and the south coast.

For any point along Falealili St/Tiavi Rd (to Vailima, the Baha'i temple, the turn-off to Lake Lanoto'o and Tiavi Falls), take either the Mulivai or the Lotofaga bus. To Togitogiga and O Le Pupu-Pu'e National Park, take the Lotofaga, Tafatafa or Falealili buses from the Maketi Fou.

If you're going to Papase'a Sliding Rock, the Tafa'igata bus will drop you several km away so it's better to take the Se'ese'e bus and let the driver know where you want to go (although they'll know, anyway). They'll drop you within two km of the rocks and provide directions to the entrance.

From Apia, fares to the western end of 'Upolu (Mulifanua and Manono-uta) or Mulivai are WS$1.50. To Si'umu or Lefaga they're WS$2 and to Aleipata, WS$3. To Faleolo Airport costs WS$1.50 and to Vailima, 60 sene. Around Apia and its environs will cost between 40 and 60 sene.

Car

The Main Coast Rd follows the coast most of the way around 'Upolu but cuts off the beautiful Aleipata district at the far eastern end. To reach this area, you'll have to take the recently asphalted Richardson Track through the centre or travel along the unpaved coast road east of Lotofaga. Three good cross-island roads pass over the east-west tending central ridge and divide the island roughly into quarters. The central of the cross-island roads begins in Apia as Falealili St, becoming Tiavi Rd (also known as *the* Cross-Island Rd) further south.

The north-eastern section of 'Upolu is the most rugged and inaccessible, and you'll need 4WD to negotiate the track to Fagaloa Bay. However, at the present rate of development, it's likely that a complete island circuit will be possible in a normal car in the next few years.

Petrol is available only in the Apia area; at Faleula about 10 km west of Apia; Vailele about five km east of Apia; and Nofoali'i, about five km east of Faleolo Airport.

The following is a rundown of vehicle rental agencies and approximate prices. All rates are in Samoan tala and include CDW insurance and unlimited mileage:

Apia Rentals
  PO Box 173, Apia – specialises in 4WD vehicles: Suzuki Samurai costs WS$100 per day plus a WS$50 security deposit and 10% GST; a Suzuki Sidekick costs WS$120 per day plus WS$100 tax and deposit. Substantial discounts are available for longer hire (☎ 24244; fax 26193).

Apia Ricksha
  PO Box 9513, Apia – for a totally different option, you can hire a three-wheeled tuk-tuk for just WS$60 per day or WS$300 per week (☎ 20679).

Billie's Car Rentals
  Retzlaff's Travel, PO Box 1863, Saleufi, Apia – a basic car without air-con costs WS$110 per day, with air-con it costs WS$138 (☎ 25363; fax 23038).

Budget Car Hire
  NPF Bldg, Apia – a basic Hyundai Excel without air-con costs WS$120 per day or WS$720 per week; a 4WD Suzuki Sidekick costs WS$168 per day and WS$1000 per week (☎ 20561).

Coconuts Beach Club Resort
  PO Box 3684, Apia – Suzuki 4WD Sidekick costs WS$138 per day, including tax, insurance and unlimited mileage (☎ 24849; fax 20071).

Emka Rentals
  PO Box 3541, Lalovaea, Apia – this no-nonsense rental agency charges WS$100 per day and WS$600 per week, plus a security deposit of WS$100. Check the car and the contract carefully (☎ 23266).

Funway Rentals
  Mr Sonny Ahkui, PO Box 6075, Pesega, Apia – a 4WD Suzuki Samurai costs WSR100 per day for up to two days; WS$90 per day for three to seven days and WS$80 per day for more than seven days. This is one of the few agencies that allows their vehicles to be taken to Savai'i (☎ 22045).

G & J Rentals
  PO Box 1707, Matafele, Apia – this one charges a flat WS$145 per day for a standard air-conditioned vehicle. They also allow vehicles to be taken to Savai'i (☎ /fax 21078).

Hibiscus Rentals
Moto'otua, Apia – standard, non air-conditioned cars cost WS$110 per day, plus 10% GST (☎ 24342).

Le Car Rentals
PO Box 3669, Fugalei, Apia – a 4WD Suzuki Samurai costs WS$110 per day for a single day, WS$100 per day for two to six days and WS$90 per day for a week or more. A WS$110 deposit is also required (☎ /fax 22754).

Mt Vaea Rentals
PO Box 94, Lalovaea, Apia – a 4WD Suzuki Samurai costs WS$100 per day or WS$600 per week, plus a WS$100 security deposit. For longer term rentals, even better rates may be negotiated (☎ 20620; fax 20886).

P & K Filo Rentals
PO Box 4310, Mata'utu-Uta, Apia – Suzuki Samurai 4WDs cost WS$110 per day and WS$650 per week, plus a WS$200 security deposit (☎ 23031; fax 25574).

Pavitt's U-Drive
PO Box 290, Moto'otua, Apia – this friendly agency charges WS$115/120 per day without/with air-conditioning, plus a deposit of WS$150 (☎ 21766).

Rentway Rentals
Saleufi, Apia – basic non air-conditioned vans and cars rent for a flat WS$90 per day, with a minimum hire period of two days (☎ /fax 22468).

Taxi

Taxis in Apia are quite inexpensive and are good for getting around after the buses have stopped running. To travel anywhere between Aggie's and the Maketi Fou will cost WS$2; to anywhere else in Apia, the charge is WS$3. The standard fare for a trip to or from the airport is WS$30. It's still possible for foreigners to get a fair price in Western Samoa, but the temptation to over-charge is great so if you know the correct fare, stand your ground. Be sure you agree on a price with the driver before you climb in or there's likely to be an unpleasant scene when it comes time to pay up. In Western Samoa, official taxi number plates begin with 'T'.

For those in a hurry, taxis are also convenient for day-tripping around 'Upolu. You'll pay around WS$40 for half a day's sightseeing for up to four or five people. This is a particularly useful option if you'd rather avoid anxiety about catching the last bus

back to Apia. The visitors' bureau sets limits on the amount drivers may charge; check with them if you feel a driver is attempting to gouge.

For a bit of low-grade entertainment, visit the taxi ranks at the Maketi Fou and watch the odd loading procedure. For some unfathomable reason, taxis must reverse into the ranks; therefore, passengers must take the taxi which appears to be at the rear of the queue.

The following are some of the taxi companies operating in and around Apia:

Blue Bird Taxis (☎ 20977)
Marlboro (☎ 20808)
Samoan Radio Services (☎ 21591)
Time Taxi Tours (☎ 24202)
Town Taxi (☎ 21600)
Tusitala Taxis (☎ 21122)
Vailima (☎ 22380)

Motorbike & Bicycle

In Western Samoa, motorbikes may be hired at Tulei's Bike Rentals on Beach Rd in Apia for WS$55 per day plus 10% GST; helmets cost an additional WS$5 per day each. A WS$200 deposit is required on the motorbikes, and you'll need a driving licence to operate one.

Despite the mountainous nature of the island, 'Upolu is a pleasant place for keen cyclists, and the north coast can be negotiated by just about anyone. Whatever sort of bike you have, when travelling through villages, beware of children, who have a habit of throwing stones at people on bikes. The tourism commission is trying to put a stop to this practice but with little success. If you are hit, take the matter to the village pulenu'u, but try to report the incident calmly and accurately, without losing your temper.

Hitching

A lot of visitors avoid having to catch buses at wicked hours of the morning by hitching. This is easy around 'Upolu but it gets more difficult towards late afternoon and evening when everyone is in their own village playing rugby, volleyball or kirikiti. Hitching is discouraged on Sunday.

To be on the safe side, women probably shouldn't hitch alone, although I've done it and haven't had any problems. It's a good rule of thumb to look for older people, a woman or children in a car or truck before climbing aboard.

Although it's a good idea to offer payment for a ride – the equivalent of the bus fare will suffice – it will normally be refused. If you insist, you may be able to persuade them to take the money, but the best bet is to watch what other passengers do (very rarely will you be the only hitchhiker aboard) and do likewise.

Savai'i Island

Nature reigns supreme on the big island of Savai'i – the largest in Polynesia outside New Zealand and Hawaii – and much of it remains uninhabited and pristine. A large part of the island's appeal lies in the natural element, but Savai'i has retained its traditional ways even better than 'Upolu, and the sense of Polynesian history is strong. Scattered across the island are numerous archaeological sites – fortifications, star mounds and ancient platforms – many of which have been swallowed by the nearly impenetrable jungle. These ancient structures and monuments are unknown to present-day Samoans, but for many, the major sites have been relegated to the realms of legend and tradition.

Savai'i also has its share of sandy beaches and traditional villages. On the north coast is the best surfing and sailboarding in the Samoas, snorkelling is possible in several places around the northern and eastern coasts, and there's world-class diving along the island's barrier reef, off the coast at Lalomalava.

If you do make the effort to visit Savai'i, you won't be disappointed, but to see the island properly and to make the most of it, you'll need time and patience. Even more than on 'Upolu, transport is infrequent and unreliable, so allow time if you wish to travel around the island. Furthermore, much of your exploration will have to be done on foot, not just on wild mountain tracks but also along the main road.

History

On all the Polynesian migrations around the Pacific, people carried with them legends of the ancient homeland, 'the largest island of the leeward group', from which all the islanders dispersed. The Hawaiians called it Hawai'i, the Maoris Hawaiki, the Tahitians Havaiki, the Cook Islanders 'Avaiki and the Samoans Savai'i. The largest island of the Hawaiian group, which was settled relatively late in the scheme of things, was named after it.

No one knows for certain which island it was, but many researchers believe it was the largest island of the leeward group of Tahiti – Raiatea; in his book *Hawaii*, James Michener takes this opinion. Others, though, subscribe to the claims of Rarotonga or Manu'a. Most Samoans, however, have no doubt that their own 'big island of the leeward group', Savai'i, is the 'cradle of Polynesia'.

It was on Savai'i, in the village of Safotulafai, that the Mau Movement was formed by Namulau'ulu Lauaki Mamoe. The group's original objective was to replace the German administration, which they thought lacked interest in Samoan concerns, with a British one set up in much the same way as the loosely defined one in the British protectorate in Tonga. This stand was later softened to merely advocate an administration which would be more sensitive to local interests and show more respect for the Samoan king, Mata'afa.

As a result of his political activism, Namulau'ulu was exiled to the Mariana Islands, never to return to Samoa. He died at sea in 1915 on the ship sent by the New Zealand administration to retrieve him. The Mau Movement, however, carried on through the New Zealand years, which were so fraught with strife that there were times when the Samoans probably wished for the return of the Germans.

During the past century, Savai'i has fallen victim to several natural disasters. The first was the eruption of Mt Matavanu between 1905 and 1911, destroying property and villages. A song composed during the eruptions reflects the people's reaction to the disaster:

Alas, how fearful! The fire burning over there...
The fire below which is swallowing Savai'i,
...Reminding us to repent of our stubborn ways.
We cannot know God's will, but the slow...lava

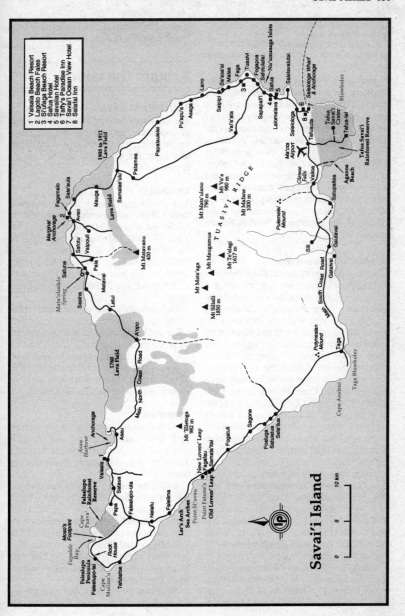

1 Vaisala Beach Resort
2 Lagoto Beach Fales
3 Si'ufaga Beach Resort
4 Safua Hotel
5 Savaiian Hotel
6 Taffy's Paradise Inn
7 Savai'i Ocean View Hotel
8 Salafai Inn

Savai'i Island

0   5   10 km

May indicate His Mercy
Because it allows...escape
It may be a warning concerning our sins –
As a result of which Savai'i has been turned to stone.

If that wasn't enough, Savai'i was the epicentre of devastation by the cyclones, 'Ofa and Val, which struck in February 1990 and December 1991, respectively. Many of the villages in the north-western corner of the island, including Falealupo-tai, Tafutafoe, Papa, Sataua, Vaisala and Asau, were either utterly destroyed or damaged beyond recognition. Clean-up operations continue but some villages have been abandoned altogether and those that remain will never be the same again. For more information, see under History in the Facts about Western Samoa chapter.

Orientation & Information

The Samoas' largest island is also its wildest. Its 50,000 inhabitants are concentrated in a string of villages along the east and south-east coasts; there are only a scattering of villages elsewhere. The vast, trackless interior of the island lies empty and distorted by recent bouts of vulcanism. A string of craters, some active, extend all along the central ridge of the island from the east coast at Tuasivi to within five km of Samoa's westernmost tip at Cape Mulinu'u. At 1850 metres, Mt Silisili is the highest point in the Samoan islands. The north coast of Savai'i is punctuated by lava fields; the western one between Asau and Sasina flowed from Mauga Afi in 1760, and the eastern one, from the eruptions between 1905 and 1911.

There isn't much of a service centre on Savai'i, and even the main populated area between Salelologa and Lano is just a cluster of 30 or so rural villages. There are hospitals at Tuasivi, Sasina, Sataua and Foaluga, but don't expect too much. At Faga, an Italian, Dr Peter Cafarelli, runs a medical clinic.

For yachties, there are anchorages at Fagamalo, Salelologa Wharf and Asau Harbour. Since the utter obliteration of Asau Airport during Cyclone 'Ofa, Ma'ota Airport near Salelologa is the only one on Savai'i. It is served by Samoa Air four times daily from Fagali'i Airstrip in Apia.

Around the Island

SOUTH-EAST SAVAI'I

The south-east coast of Savai'i is the centre of population, government and commerce for the island. It is also the arrival and departure point for all flights and inter-island ferries.

Information

You can change money in the air-conditioned Bank of Western Samoa, also in Salelologa; it's open Monday to Friday until 3 pm. The post and telephone office is a bit out of the way about 500 metres outside Salelologa village, towards the airport. Beside the Big Island CCK, the largest store on the island, you'll find the new OK Laundromat.

The main police station and immigration offices are in Tuasivi, as are the main post office and headquarters of other governmental functions on the island.

For travel arrangements to and from 'Upolu or transport around the island, try the Savai'i Travel Centre in Salelologa, a private agency operated by the Savaiian Hotel.

Salelologa

The wharf area of Salelologa is, for the most part, quite uninspiring and will probably give you a poor first impression of the island. Try to ignore it – everything gets better from there.

Beside the market, the only real points of interest in the Salelologa area are the blowholes on the lava coast south of the wharf. Most people see them as they arrive on the ferry from 'Upolu. Naturally, they're at their best in high winds and surf, so on calm days, you won't have as grand a show. The route is fairly straightforward; just follow the coast south from the wharf.

There are two ancient star mounds just north of the Main Coast Rd, about 200 metres west of its intersection with the wharf road, and across the street there are two platform mounds. They're overgrown and difficult to find, so you may need directions from locals. If the first person you ask looks blank, keep trying. Eventually you'll find someone familiar with them.

John Williams Monument

In front of the Congregational church at Sapapali'i is the stone monument commemorating the landing of the former British iron-monger turned missionary, Reverend John Williams, who arrived on his makeshift vessel, the *Messenger of Peace* in 1830.

At that time, Malietoa Vainu'upo, one of the most powerful chiefs on Savai'i, and the chiefs of A'ana district were embroiled in a war. Williams left behind eight missionary teachers who were successful at converting the victorious Malietoa. It is believed that he accepted the Christian message as the fulfilment of an ancient prophecy of a new religion by the goddess Nafanua.

Following a civil war, Nafanua had been given the task of dividing up the power between the districts. Regarding government, she had determined that only a 'tail' of the true spiritual government existed and that the people would have to wait for the 'head' to come from heaven. Thanks to the Malietoa's example and influence, many Savai'ians were encouraged to convert.

Nu'umasaga Islets

These two islets near Sapapali'i are said to be the result of a stone-throwing contest between twin sisters on the mainland. The contest went on for so long that two islets appeared above the surface of the water. The name, appropriately, means 'twin islands'.

Tuasivi Ridge

The Tuasivi ridge begins near the village of Tuasivi and rises in a series of craters that form the spine of Savai'i, ending just inland of the village of Falealupo-tai. As you approach on the ferry, the *olo* (barricade) formed by it will be obvious, looking very much like a series of artificial mounds climbing skyward. From the sea upward, the craters visible from the sea are Asi, Misimala, Vaiala, Vaiolo, Afutina and Masa.

In Samoan, the word *tuasivi* means 'ridge', so to say 'Tuasivi ridge' is actually a bit repetitive. The Samoans called it the enchanted ridge because they believed it possessed supernatural powers to harm and kill those who dealt with it improperly: pregnant women had to walk up to it three times before proceeding across it or the child would die; any person too sick to walk across it and had to be carried across was sure to die.

The crater of Mt Asi, the one nearest the sea, is said to be the mark left when an inland mountain wandered towards the sea to fetch some water to make palusami. Asi didn't want to be second from the sea so he threw a breadfruit in the other mountain's face as it approached; where it fell, a crater was formed.

There are two ancient terraces and a platform atop Mt Asi, as well as a good view out to sea.

Beaches

All along the east coast between Salelologa and Pu'apu'a, there are nice beaches and good snorkelling. Most of the villages will charge custom fees of about WS$1 per person to use their beaches. The best are at Faga and Lano, but part of Lano Beach, the nicest part in fact, is closed because too many careless bathers were leaving rubbish and bottles lying around on the sand.

The area also has numerous freshwater pools and springs for either bathing or rinsing.

Pu'apu'a

In the village of Pu'apu'a are two freshwater bathing pools maintained by the local women's committee. The pool on the eastern side of the road is for women and the one on the western side, for men. If you'd like to have a swim there, the locals will be flattered that you chose their pool, but it's still best to ask villagers' permission before jumping in.

Just south of Pu'apu'a are several other

springs, including Vaimanuia, whose name means 'healthy waters'.

Tafua Savai'i Rainforest Reserve

The new Tafua Savai'i Rainforest Reserve occupies much of the Tafua Peninsula, Savai'i's south-easternmost extremity. In addition to one of Samoa's most accessible and beautiful stands of rainforest, it also contains beautifully rugged stretches of lava coast, which is studded with cliffs, sea arches, lava tubes and blowholes. On the western coast of the peninsula is a track leading south to the lovely Aganoa dark sand beach. There were once rest fales here, but everything was badly damaged during the recent cyclones.

The centrepiece of the reserve, however, is the extinct Tafua Savai'i crater, which rises above the village of Tafua-tai. This forest-choked crated harbours a colony of flying foxes; from the crater rim, they may be seen circling above the treetops in the afternoon. The reserve is also one of the only remaining habitats of the *manume'a* or Samoan tooth-billed pigeon, believed by some zoologists to be the closest living relative of the dodo (it does bear a vague resemblance!).

To reach the crater, go to the village of Ma'ota and turn south off the Main South Coast Rd. There's a WS$5 per person custom fee to enter the reserve. After five km (just over an hour on foot), turn left along a track leading toward the northern rim of the crater. On foot, it will take about 10 minutes from the Tafua-tai road to the crater base; then it's an easy five to 10-minute stroll up to the rim.

Alternatively, continue a further two km south to Tafua-tai village on the coast. From there, a 20-minute track will take you up the steeper and higher southern slope of the crater. This worthwhile walk ends at a rest fale on the southern rim, which affords a far-ranging view of the island's southern coastline and up to the crater-studded highlands.

Places to Stay – bottom end

The *Salafai Inn* (☎ 51111), PO Box 1193, Apia, beside the market in Salelologa, is the only real budget accommodation on Savai'i. It was officially closed during my last visit, but that was reportedly only temporary and at any rate, I did meet travellers who'd managed to get a room there. It looks terrible from the outside but inside it's clean and airy. Upstairs, there's a great TV room, bar and lounge. Drinks and food can be bought in the shop downstairs or at the market next door. Single/double rooms with shared facilities (cold water only) cost WS$18/25. If you can't take the heat, one air-conditioned unit is available for WS$45. Meals can be arranged at extra cost.

Places to Stay – middle

The premier place to stay on Savai'i is the *Safua Hotel* (☎ 51271; fax 51272) in Lalomalava. The proprietor, Moelagi Jackson, is as interesting as any of the sites on the island and visitors to Savai'i should make a point of meeting her. You'll rarely find such an excellent chance to gain the insights into Samoan ways and history that she can provide and you'd be hard-pressed to find a more knowledgeable, vivacious and charismatic individual.

The idea behind the Safua is to provide opportunities for visitors to experience a bit of the Samoan lifestyle – Moelagi will even arrange a Samoan tattoo, if you'd like one! The rooms consist of fale-style bungalows, all with attached showers and toilets. The dining room and lounge is a large and airy thatched shelter.

For victims of the 'Safua Hotel Bug', as Moelagi calls the local strain of Polynesian paralysis, there's a library of paperbacks and reference books. She claims to have been forced to evict some long-stayers or send them elsewhere to prevent them becoming part of the furniture! Given the circumstances, it's difficult to avoid this particular malady.

Single/double fales cost WS$93/110 plus WS$25 for each extra person. With the three-meal plan, the rate is WS$150/200. This includes three *immense* and incredible Samoan-style meals.

Dormitory style accommodation can also

be arranged for WS$30 per person, including breakfast and tent space costs WS$10 per person. If you stay more than four days, there's a 15% discount and if you settle in for more than 15 days, the discount increases to 25%. If you'd prefer to stay in a village, Moelagi will arrange accommodation in private homes, including meals, for WS$30 per person. In addition to their typically fabulous meals, they stage a fiafia on Friday and Saturday nights and an umu feast at midday on Sunday.

Another favourite travellers haunt is the friendly *Si'ufaga Beach Resort* (☎ 53518; fax 53535), PO Box 8002, Tuasivi, which is at the village of Faga immediately north of Tuasivi. It's run by Italian Dr Peter Cafarelli and his wife Alauni (and their 11 children). The hotel consists of six self-contained fales, each with showers, loos and cooking facilities, strewn about a large grassy lawn. Camping is also permitted. The real drawing card, however, is the white and sandy Si'ufaga Beach across the road, which is safe for swimming and snorkelling.

Single/double/triple fales cost WS$90/100/110; campers pay WS$15 per person. If you book in advance, complimentary pick-up service is available from the wharf or airport. For staples, there's a small shop at the hotel, but they'll provide transport to the supermarket in Salelologa upon request.

Across the road and about 200 metres south of the Safua Hotel is the newly constructed *Savaiian Hotel* (☎ 51206; fax 51291), PO Box 5082, Lalomalava, Salelologa. It's intended to be eastern Savai'i's answer to up-market tourist accommodation, but the main building is reminiscent of a primary school. Fortunately, the pathetic artificial beach is offset by a swimming pool. Single/double rooms with air-conditioning, cooking facilities and hot showers cost WS$95/115; prices include complimentary transfers to and from the wharf or airport. Breakfast costs WS$10 and set dinners, WS$25. On Friday and Saturday nights, there's live music and dancing in the restaurant/bar.

Convenient to the wharf and the market in Salelologa is *Taffy's Paradise Inn* (☎ 51321; 20263), a small and slightly shabby seven-room guesthouse. Single/double rooms cost WS$38/75 but discounts can be negotiated if they're not busy. Breakfast costs WS$8 to WS$11, depending on what you have; set-menu lunches are WS$10 and dinners are WS$15.

Just down the road, also in Salelologa, is the new *Savai'i Ocean View Hotel* (☎ /fax 51258), PO Box 195, Apia, which has recently had a second storey added on. Comfortable single/double rooms with facilities cost WS$88/112, plus 10% GST. Bookings may be made through Retzlaff's Travel in Apia.

Places to Eat

The earth-shaking buffet meals served at the *Safua Hotel* are among the best in Western Samoa. You'll get real Samoan fare and more of it than anyone could hope to finish. Prices are a bit high for most budget travellers, but if you can manage it, forego something else and eat at least one meal there. On Sundays, don't miss the umu feast. Get up early and watch the preparation of the umu, which begins at 6.30 am. The meal is served after church.

Safua guests whose budget doesn't stretch to the hotel meals have another option in the *Lalomalava Trading Company* diagonally across the street from the hotel. They serve café meals and takeaways from 6.30 am to 7 pm Monday to Saturday and on Sunday from 5 to 7 pm.

In Salelologa, the only formal eating establishment is the *Chan Wong Restaurant* which, as its name would imply, serves Chinese food. It's rather grotty appearance belies the quality of the food, which is quite good.

At the intersection of the wharf road and the Main Coast road in Salelologa is a general store, which has a milk bar serving fish & chips and other greasy snacks. Inside the market are a number of food stalls serving very passable local dishes for rock-bottom prices. Behind the market is a whole bank of little general stores where you'll find inexpensive staple items.

NORTH-EAST SAVAI'I

Between Pu'apu'a and Samalae'ulu, fast-growing eucalypts are being planted as part of a reforestation project. As you travel along this stretch of road, notice the great views of far-off craters and the volcanic landscapes of the island's interior.

Lava Field

The Mt Matavanu eruptions of 1905 to 1911 created a moonscape on the north-eastern corner of Savai'i as the flow of hot lava 10 to 150 metres thick, rolled across plantations and villages destroying everything in its path. Between Samalae'ulu and Sale'aula, the Main Coast Rd crosses the lava field and passes a couple of interesting sites.

Just east of the road is the village of Mauga, the name of which means 'mountain'. It is built in a circular pattern around a nearly perfect crater. After the eruptions, the intense heat and the porous rock caused a scarcity of fresh water in the area. The priest in the village felt inspired to instruct the villagers to dig in the bottom of the crater to find water. After many days of exhausting labour, they reached the water table and the town well has been located in the crater ever since.

Just north of Mauga, about 100 metres east of the road, in a large hole in the lava, is the partially built Methodist church that 'miraculously' survived the lava flow while the Mormon and Catholic church buildings were destroyed. Many people attribute its survival to the fact that it was constructed of cement.

Further along the road, less than one km east of Sale'aula, is another 'divinely protected' site, the Virgin's Grave. Legend states that a novice Catholic nun from the convent in the village of Lealatele had been buried there in the usual manner beneath a raised concrete headstone. When the lava ploughed through, the church adjoining the site was destroyed, but as it approached the girl's grave, the stream of molten rock parted

and flowed around it. Geologists, however, have determined that the miracle may be attributed to a coincidentally placed steam vent which interrupted the lava flow.

The grave can still be seen in a pit two metres below the surface of the lava field and about 100 metres north of the road near a rest fale. It's been completely left alone since the eruptions and, today, beautiful plants and wildflowers grow around it. If there's an attendant at the site, you'll be asked to pay a WS$1 custom fee.

Fagamalo

There is a marginal anchorage at Fagamalo but the primary interest of the place will be to surfers and sailboarders. The wind and waves here are excellent for sailboarding. There's now bungalow accommodation on the beach just west of the village; see under Places to Stay later in this section.

At nearby Avao, three km west of Fagamalo, is the site where, in 1834, early missionaries first translated the Bible into Samoan. The pulpit of the Congregational church is carved from the stump of the tree which shaded the translators as they worked. There's also a monument to their efforts at the site where the tree actually grew.

Safotu

The long, strung-out village of Safotu is interesting in that it has three large and prominent churches in a row near the centre, one of which is painted with rather unusual colours. The large and sparkling white one is a landmark to sailors. To the west of the churches, near the sea, are a series of fresh-water pools for bathing or swimming. Some are for men and some for women so be sure to ask rather than make assumptions.

About two km to the east of Safotu is a nice secluded beach between headlands and away from the population. It's a particularly good place for a Sunday swim.

Mt Matavanu Crater Walk

One of the most easily accessible and dramatic natural features of Savai'i is Mt Matavanu, the errant crater that sent a flow

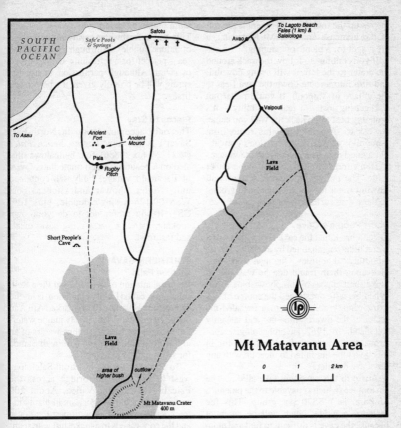

Mt Matavanu Area

SOUTH PACIFIC OCEAN

To Asau

Safe'e Pools & Springs

Safotu

Avao

To Lagoto Beach Fales (1 km) & Salelologa

Vaipouli

Ancient Fort

Ancient Mound

Paia

Rugby Pitch

Lava Field

Short People's Cave

Lava Field

area of higher bush

outflow

Mt Matavanu Crater 400 m

0   1   2 km

of destruction from the heart of the earth to the north-east coast of the island. From Safotu, it's a pleasant day walk but can be done in about five hours if you can catch a lift as far as Paia village.

Once you get to Paia, you may want to stop and have a look at the ancient fort and mound atop the hill there. The mound is about four metres high and has several fales on top. The fort, which is surrounded by a ditch, is just to the north of the mound. It's not terribly dramatic but may be of interest to archaeology buffs. Expect to pay a custom fee of WS$1 to pass through Paia en route to

the crater, but be sure to pay only the pulenu'u.

From Paia, follow the plantation road south. Ask the locals if you're unsure about which one to take, as there are three roads entering the village from Safotu. After a little more than an hour of walking, you should enter the lava field. Nearly another hour on, the lava field gives way to heavier bush and clumps of acacias. At the point where the road begins to dip for the first time, you'll see a trail to the left leading uphill through a forest (if you reach the end of the road, you've gone too far). Several hundred metres up the trail from this point is the rim of the immense crater of Mt Matavanu, a great spot for a picnic or camping.

If you continue to follow the track around the crater to the left, it will swing downhill and turn into a route down the lava field to the village of Vaipouli. If you'd rather not risk getting lost – a real possibility – it's probably best to go back the way you came. Access to the crater up this route from Vaipouli is also possible, but don't go without a good map or a guide from the village.

Don't forget to carry water along either route. The porous volcanic rock allows all flowing water to seep through underground so there's no surface water to speak of.

Short People's Cave

Legend has it that the cave above Paia was a secret hide-out inhabited by a tribe of dwarfs with magical abilities. One man who stumbled upon them found that he was able to make food appear by simply wishing for it. When his wife questioned the source of this extraordinary ability, the man revealed the secret of the dwarfs' hide-out and instantly fell dead. In 1962 an archaeologist confirmed the existence of a dwarf footprint in this lava tube but failed to meet up with any tiny cave dwellers.

A trip to this cave will take all day. The custom fee, which is payable to the pulenu'u of Paia, is WS$20 per group. This fee includes a guide which will be essential because the cave is difficult to find and quite dangerous inside. If you don't have a torch, you'll need to hire kerosene lamps before heading up; the pastor, the pulenu'u and the family living in the highest fale in town all charge around WS$5 per day.

To reach the cave, walk up the road from Paia (see map) for about an hour. Upon entering, you'll come to a room that appears to be furnished with stone tables. From there, one cave leads off to the left and another to the right. The left cave goes the furthest – more than one km – and involves swimming across five small pools and down underground waterfalls. The right cave goes only about 50 metres.

Mata'olealelo Spring

This ample freshwater spring in the village of Safune bubbles up through a pool into the sea – perfect for a refreshing swim-jet type of swim. Although permission to use the spring will be proudly given, it's best to ask first.

Places to Stay

The only accommodation in North-East Savai'i is the new *Lagoto Beach Fales* (☎ 21724; fax 20886), four bungalows situated on a beautiful beach immediately west of Fagamalo village. Fully self-contained units (toilet, shower and kitchen) cost WS$100/125 a single/double, plus 10% GST. If you prefer not to do your own cooking, there's a bar serving basic meals and fast food.

SOUTHERN SAVAI'I
Olemoe Falls

On the plantation of Mea'ole and Pu'a Keil, sometimes called Letolo Plantation, is idyllic and secluded Olemoe Falls (marked Afu Aau on the Hema map). This lovely jungle waterfall plunges into the crystalline waters of an idyllic deep blue pool, the best in all Samoa for swimming and diving.

To reach it, take the bus from Salelologa west to just past the bridge across the Falealila River near Vailoa. About 200 metres west of the bridge, a small plantation track leads inland. Follow it past the house and the copra sheds to a makeshift gate spanning a break in the stone wall on your right. Pass through the gate and follow the track to a second gate. Once through this gate, follow the plantation rows east through the coconut trees and cow pastures to the line of bush and a barbed wire fence. Where the fence is broken, a track leads steeply down to the river. Just upstream are the falls and pool.

The track leads around to the western side of the pool, where you can dive from the cliffs into three metres or more of water. Be sure to ascertain the depth, however, before plunging in! Dry weather could conceivably lower the water level and make for disastrous diving. With snorkelling gear, you can look

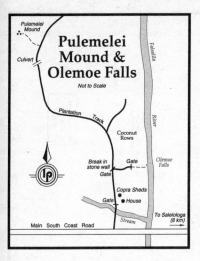

Pulemelei
Mound &
Olemoe Falls

Not to Scale

Pulemelei Mound

Plantation Track

Coconut Rows

Break in stone wall   Gate   Olemoe Falls
Gate

Copra Sheds
Gate   ● House

To Salelologa (8 km)
Stream

Main South Coast Road

Falealila River

for the freshwater prawns which inhabit the pool; there are also pools further downstream where you can observe them without a mask.

Remember that you're on private property here. Don't leave rubbish lying around or disturb any of the crops or animals. The Keils welcome visitors who wish to use the pool for swimming but abuse of the privilege will make things difficult for future travellers.

Pulemelei Mound

Polynesia's largest ancient structure, Pulemelei Mound (marked on the Hema map as Tia Seu Ancient Mound), is found not far from Olemoe Falls, also on the Letolo plantation. This large pyramid measures 61 metres by 50 metres at the base and rises in two tiers to a height of more than 12 metres.

It is almost squarely oriented with the compass directions. The main approaches to the summit are up ramps on the eastern and western slopes. Smaller mounds and platforms are found in four directions away from the main structure. There is a relatively large platform about 40 metres north of the main pyramid and connected to it by a stone walkway.

Unfortunately, this impressive monument is naturally obscured by jungle growth, so unless it has been cleared recently, it is extremely difficult to locate. However, the fact that relatively few travellers have actually found it seems to make it all the more intriguing. Move over, Indiana Jones!

After visiting Olemoe Falls, keep following the main plantation road inland. About 200 metres past the break in the stone wall where you turn off to the falls, there is a fork in the road. Follow it to the left and keep going for about another 1½ km until you cross a culvert perpendicular to the road. Standing on the culvert and looking ahead along the road, you're looking straight at the pyramid, although it won't be obvious at the time.

About 120 metres beyond the culvert, an overgrown track leads off to the left. Follow it for about 150 metres to the top of a hill and look around. You'll be standing on the summit of Pulemelei Mound.

Given its similarity to religious structures in Meso-America and the mid-western USA, archaeologists have difficulty believing that Pulemelei was used for pigeon-snaring, as oral tradition seems to imply all the ancient Polynesian monuments were. The complexity of its design and the effort expended in its construction leads them to believe that it may have had religious or other significance. Another theory postulates that it was used for strategic purposes since, when cleared, it affords a view right down to the coast.

Satupaitea

The long narrow village of Satupaitea lies on a loop road about two km south of the South Coast Rd. There's nothing of overwhelming interest, but taken as a package, it's an unusual village. It lies beside a foul-smelling inlet which at low tide becomes a mucky paddock for oyster-foraging pigs. Locals maintain that these 'aquatic pigs' produce some of the richest and best-tasting pork in Samoa.

While you're there, also take a look at the Peter Turner monument in front of the colourful Methodist church. You can also see

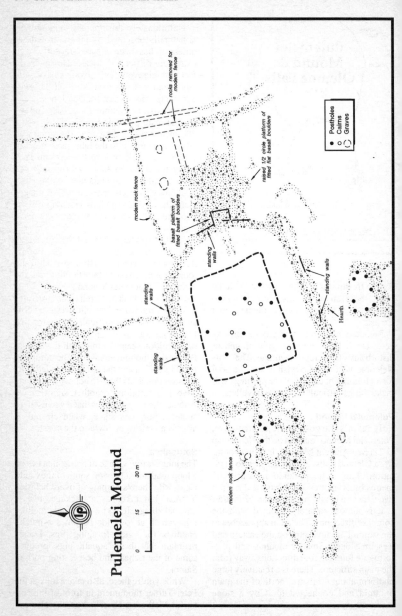

Top: Church before the cyclone at Falealupo-tai, Savai'i (DS)
Middle Left: Cyclone-damaged church at Falealupo-tai, Savai'i (DS)
Middle Right: Piula Methodist church, 'Upolu (GC)
Bottom: Ulutonia Congregational church, 'Upolu (GC)

Top Left: New growth on the 1905-1911 lava field, Savai'i (GC)
Top Right: Poinciana tree, Savai'i (DS)
Middle: Hibiscus (SC) & Fatumea Pool, 'Upolu (GC)
Bottom: Wild coleus & tree fungus (DC)

several springs bubbling up in the middle of streams beside the road. They don't appear too health-promoting, but local children seem to like them, anyway.

Gataivai

The beautifully-situated village of Gataivai sits beside a veritable water garden of cascades. Here, the waters of Samoa's greatest river rush down to their climax at Mu Tagoa Falls, where they plunge five metres into the sea. The approach to the falls is from the sub-village of Gautavai, which is beside the South Coast Rd on the opposite bank of the river.

Sili

If for some reason you're going to the village of Sili (wonderful name, isn't it?), bear in mind that the suspension bridge over the river has collapsed. Access to the village will require wading across the river.

Taga Blowholes

This is not just another set of blowholes. I've never seen anything like them anywhere else in the world and to miss them would be to miss what is one of the most impressive natural features in Samoa.

At the village of Taga, pay the WS$1 custom fee and walk down the hill and west along the coast for about 10 minutes. You'll then emerge from the coconut plantation for a clear view across the black lava coast. Here are the roaring blowholes; surf-powered dynamos that provide you with hours of entertainment trying to second guess them. Often, locals who are familiar with their behaviour will demonstrate the incredible power of the surf by tossing in a coconut at just the right moment to send it flying up to 90 metres into the air.

About five km north-west of Taga, just north of the road, is a large jungle-covered Polynesian mound which is thought to date back at least 1000 years, possibly to the period of Tongan domination. It is fashioned of coral and lava blocks and is divided on top by a low wall. Its use is unknown but is thought to have served a religious purpose or

was simply a platform to support the home of a noble.

Lovers' Leap

The sheer cliff called (New) Lovers' Leap is just north-west of the village of Fagafau. It's a nice view down to the sea but don't go too far out of your way to see it. The story goes that a woman from Tutuila married a man from this corner of Savai'i. When he died, the broken-hearted woman and her daughter were so badly treated by the villagers that they leapt into the sea and were turned into a turtle and a shark. For the slightly mangled sequel to this story, see under Turtle & Shark Point in the Tutuila chapter.

There are actually two Lover's Leaps. The old one lies about 1½ km south-east of the new one, which was deemed better for photography.

Sea Arches

Near the village of Falelima, the coastal lava flows have been sculpted by roiling surf into dramatic shapes and terraces. If you're mesmerised by roiling surf, this area is great for a few hours of maritime contemplation. At Km posts 175 and 181 along the Main Coast Rd are two impressive natural sea arches, caused by the pounding waves. About 300 metres east of the large arch at Falelima is an odd blowhole which shoots blasts of warm air. It's known as – you guessed it – Moso's Fart.

Mt Silisili

With some planning, it is possible to climb 1850-metre Mt Silisili, the Samoas' highest point. The peak is nondescript – really little more than a volcanic knob, much like scores of other little volcanic knobs in the area, and it's difficult to pick out as the highest.

The most convenient route up is from A'opo village on the 1760 lava field, but the villagers have been known to make life very difficult for visitors with hassles and exorbitant custom fees. At the present time, this route is probably best given a miss.

An alternative route leads up plantation roads from Sala'ilua on the south-west coast.

The climb is not difficult but the chances of getting lost increase the further you go from the end of the road. One group of Japanese climbers built some cairns at the end of the road to steer you in the right direction, but they're now well overgrown, so it's still best to hire a guide for the trip. The problem, of course, is finding one who actually knows the way!

If you're set on making the trip, allow at least three days up and down and wear strong boots. You'll also need to carry all the food and water you'll need, one change of warm clothing and a sleeping bag – and provide supplies for the guide. Because temperatures are normally mild, just a tent fly or a light tarp will suffice as a rain catchment or a shelter at night.

Don't forget to carry topographical sheets from the Department of Lands & Surveys in Apia, which are available for WS$5 each. Although they aren't perfect, they'll prove indispensable for this trip.

NORTH-WEST SAVAI'I
Falealupo Peninsula

The Falealupo Peninsula figures prominently in local legend. The natural beauty of the area belies the dark significance it holds for Samoans, who believe that the gateway to the underworld of the aitu (spirits) is found at the place where the sun sets in the sea. According to tradition, there are actually two entrances, one for chiefs and the other for commoners. One entrance is through a cave near Cape Mulinu'u and the other is on the trail made by the setting sun over the sea. During the night, these spirits wander abroad, but at daybreak they must return to their hellish home or suffer the unpleasant consequences of being caught out by daylight.

To get onto the Falealupo or Tafutafoe roads, foreigners have to pay a custom fee of WS$2 per person or WS$5 per vehicle.

Falealupo Rainforest Reserve Once a showcase for rainforest preservation in Samoa, the Falealupo Rainforest Reserve on the northern side of the peninsula was heavily damaged in the cyclones. Many of the larger trees were knocked down, causing growth of additional sun-loving undergrowth. This was, however, clearly a part of the natural cycle – 'Ofa and Val weren't the first cyclones to happen along. One problem lies in the fact that this was one of the last stands of rainforest on Savai'i. Another problem concerns the attitude of local people and government; if they decide that cyclone-damaged rainforest might as well be cleared for settlement or agriculture, the consequences could be significant.

Falealupo-tai Sadly, the once bright and magnificent village at the western tip of the Samoan islands is no more, having been annihilated by the wrath of cyclones 'Ofa and Val, which struck here with a particular vengeance. Although there are a few hangers on, for practical purposes the village has been abandoned. However, the former Swedish school is now being renovated with Swedish aid, so there's hope that some sort of revival will be possible. The ruin of the old Catholic Church, which now sits amidst a garden of weeds, has been left standing as a monument to the power of the cyclones.

Rock House About 300 metres inland from the village of Falealupo-tai are the two closely associated lava tubes known as Rock House. Inside is a very crude stone armchair, and there are stone benches around the sides.

Legend says that the Rock House is the result of a competition between the men and the women of Falealupo-tai. They staged a house-building contest to find out which sex was more adept at it. At the end of the first day of construction, the men were winning so the women decided to stay up and work through the night while the men were asleep. The women won, of course, and the men were so angry about it that they never finished their house, leaving the hole in the ceiling that is still in evidence.

If someone is there to collect it, you'll be asked to pay a custom fee of WS$5 per group to visit the Rock House.

Moso's Footprint The ancient one-metre by three-metre rock enclosure called Moso's Footprint is found in the uncharacteristic scrubby bush along the road that winds north and then east from Falealupo-tai back towards the Main Coast Rd. The footprint was said to have been made by the giant Moso when he stepped from Fiji to Samoa. There is said to be another 'footprint' on the Fijian island of Viti Levu which marks his point of departure.

The scientific explanation is a bit more complicated. When lava cools and contracts, it breaks into blocks. These blocks are often lifted and moved by tree roots growing down into the joints. Once they're on the surface, a cyclone could easily clear them away, leaving regularly-shaped indentations in the crust. Hence, Moso's Footprint.

Because Moso's Footprint was in plain view just a few metres north of the road, someone decided to build a ridiculous dog-house-like structure over it. The idea was that foreigners would pay someone WS$5 to unlock it so they could take a look. This is one custom fee that I feel is inappropriate – the doghouse has actually ruined the site. Unless you have a particular interest, you may want to give it a miss.

Papa This friendly little village along the rugged north coast of the Falealupo Peninsula is well off the beaten track, but like other villages in the area, it was also destroyed in the cyclones. Nevertheless, it still has a decent swimming beach that can be used for a custom fee of WS$1.

Sataua

To see Sataua today, you'd never guess that just prior to Cyclone 'Ofa, it was awarded the title of the 'tidiest town in Samoa'. Now it is devastated, having been hammered in the cyclones by high surf and winds of up to 260 km/h. Because all the buildings collapsed during the storm – even the solid-looking Mormon church was reduced to a ruin – people smashed openings in their water cisterns and crawled inside to shelter from the wind, rain and waves. The clean-up

has been slow, but the fact that Sataua remains, however battered, certainly is a tribute to the tenacity of its people.

Asau & Vaisala

Asau, which is the main anchorage on Savai'i and service centre for the western end of the island, lies at the end of the paved road and serves as a departure point for trips across the 1760 lava field. Its importance, however, was challenged by Cyclone 'Ofa, which reduced its airport to so much sand and coral rubble; not a trace remains. The village also suffered in the cyclones – take a look at the house slowly crumbling into the sea beside the new harbour. At nearby Vaisala, note the new salt marshland which appeared during the cyclones on the site of the former football pitch.

An interesting place to visit is the old harbour and petrol storage tanks three km north-east of the village, where you can swim and look for tropical fish and sea turtles in the clear, ultra-green water.

Places to Stay & Eat

The *Vaisala Beach Resort* (☎ 58016; fax 58017) is at Vaisala on the north-west coast. It clings to a slope right above a lovely white sand beach and although much of its charm disappeared in the cyclones (all the thatched

buildings and coconut trees were levelled), it's nice and fairly low key. During reconstruction, rooms will cost WS$77/88 single/double, but once it's completed, the prices will increase to WS$130/145, including GST.

The hotel also has the north-west's only formal bar/restaurant but it's considerably less charming since the cyclones pulverised their old thatched building. The new restaurant is a stark concrete affair that should withstand just about any blow. Set-menu meals are available for WS$20 for breakfast, WS$35 for lunch and WS$40 for dinner.

Getting There & Away

Air
From Fagali'i Airstrip in Apia, Polynesian Airlines flies to Ma'ota Airport four times daily: at 7 and 8 am and at 3 and 4 pm, returning to Fagali'i 30 minutes later. The fare is WS$35 each way or WS$57 return. For bookings, ring Polynesian Airlines Internal Service (☎ 21261) in Apia.

Boat
The Western Samoa Shipping Corporation operates a vehicle and passenger ferry between Mulifanua Wharf on the western end of 'Upolu and Salelologa, Savai'i. In theory, it runs at least three times daily. On weekdays and Sunday, it sails from Salelologa at 6 am, 10 am and 2 pm and from Mulifanua at 8 am, noon and 4 pm. On Saturday, it sails from Savai'i at 6 am and 10 am and from Mulifanua at 8 am and noon.

However, it frequently misses a run so passengers often face long waits on the dock. The fare is WS$6 each way and the 22-km crossing takes one to 1½ hours.

Getting Around

To/From the Airport
Whenever a plane arrives, nearly every taxi on Savai'i is waiting for it, so there'll be no problem finding transport, but they are expensive. To Salelologa, they charge WS$6; to Safua, WS$15; to Tuasivi, WS$22; and to Vaisala, around WS$45.

All Savai'i hotels (except the Salafai Inn) offer airport transfers, provided you book in advance. Most are free but the remote Hotel Vaisala charges WS$50 return.

The public buses are convenient for getting to Salelologa from the airport but if you're travelling to Safua, Tuasivi or further north, you'll have to change buses at Salelologa.

Bus
The buses of Savai'i, which rarely have glass in their window frames or doors in their doorways, are crowded, vibrantly coloured affairs that blare reggae music and awaken all the senses.

The market near the wharf is the main terminal for regular buses to Lalomalava, Tuasivi, Palauli and Gataivai. Less frequently, they go to Safotu or Sasina on the north coast and Asau in the north-west. There is no public transport across the lava field between Asau and Safotu so travelling between the two by bus will require passing through Salelologa.

Way out on the north-western end, buses run regularly between Asau and Falelima. There's even a rumour of a once-daily bus out to Falealupo-tai from Asau at 6 am, and locals will verify it again and again. However, I've tried repeatedly to connect with it and there was never any sign of such a bus at 6 am or any hour of the day. If you're headed in that direction, consider it a possibility but don't rely on it.

Ferry passengers will have the most luck connecting with buses to out-of-the-way destinations – that is, beyond the cluster of villages along the south-eastern coast. Buses bound for the north and west coasts depart as soon as the ferry comes in and then aren't seen again until the ferry returns. When the ferry is late or cancelled, the buses are, too, so anyone awaiting a bus away from the wharf area will have no idea when or if a bus is likely to pass.

The fare from Salelologa to Palauli and Lalomalava is only 40 sene. To either end of the main road – Asau or Safotu/Sasina it's WS$4. The trip to the blowholes at Taga costs WS$2.

Boat

There are no ferries travelling between ports on Savai'i, so if you want to cruise around Savai'i, you'll need a private yacht. Yachties wanting to cruise around Savai'i must first obtain a cruising permit from the immigration office in Apia. If you're planning to leave Western Samoa from Savai'i, you should have checked out of the country in Apia before leaving 'Upolu.

Car & Motorbike

Only two Apia car hire agencies – G & J Rentals and Funway Rentals – allow their vehicles to be taken to Savai'i on the ferry, but if you want to drive around Savai'i, this is the only practical way to go. For information, see Getting Around at the end of the 'Upolu chapter.

Hitching

Every Savai'i traveller will probably have to resort to hitching at one time or another. Most of your rides will only take you from one village to the next, but it will get you around eventually. Hitching is relatively easy prior to mid-afternoon, when the daily kirikiti and volleyball matches begin in the villages. Be prepared to pay a tala or two (not

---

Busing it on Savai'i

On the big island of Savai'i, public transport is limited and buses seem to operate on a schedule known only to their drivers. For example, in Asau I visited the owner/driver of one vehicle to find out what time the following morning the first bus to Salelologa would leave. He told me that passengers should be waiting at the petrol station at 3 am:

I turned up at 2.30, however, because the previous day I'd missed the '6 am bus', which for some reason had departed at 5.40 am. Of course there was no one else waiting when I arrived at the petrol station and when the 3 am bus finally turned up at 4.30 there was still no one else waiting. I soon learned why. Instead of taking off for Salelologa, it set off in the opposite direction.

We pulled up in front of a house. The driver got out, knocked on the door, and the lights came on. There was evidence of people bustling around inside and then, 15 minutes later, two girls emerged with baskets and luggage and boarded the bus. We proceeded to another house and the same thing happened. Then another house and another...The first and only bus of the day from Asau to Salelologa was providing a wake-up and pick-up service for its passengers! At 5.45 am we finally set out for Salelologa.

The bus was scheduled to return to Asau at noon (leaving only three hours in Salelologa), so at precisely 12, I was waiting beside the road. Two hours passed, then three. The ferries between Savai'i and 'Upolu had been undergoing repairs so there was no way of knowing if the arrival of a ferry would provide a bus or not.

It looked as if the bus were never going to turn up and everyone I asked had a different answer. Since traffic is thin anytime after about 2 pm, I realised it was time to begin hitching. After several short rides and many km of walking between them, I arrived back in Asau, by which time it was well after dark.

Later I learned from a friend that the driver of the Asau bus had decided to stay in Salelologa playing pool and drinking with his buddies that night and that no afternoon ferry had ever arrived.

The moral of the story is that you shouldn't set out between any two points on (or away from) Savai'i without leaving your options open. If you have a plane to catch in Apia the following day, don't count on the bus getting you to the wharf or the airport, and for that matter, don't depend on the plane or the ferry getting you back to 'Upolu in any reasonable amount of time either. Go back a day early – or even two days early – if you'd rather not risk missing an international flight. The mellow Polynesians are just that – mellow – and they realise that if the bus/boat/plane doesn't go today, it may go tomorrow, or the next day, or...

At any rate, welcome to paradise! ■

per person – this will suffice for a group of two or three) for a ride of a longer distance. Payment should be proportional to the length of time you're aboard and a good rule of thumb (pun unintentional) is to offer the equivalent of bus fare for that distance travelled.

Some stretches of the coast road, especially the north coast lava field and the stretches between Taga and Sala'ilua or Falelima and Samata'itai see very little traffic. At times, hitching will seem more like walking; you may find yourself hoofing for long stretches before someone comes by.

The most difficult section of the trip around the island is the 28-km stretch across the lava field between Asau and Sasina. The road is just a rough track and carries very little traffic. Forest service vehicles carrying workers cross it on workdays – east to west in the morning and west to east in the evening – and they're probably the best hope you'll have of hitching across it. The most persistent travellers normally wind up walking it.

Organised Tours

For organised sightseeing and cultural tours around the island, you can't beat Safua Tours at the Safua Hotel. Warren Jopling, the tour organiser, guide and resident geologist, has spent many years on Savai'i and knows the island as well as anyone. Because tour departures are guaranteed – that is, Warren is happy to go even if there's only one person interested – these tours are especially convenient for individual travellers. Half-day tours cost WS$45 per person and full-day trips are WS$85 or WS$90.

Safua's Tours are not the 'see-Samoa-through-the-window' variety you get on

'Upolu. Many are hands-on experiences and Moelagi or Warren will accompany you on all sorts of adventures and cultural experiences. Particularly interesting is the tapa tour, visiting the home of a local woman who will demonstrate tapa-making from start to finish, but any sort of cultural interests can be accommodated, including Samoan dancing, woodcarving, weaving, tattooing, language courses or even kirikiti.

There are four basic day tours, but these are flexible and can be altered according to individual interests. One takes in the Saleaula Lava Flow and several of the villages along the north coast. Another includes a trip along the south coast to Taga, with stops at Gataivai, Pulemelei Mound, a swim at Olemoe Falls and a visit to a tapa maker who will demonstrate the art.

The third possibility takes you to the western end of the island, including the Taga blowholes, sea arches, Asau Harbour and the Falealupo peninsula, which was decimated by the cyclones 'Ofa and Val. Lastly, you can spend a day exploring the Tafua Peninsula on foot, climbing the Tafua Savai'i crater and visiting caves, beaches, sea arches and blowholes.

Other possible full-day tours include exploration of the Short People's Cave and drives right around the island.

Half-day tour possibilities include abbreviated trips to the north coast, Tafua Savai'i Rainforest Reserve, Pulemelei Mound and Olemoe Falls, Aganoa Beach and the Mt Matavanu Crater. In addition to these standard tours, customised trips and expeditions may also be organised; they've even arranged climbs of Mt Silisili and jungle treks in search of ruins.

American Samoa

Introduction

...the rain fell with a cruel persistence. You felt that the heavens must at last be empty of water, but still it poured down, straight and heavy, with a maddening iteration, on the iron roof...

'If it would only stop raining for a single day...'

In his short story *Rain*, Somerset Maugham captures the overwhelmingly dreary mood of Pago Pago. Although it does have a fair number of fine days, the steep and rugged mountains that surround Pago Pago Harbor act as a funnel, capturing stray rain clouds as they pass the entrance and thrusting them onto Rainmaker Mountain, which in turn extracts every drop and dumps it on the harbour area. But potential visitors shouldn't be discouraged; the rest of Tutuila Island, away from the main area of settlement and the harbour microclimate, enjoys more agreeable weather.

And there's more to American Samoa than Tutuila. Off the eastern end of the main island is tiny 'Aunu'u, with its traditional village, its fiery red quicksand lakes, its beautiful crater and wild, roiling surf. A hundred kilometres to the east are the breathtaking islands of the Manu'a group – three small, dramatic outcrops that epitomise every traveller's dream of the South Seas. In the farthest reaches of the territory are remote Swains Island, actually one of the Tokelau Islands, and Rose Atoll, a US wildlife refuge.

American Samoa is subsidised almost totally by the US government which, for better or worse, has turned it into a welfare state. At least half the workforce is employed by the government, either federal or territorial, and much of the other half is comprised of Western Samoans, Tongans, Koreans and Chinese who are involved in the tuna-fishing industry.

For the visitor, American Samoa provides a unique cultural study and a distinct counterpoint to the sublime appeal of its historical 'other half', Western Samoa. It will be obvious to anyone who travels to American Samoa that it is in a state of transition and searching for an identity. It is still trying to decide whether it is Samoan or American or whether some sort of compromise between the two will produce an entirely new social structure.

While most American Samoans consider themselves fortunate to have access to the health care, technology and educational opportunities inherent in their political connections with the USA, it's clear that with the benefits package come a host of destructive forces. Among them are an undermining of tradition and loss of cultural identity that, in so many places, has resulted in violence and despair.

Largely due to all this outside input, which some American Samoans would rather be without, the social structure on the island is changing. People are abandoning their traditional foods for imported tinned and frozen foods; traditional aiga structures are breaking down; the environment is being sacrificed to American 'throwaway' technology; and outside governmental values and influences are usurping control of the islands' cultural destiny. In the face of such trends, it's not surprising that many are tempted by the 'American dream' over the crumbling vestiges of fa'a Samoa.

Fortunately, a few enlightened American Samoans seem to believe that a more positive balance can be struck and indeed, there are laws in place aimed at limiting outside influence. Americans cannot immigrate at will from the USA; non-Samoans may not own land; and foreign companies and franchises may not compete with private Samoan businesses.

Thanks to these regulations, American Samoa has not suffered the exclusive condominium developments, high-rise cities and large-scale ruination that Hawaii has experienced at the hands of outsiders.

Having said all that, it's also a friendly and

beautiful place to explore. It may appear a bit grimy and uncared for around the main harbour area, but beyond Pago Pago are the mountains, beaches, rugged coasts and isolated villages that poignantly remind you in what part of the world you're travelling.

Facts about American Samoa

HISTORY

The formal annexation of eastern Samoa on the part of the USA took place on 17 April 1900, by a deed of cession signed and agreed to by all the chiefs of the islands involved:

The island of Tutuila of the Samoan group, and all other islands of the group east of longitude one hundred and seventy one degrees west of Greenwich, are hereby placed under the control of the Department of the Navy, for a naval station.

The Secretary of the Navy will take such steps as may be necessary to establish the authority of the United States, and to give the islands the necessary protection.

Under the jurisdiction of the US Department of the Navy, the territory became a naval station headed by Commander Benjamin F Tilley of the USS *Abarenda*. The USA agreed to protect the traditional rights of the indigenous Samoans in exchange for the military base and coaling station. The territory's inhabitants acquired the status of US nationals but were denied the vote or representation in Washington.

In 1905 the military commander of Tutuila was given the title of governor, and the territory officially became known as American Samoa.

The original deed of cession included only the islands of Tutuila and 'Aunu'u, leaving the Manu'a Islands under the control of the Tu'i Manu'a, the hereditary chief of that eastern group and the holder of perhaps the most revered title in Polynesia. In 1904, however, he also signed a deed of cession. When he died, on 2 April 1909, he stipulated in his will that the title die with him in order that no other Tu'i Manu'a ever be subservient to a foreign power.

Swains Island, an atoll more than 300 km north of Tutuila in the Tokelau Islands, was acquired in 1876 by a US citizen, Eli Jennings. It was added to American Samoa by joint congressional resolution on 4 March 1925. The two later cessions were formally recognised by the US Congress on 20 February 1929.

At this point, a commission was established to recommend a form of government for the territory, but nothing immediately came of it, and American Samoa remained under naval jurisdiction until 1951 when control was transferred to the US Department of the Interior.

During the years that followed, a constitution was drafted, discussed and amended. It was finally approved by the people in 1960. Stipulations included the official protection of American Samoans from alienation of their lands, the destruction of fa'a Samoa and the undermining of their language by outside interests. It set up territorial government and granted legislative powers to the fono, the territorial legislature.

At this point, American Samoa still retained its very traditional social structure and subsistence economy, and the governor at the time recommended restraint on the part of the Americans in dragging the territory too quickly into the North American version of the 20th century.

In the early '60s, however, an influential North American magazine published an article entitled 'America's Shame in the South Seas', which examined the simple subsistence lifestyle enjoyed by the American Samoans and determined it to be poverty by US standards. Americans became outraged and demanded that something be done about the situation.

In response, President Kennedy appointed H Rex Lee, a Mormon, to the governorship and instructed him to oversee the wholesale modernisation of the territory. Funds were appropriated by Congress, and almost overnight, American Samoa became a US construction project, overtaken by haphazard and insensitive development.

Roads were built and European-style homes replaced traditional fales, electrification and sewage treatment projects were implemented and harbour facilities, schools and a tourist hotel were constructed. In addition, an international airport, a public auditorium, a hospital, the tuna canneries and TV transmission from the mainland were laid down. Suddenly, all the problems experienced on the US mainland– alcoholism, crime and juvenile delinquency, to name a few – began to surface in American Samoa. By the time Governor Lee left office in 1967, Samoan leaders were already lamenting the downfall of their society and the creation of a directionless welfare state.

Between 1967 and 1975, lack of sufficient funds from Washington to maintain all the new amenities caused the whole system to fall into disrepair or go awry for one reason or another. In a series of referendums, the American Samoans voted to continue under the direction of appointed governors. However, under a bit of coercion from Washington, a subsequent referendum determined that the American Samoans were ready for democratically elected leadership and some measure of autonomy. Gratefully, the US government attempted to wash its hands of the mess it had created in the territory.

The first elected governor was Republican Peter Tali Coleman, who had served for a time as the only Samoan appointed governor in the earlier years. Four years later, he was elected to a second term but was barred from seeking a third consecutive term in the next elections. In November 1988 he ran against the interim governor, A P Lutali, and won – 5261 votes to Lutali's 4344 votes.

Of recent interest, the elected congressional representative to Washington, Fofo Sunia, was indicted on 6 September 1988 on multiple counts of payroll fraud amounting to US$130,000. The money was bilked from the federal government for personal use by adding family members to the federal payroll.

Overall, American Samoans, accustomed to traditional dog-eat-dog competition between aiga and seemingly admiring of those who can get away with profitable mischief, were initially sorry to see him found out. The territory suffered a major setback,

however, as far as the USA's perception of the affair, and it will take many years for the government to regain the credibility lost because of this fiasco.

In the November 1988 elections, Sunia was replaced by Democrat Faleomavaega Eni Hunkin Jr, who advocates a loosening of ties between the USA and American Samoa. To quote Hunkin: 'I am a Samoan first, an American second. You cannot serve two masters.' In the hopes of putting a stop to the imminent breakdown of fa'a Samoa in the territory, he would like to see enacted a policy of free association based on the Cook Islands-New Zealand model.

In 1990 and 1992, Hunkin was re-elected to second and third terms. The 1992 elections also saw the replacement of Republican incumbent governor Peter Coleman with Democrat A P Lutali, who had previously served from 1985 to 1989.

In December 1991, American Samoa was badly hit by Cyclone Val (see under History in the Facts about Western Samoa chapter), which caused US$25 million worth of destruction, damaging 60% of the homes on the islands and destroying 95 % of the subsistence crops.

GOVERNMENT

American Samoa is an unincorporated territory of the USA, but it is not under the jurisdiction of the US constitution, and operates under a constitution that has not yet been sanctioned by the US Congress. For American Samoa, remaining outside the US constitutional realm has its obvious advantages, which include freedom from business competition and immigration from the mainland and the continuation of the traditional Samoan system of matais and land rights.

The people of American Samoa are nationals of the USA and are permitted to migrate to the mainland at will (more than two-thirds of American Samoan high-school graduates migrate to the mainland), but they are not permitted to vote in national elections and have only a non-voting representative in the US Congress who is elected every two years. Any American Samoan who chooses may become a US citizen upon meeting the requirements of citizenship.

Territorial government is patterned loosely on that of the USA, with legislative, executive and judicial branches. The legislative branch, the fono, is divided into a senate and a house of representatives, which have 18 four-year-term and 21 two-year-term members, respectively. It is the responsibility of the fono to enact the laws of the territory. All legislation must be approved by the governor before being put into effect. The US Office of Territorial & International Affairs, an agency of the Department of the Interior in Washington, ultimately holds veto power over any law passed by the fono.

The governor, lieutenant governor and heads of executive departments make up the executive branch. In August 1976 the people decided by referendum to change the office of governor, a position previously appointed by the Department of the Interior, to an elected office. The governor has the right to veto legislation approved by the fono, but officials in Washington retain the right to veto anyone and anything they choose.

The main power of the judicial branch rests with the high court, which is presided over by a chief justice appointed by the Secretary of the US Department of the Interior, and has jurisdiction throughout the territory. In addition, there are five district courts, a traffic court, a small claims court and a matai title court.

Cases in the high court are conducted in both Samoan and English before a panel of judges including the chief justice and three other judges. Criminal cases are tried by a judge and a six-person jury. Matai title issues are heard by a panel of three associate judges. Judges from other areas of the USA and US territories occasionally assist in difficult cases and in decisions particularly requiring neutrality.

Local government is overseen by three district governors and 15 county chiefs. Village governments consist of the traditional hierarchy of pulenu'u and matai.

American Samoans pay taxes to their territorial government under the same tax structure as that of the US federal government.

Territorial Seal

The official seal of the territory of American Samoa is an interesting design that tries to mesh some of the traditional aspects of Samoan culture with the reality of the present.

It contains an illustration of a fue (fly whisk), which represents wisdom, and the to'oto'o – the staff signifying authority. Both of these items are symbols of the rank of the tulafale (talking chief). Below these items is an 'ava bowl symbolising service to the matais, and the background is a siapo pattern. Around the outside is the date 17 April 1900, the day American Samoa was taken over by the USA, and the words *Samoa Muamua le Atua* meaning 'Samoa, Let God be First', effectively illustrating the degree to which the Christian missionaries were successful here.

ECONOMY

The mainstay of the American Samoan economy is government, with nearly half of the total workforce of the territory employed in public service. Most of the operating budget of the territorial government is provided by Washington, and US contributions are increasing annually.

The bulk of private sector employment is provided by the fishing industry, which is centred on the Starkist and Samoa Packing tuna canneries across Pago Pago Harbor from Fagatogo. Together they pack and can 95% of American Samoa's exports. The actual value of fish products exported annually – including tinned tuna, pet food and fish meal – is nearly US$100 million.

In the late 1980s, Samoa Packing, the large US corporation that purchased Van Camp in 1954, was sold to an Indonesian firm. Starkist, by far the larger of the two canneries, arrived in 1963. Today most of the tuna is provided by more than 180 large Korean and Taiwanese long liners and 60 or so purse seiners from the US mainland. (During the recent cyclones, nearly a dozen of these were destroyed; they're now just more junk languishing in the harbour.) Altogether, the fish processed in American Samoa represent the majority of the South Pacific tuna catch, primarily because US federal regulations against the offloading of fish from foreign vessels and high US import tariffs do not apply if more than 30% of their value is added in American Samoa.

In a push towards diversification of the private sector, the American Samoan government is encouraging new business developments, including a large industrial park at Tafuna near the airport, which will train and employ American Samoan residents. The current problem with such programs is that American Samoans would rather remain unemployed and wait for more prestigious and high-benefit white-collar or government jobs. Most private sector employees and labourers in the territory are of Oriental, Western Samoan or Tongan origin.

Although the importance of subsistence plantations is steadily declining, many plantation owners have become involved in commercial production of market crops. On the island of Ofu, an experimental farm has been established to provide a greater variety of produce and to try to eliminate crop diseases in the territory.

While tourism was on the increase a few years ago, things have now slowed right down. Presently, most of the tourism in American Samoa is related to overseas family visits, shopping trips from Western Samoa, business travel and cruising yachts which stop in Pago Pago to stock up on inexpensive food and supplies. The lack of dependable international airline transport in and out seems to be a main factor in the decline in tourism. In addition, the absence of a luxury resort (or even a decent hotel) puts off traditional tourists, and the lack of viable, inexpensive accommodation tends to keep budget travellers away, as well. However, there are currently plans to develop a luxury business hotel somewhere in the harbour area.

Facts for the Visitor

VISAS & EMBASSIES

The territory of American Samoa has its own immigration laws, which are different from those of the US mainland, so fortunately, intending visitors will be spared the odd questions asked on a regular US visa application form!

No visas are required of visitors to American Samoa but US citizens need proof of citizenship and everyone else must have a valid passport. Everyone, including US citizens, must have an onward ticket. Crew arriving on yachts must either hold an onward ticket or have the captain's guarantee of responsibility for all crew members' departures. Western Samoan citizens, who were once permitted to pass freely between the two Samoas, are now required to hold a permit to enter and may no longer remain indefinitely in American Samoa.

Normally, stays of 30 days, extendible to 90 days, are initially granted to tourists and business travellers. Anyone wishing to remain longer or to work in American Samoa must secure permission to stay. Applications for length of stay extensions, work permits and long-stay permits must be organised through the immigration office in the Executive Office building in 'Utulei. Advance enquiries should be directed to the Chief Immigration Officer, PO Box 7, Pago Pago, American Samoa 96799.

All American Samoan diplomatic affairs are handled by the USA.

Immigration Problems

In late 1992, there was an odd blip in immigration policy and the ridiculous happened, as the following reader's letter explains:

After the November 1992 election, the new Attorney General, appointed by the new governor A P Lutali, decided to take away all visitors' passports (except US passports) upon arrival at Pago Pago International Airport. The reason behind this was to prevent Western Samoans from entering American Samoa with a three-day permit visa and staying permanently. The passports were to be returned to travellers at the airport before their departure, but naturally this caused a lot of anxiety among foreign travellers.

Visitors during this period report that they weren't able to change money at the bank without first trekking out to the airport to retrieve their passports – and then having to return them to the airport afterwards! Hopefully this sort of thing won't happen again but if it does, I can only recommend that you stand your ground and refuse to give up your passport. If they insist, perhaps threaten to take the matter to your embassy in the USA.

Foreign Consulates in American Samoa

There are no consulates or embassies in American Samoa and there is currently no place in American Samoa that will issue visas for the USA. According to the US Immigration & Naturalisation Service, there is not likely to be such a place anywhere in the Pacific islands in the near future.

CUSTOMS

Customs and immigration are handled at the airport or at the port facility in Fagatogo. Be prepared for fairly thorough customs searches. All the immigration officers attended an illicit substances seminar in Hawaii recently and they've quite zealously adopted the typical US paranoia regarding such things.

If you're arriving by yacht, raise the quarantine flag upon entering Pago Pago Harbor and anchor. If customs officials don't turn up in an hour or two, radio the harbour authorities for instructions. The customs fee is US$50 – that is, US$25 to check in and the same to check out. They charge an additional overtime fee to check you in on weekends.

US citizens returning to the mainland from American Samoa are permitted a duty-free allowance of US$800 rather than the usual US$400, provided it all originated in American Samoa.

MONEY

There are two banks in Fagatogo, the Bank of Hawaii and the Amerika Samoa Bank near the wharf, but currently, only the former will exchange foreign currency. Banks are open from 9 am to 3 pm Monday to Friday, with a service window open until 4.30 pm on Fridays. The Nu'uuli branch of the Amerika Samoa Bank is open from 9 am to noon on Saturdays.

There is no exchange office at the airport, so if you'll be arriving at night or on weekends, make sure you have some US currency or travellers' cheques from elsewhere.

Currency

The US dollar is the currency used in American Samoa. If you're not already familiar with US currency, notes come in denominations of 1, 2 (rare), 5, 10, 20, 50 and 100 dollars and coins in circulation come in denominations of 1 (a penny), 5 (a nickel), 10 (a dime), 25 (a quarter) and 50 cents (somewhat rare). There is also a one dollar coin, but it's not in common usage outside of Nevada and other casino areas.

In addition, US dollar travellers' cheques are accepted at most shops, restaurants and hotels. Japanese yen, Deutschmark, Swiss francs, pounds sterling and Canadian, New Zealand and Australian dollars may be exchanged for US dollars for a small commission at the Bank of Hawaii on the malae in Fagatogo.

Exchange Rates

WS$1	=	US$0.39
A$1	=	US$0.71
NZ$1	=	US$0.58
C$1	=	US$0.72
UK£1	=	US$1.49
FF 1	=	US$0.18
DM 1	=	US$0.60

Credit Cards

Visa, American Express and MasterCard are accepted at the Rainmaker Hotel and at tourist-oriented shops and restaurants on Tutuila. The American Express representative in Pago Pago is the Samoan Holiday & Travel Centre (☎ 633-4692), upstairs in the Lumana'i building (above the Bank of Hawaii and the post office). Its address is PO Box 968, Pago Pago, American Samoa 96799.

Costs

Budget travel in American Samoa is difficult but not impossible for those who aren't averse to a bit of inconvenience. There are a couple of inexpensive and out-of-the-way places to stay where you'll pay US$20 to US$30 per night but the cheapest place that actually calls itself a 'hotel' is a grotty and unappealing establishment that charges US$35 a single. Formal home stays may be arranged through the tourist office for US$25 to US$45.

Camping on Tutuila will require some searching for a secluded spot or a long walk from populated areas, but it is possible. Be sure to ask permission of locals before pitching a tent in an area where you're likely to be noticed. On Aunu'u, the Manu'a Islands and other outer islands, there are lots of isolated places to camp and although you'll probably have to carry water, it's certainly the cheapest way to go.

Reasonable fast food is available for US$2 to US$3 for breakfast or lunch and US$5 for dinner. Inexpensive vegetables and fruits are available in the market in Fagatogo, but nontropical produce may only be found in the supermarkets and is outrageously priced – US$7 for a cabbage and US$3 for a bunch of carrots! Alcohol products are quite expensive in comparison to those on the US mainland.

Petrol prices are comparable to those in the US proper and are therefore low when measured against Australian and European standards.

Consumer Taxes

There is a 2% territorial sales tax on consumer goods but it's not worked into the posted prices. Take this into consideration when you're down to your last few cents and want to pay in exact change.

Tipping
In Pago Pago some tipping is acceptable for exceptional service at finer restaurants, but otherwise, it's not the custom.

TOURIST OFFICE
The amazingly well-staffed American Samoa Office of Tourism (☎ 633-1091; fax 633-1094) is housed in the white weatherboard building opposite Tedi of Samoa in Fagatogo. Government offices and agencies in the territory exist primarily to provide employment, not service, so don't expect a great deal of help here. They can, however, provide you with a nice map of Tutuila and the harbour area and a pack of interesting brochures.

The tourist office has also established an official home-stay programme known as *Fale, fala ma ti*, which means 'House, mat and tea'. In theory, it provides the option of staying with Samoan host families for US$25 to US$45 per night. Their current list includes places in the Pago Pago area as well as Tula, Leone, Futiga, Vatia and Amalau. Unfortunately, you'll sometimes find that the prospective host family has forgotten they ever signed up for the program so you may have to try more than one before coming up with something. For information and the most current listings of participants, contact American Samoa Office of Tourism, P O Box 1147, Pago Pago, American Samoa 96799.

POST & TELECOMMUNICATIONS
Post
The post office is near the malae in Fagatogo on the ground floor of the Lumana'i building, the same building as the Bank of Hawaii occupies. It is open from 8 am to 4 pm Monday to Friday and from 8.30 am to noon Saturday. There are other post offices in Faga'itua and Leone, both in rural Tutuila. Because US stamps are used and US postal rates apply, travellers from the USA will find it particularly inexpensive to post parcels

home from American Samoa. The zip (postal) code for all of American Samoa is 96799.

Mail delivery to Pago Pago from the US mainland is inconsistent, thanks mainly to the airlines, which place a weight limit on mail allowed to be carried on each run from Honolulu. When that limit is reached, all remaining mail is placed in a storeroom awaiting the next flight. Things can pile up and since items placed in the storeroom don't necessarily emerge on a 'first-in, first-out' basis, Honolulu becomes a sort of limbo for American Samoa-bound mail.

Items that don't have to pass through the USA (ie from Australia, New Zealand or other South Pacific islands) will normally fare much better. North America-bound post also seems to move along with a minimum of difficulty.

Receiving Mail Visitors who wish to receive correspondence here should have mail addressed to themselves, General Delivery, Pago Pago, American Samoa 96799. Those arriving on a yacht should have the name of the vessel included somewhere in the address. The general delivery pick-up window is open from 9.30 to 11 am and from 1 to 3 pm Monday to Friday and from 9 to 11 am on Saturdays.

Yacht people receiving general delivery post here should have the attendant check under the name of their yacht as well as under their surnames, as mail is normally filed under the name of the vessel if it is available.

Telephone
The communications office is in Fagatogo not far from the tourist office. It is open 24 hours a day for both local and international calls; cable and fax services are also available.

During prime hours, station-to-station calls to the US mainland, Hawaii and Canada cost US$8 for the first three minutes and US$3.50 for each minute thereafter. Operator-assisted calls are considerably more. To Australia, New Zealand and the rest of the Pacific, the charge is US$5.25 for the first

comes from Hawaii on a week-delay basis, complete with advertising for Honolulu fast-food restaurants and shopping malls. In addition, Cable News Network is broadcast via satellite during daylight hours.

WORK
For employment purposes, American Samoans will always be considered before foreigners, although teachers and medical personnel are currently in demand and will probably have more luck than unskilled labourers. Foreigners, including US citizens, may not purchase land or controlling percentages of businesses in American Samoa. However, land may be leased to outsiders for up to 55 years. Work permit applications are best handled from abroad; enquiries should be directed to the Chief Immigration Officer, PO Box 7, Pago Pago, American Samoa 96799.

HEALTH
The LBJ Tropical Medical Center was once the best hospital in the Pacific islands but unfortunately, recent bouts of corruption and mismanagement of funds, among other things, have resulted in a significant drop in standards.

Under the best of conditions, there are emergency doctors on duty at all hours and the clinic is open from 8 am to 4 pm weekdays. Office visits cost only US$2 per initial visit and US$1 for each subsequent visit. Gamma globulin shots (against hepatitis) are available for US$2.

The hospital has the only prescription pharmacy in American Samoa. The emergency telephone number is 911, as it is throughout the USA.

ACTIVITIES
Watersports
Although the Pago Pago harbour region isn't exactly the nicest, cleanest or safest area to engage in water activities, there is a reasonable beach at 'Utulei where the locals swim. It's probably best not to go into the water this close to the harbour with any open wounds, however, due to high levels of contaminants,

---

three minutes. To Europe, it's about US$12 for three minutes station-to-station. On weekends and evenings, all charges are discounted.

ELECTRICITY
Power is supplied mainly from the Tafuna and Satala power plants on Tutuila. The current in the outlets is 110 V, so US plugs and appliances may be used.

LAUNDRY
In American Samoa there are good old Western-style laundrettes, which are open from Monday to Saturday and occasionally even on Sunday. For specifics, see under Information in the Pago Pago section.

MEDIA
The *Samoa News* is published daily Monday to Friday and the *Samoa Journal* is published twice weekly on Tuesday and Thursday. Both contain minimal news of international interest but they cover both local and sports news in detail. There's also a new weekly consumer paper, *Pacific Hotline*, which is mainly an advertising medium with classified ads, consumer advice and other titbits of information (if not for this paper, I wouldn't know how to prepare lamb flaps in cheese sauce!). It's available free in shops.

Radio programming on 10,000-watt WVUV at 648 AM is available 24 hours a day, with brief news programs hourly. Broadcasts are in Samoan and English.

There is one TV station, KVZK, which broadcasts on three channels from 3.30 pm to midnight from a transmitter atop Mt 'Alava above Pago Pago Harbor. Most of its programming is standard US stuff, which

sewage and garbage that find their way into the harbour.

If you want to snorkel or swim at any of the more remote village beaches, be sure to ask permission before doing so.

Surfing & Windsurfing Thanks to the strong winds funnelled up the harbour, especially during the winter months, conditions are favourable for windsurfing but the hazards are obvious. Watch out for cargo ships, long liners and yachts (between August and October they're everywhere!), and again, don't fall into the water if you have open wounds. A serious infection could result. Currently, there are no sailboard rental agencies in the area, but ask at Atamai Marine either in Faga'alu or beside the wharf for the name of someone who might have a board to rent for the day.

The best surfing is found just beyond the reef near Faganeanea and Faga'alu, but if the trade winds are blowing, surfing will be impossible. The rest of the time, it is merely very risky.

Because of heavy breakers and shallow reefs along the coast near Faga'alu, snorkelling is possible but marginal and dangerous, especially when the south-easterly trade winds are blowing. Far better areas for diving and snorkelling may be found along the south coast near the eastern and western ends of Tutuila and all along the north coast of the island in 10 to 30 metres of water.

Diving Long-time resident Chuck Brugman, together with Atamai Marine (in Faga'alu), operates Dive Samoa (☎ 633-2010, 633-2183), PO Box 3927, Pago Pago. He operates worthwhile fishing, snorkelling and diving charters to particularly interesting areas offshore from Tutuila. On a trip with Chuck you will have access to his vast store of knowledge about dive spots and marine life in American Samoa as well as his considerable diving expertise. Single-tank dives off the south coast of Tutuila (certified divers only) cost US$30, with a minimum of two divers. Two-tank dives cost US$50 per person. Due to the distance involved, dives on the north coast will cost slightly more. Snorkellers pay only US$25 for a day trip.

Fishing Charters Chuck Brugman (see under diving) also offers deep-sea fishing trips for tuna, wahoo, masimasi (dolphin fish) and other local big-game fish for US$50 per person with a minimum of three participants. All equipment is provided. To book in advance write to Chuck Brugman/Atamai Marine, PO Box 3927, Pago Pago, American Samoa 96799.

Another option is to go with Mike Crook (☎ 622-7413) on his vessel, *Leilani*. Charters for up to six people cost US$200 for up to five hours and US$350 for 12 hours. Prices include bait and use of equipment. For advance bookings, write to Mike Crook, PO Box 3700, Pago Pago, American Samoa 96799.

Some yachties also give diving lessons: if you're there between July and October, check around the wharf area.

BOOKS
If you'll be travelling only to American Samoa, you'd be wise to carry with you any books you'll be wanting to read there. In the entire territory there are only three places to buy books – the Wesley Bookshop in Fagatogo, Malaloa Duty Free in Malaloa (between Fagatogo and Pago Pago) and the Rainmaker Hotel Gift Shop. The Wesley Bookshop does have a good selection of books about Samoa but neither of the others bothers to stock anything but pulpy romance and spy novels. I scoured the island for a copy of the short story *Rain*, by Somerset Maugham, the most famous fictional piece ever written about the place, but it was nowhere to be found. Bibliophiles be warned! Used paperbacks may be bought or traded at the Malaloa Duty Free, which is also a good place to buy inexpensive Kodak film.

The yacht club in 'Utulei also has a box of reading material dumped by yachties whose boats were filled to overflowing with things they'd already read. This is a good source of nautical and Pacific-related literature, if that is where your interests lie.

Libraries

American Samoa has two reasonable lending libraries, one at American Samoa Community College in Mapusaga and the Feleti Pacific Library in 'Utulei near the Rainmaker Hotel. In either case, you'll have to convince them that you're a resident in order to get a library card. There's no sign on the Feleti Pacific Library, so ask someone to point it out for you. The college library has an extensive Pacific collection, but the books don't circulate so research must be done on site.

THINGS TO BUY
Handicrafts

There are a few items for sale at the airport shop but these are mostly for the benefit of transit passengers. The Women's Handicraft Fale across the street from the malae and beside the fono is probably the least expensive of all the shops selling handicrafts and also offers the greatest variety.

The fale is a traditional open-air building where local artists come to sell their work. The artists are always happy to discuss their work with visitors who may not be familiar with methods and myths represented in Polynesian art. Masks and carvings are available for from US$7 to US$40 depending on size, siapo cloth will cost around US$5 for one square metre, and nice (if a bit kitsch) shell necklaces sell for US$2 to US$3 each.

In Pago Pago village are the Senior Citizens' Handicraft Fales, which serve as outlets for work done by older Samoans. In theory, it's open from 8 am to 3.30 pm Monday to Friday, but it's not always attended.

Luana's Handicrafts (☎ 633-2183) in the Samoa News building beside the Wesley Bookshop between 'Utulei and Fagatogo offers high-quality but also rather pricey articles from all over the Pacific Islands.

For inexpensive clothing and basic household goods, you can't beat Spencer's in Pago Pago.

Tutuila Island

Like a sinuous green dragon slinking through the sea, the island of Tutuila, 30 km long and never more than six km wide, has numerous bays and indentations where deep and fertile valleys plunge into the sea. The most prominent of these is Pago Pago Harbor, the safest and most renowned harbour in the South Pacific, which nearly divides the island in two.

Tutuila is by far the largest of the seven islands of American Samoa, comprising 145 of the territory's 197 sq km and with more than 90% of its 35,000 inhabitants.

The dramatic landscape of Tutuila is characterised by steep, rugged and lush forested mountains which branch out from the central ridge and dominate the wild topography, confining most of the development to a narrow strip along the south coast and the level area between the airport and the village of Leone. This is the only flat land in the entire territory.

The north coast is so wildly eroded that only a few tributary roads connect it with the island-long highway that follows the south coast. Matafao Peak, just west of Pago Pago harbour and above Fagatogo, is the highest point, at 653 metres. Immediately to the east of the harbour is 524-metre Mt Pioa, more commonly known as the Rainmaker Mountain for its habit of capturing precipitation in large quantities and dumping it unsparingly onto harbour-area settlements.

Tutuila's most important feature these days is Pago Pago Harbour, which is all that remains of the volcanic crater that created Tutuila in the first place. Sometime in the dim geological past, one wall of the crater collapsed and the sea came rushing in creating a nearly perfect shelter from the wrath of the sea at large. During the days of the big sailing ships, however, it was of little value. Without motors, the ships were unable to turn around in such a confined area and the most common anchorage in those days was Leone Bay near the western end of the island.

The first missionaries landed at Leone (now American Samoa's second-largest village) and built the most ornate church in the territory.

On 1 November 1988, Ronald Reagan signed a bill creating the new American Samoa National Park, which includes much of the island of Ta'u and part of Ofu in the Manu'a group and also a sizable portion of the northern slopes of Tutuila. The words 'national park' alone are sufficient to attract tourists to an area and American Samoa is hoping that its new park will do just that. As yet, however, disputes over traditional land rights have held up development of the park and the conflicts don't look like they'll be resolved in the near future.

Apart from the park, Tutuila has the usual gamut of palm-fringed white beaches, jungle waterfalls, colourful reefs and quiet villages that the world has come to expect of South Pacific places. Visitors will also find archaeological sites, pleasant bushwalks, sites made famous by history and legend (or a bit of both) and an ancient culture in transition, careering headlong into the modern world.

History

The Samoans believe that Tutuila was the last island of the archipelago to be created by Tagaloa, and once it came into existence, he asked Tutu and Ila to set about peopling it. Archaeological evidence tells us that the first settlements on Tutuila appeared around 600 BC, near the villages of Tula and Aoa on the island's far eastern tip. It is believed that early Samoan authorities used Tutuila as a place of exile for wrong-doers banished from 'Upolu.

PAGO PAGO

For most visitors, the crowded stretch of highway between the airport and the Rainmaker Hotel is all there is to American Samoa, and while such a judgement is unfounded, it is true that most of the territory's activity is nearby.

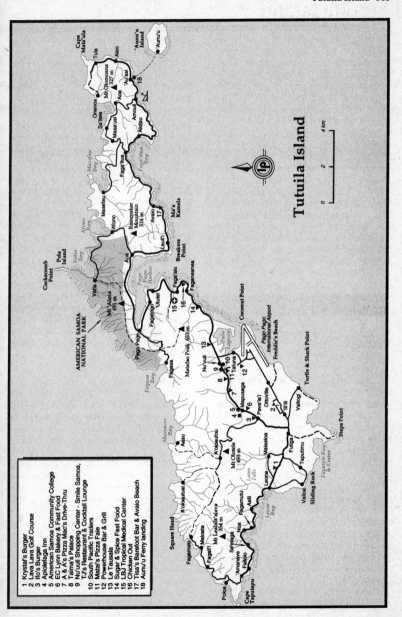

Tutuila Island

0   2   4km

1 Krystal's Burger
2 Lava Lava Golf Course
3 Ifo's Burger
4 Apiolefaga Inn
5 American Samoa Community College
6 EC Lynn Bakery & Fast Food
7 A & A's Pizza Mac's Drive-Thru
8 Taima's Palace
9 Nu'uuli Shopping Center - Smile Samoa,
   TJ's Restaurant & Cocktail Lounge
10 South Pacific Traders
11 Mata'ls Pizza Fale
12 Powerhouse Bar & Grill
13 Le Tausala
14 Sugar & Spice Fast Food
15 LBJ Tropical Medical Center
16 Chicken Out
17 Tisa's Barefoot Bar & Avalo Beach
18 Aunu'u Ferry landing

The capital of American Samoa is actually the village of Fagatogo, but the several small villages around the harbour area that contain the territorial government, all the industry and most of the commerce in American Samoa are known collectively as Pago Pago, after the small settlement at the head of the harbour. The Rainmaker Hotel itself is in 'Utulei and the canneries are in Anua, both of which are other villages of 'metro' Pago Pago.

The harbour area certainly isn't representative of the romantic image most people conjure up when they think of the South Pacific. Yes, there are coconut trees and something that resembles water, but the similarities stop there. In fact, some have speculated that Pago Pago Harbor is shaped like an elbow, because Pago Pago itself has often been referred to as the 'armpit of the Pacific'. Thanks primarily to the tuna canneries across the water from the main settlement, which spew forth a steady stream of noxious fishy farts, and the very casual garbage disposal system (rain – which ensures that it all winds up in the harbour and everywhere else en route), Pago Pago deserves its reputation.

Visitors should not despair, however; the Pago Pago area is a duty-free port, so prices on imported goods are cheaper here than in other parts of the South Pacific. And it's really only horrid under close scrutiny; from a distance, Pago Pago has one of the world's most beautiful settings.

Furthermore, around Tutuila, there's still plenty to see and do and fortunately, just as all the USA isn't Newark and all England isn't Coventry, all Tutuila isn't Pago Pago! What *is* Pago Pago is the area along the south coast between Faga'alu and Breakers Point. This area is relatively compact, so if you're willing to dodge the considerable traffic and don't mind being caught in sudden downpours, it's not difficult to walk between any of the points of interest in the harbour area.

Information

Tourist Office The new tourist office in Pago Pago (☎ 633-1091; fax 633-1094) is at Fagatogo opposite the Tedi of Samoa shopping centre. They're not a great deal of help but they seem well-intentioned and you can get a map of Tutuila and the harbour area. The office is open from 8 am to 4 pm Monday to Friday. It's closed on weekends and holidays.

Money You can exchange foreign cash or travellers' cheques at the Bank of Hawaii beside the post office in Fagatogo. Banks are open from 9 am to 3 pm Monday to Friday, with a service window open until 4.30 pm on Fridays.

Post & Telecommunications The post office is near the malae in Fagatogo on the ground floor of the Lumana'i building, in the same building as the Bank of Hawaii. It is open from 8 am to 4 pm Monday to Friday and from 8.30 am to noon Saturday.

The telephone office is in Fagatogo, on the malae near the tourist office. There is no sign identifying it as such, but anyone will be able to direct you. It is open 24 hours a day, seven days a week, for both local and international calling. In addition, cable and fax services are available.

Laundry Fagatogo has two laundrettes. Mary's, across the street from Herb and Sia's Hotel, is open from 1 pm to 8 pm Sunday and from 7 am to 10 pm Saturday. On weekdays it's open from 7 am to 10 pm, except between noon and 4 pm. Mary charges 50 cents to wash and 75 cents to dry.

JMPL's Laundrette is also open seven days a week, but on Sunday you may have to wait until the proprietor gets home from church. On Sundays during cruising season, the place becomes a yachtie social centre. Don't miss the ice cream while you're waiting for your wash. At 50 cents for a big double scoop, it's one of the best deals in town.

There are other laundrettes scattered around the island: in Pago Pago, 'Au'asi, Tafuna and on the road between Pava'ia'i and A'oloaufou.

Mt 'Alava Cable Car

One of the world's longest single-span cable-car routes begins atop Solo Hill at the end of Togotogo Ridge above 'Utulei village and ascends 1.8 km across Pago Pago Harbor to 487-metre-high Mt 'Alava. It was constructed in 1965 as a service access to the TV transmission equipment on the mountain.

During a Flag Day military demonstration in 1980, a US Navy plane hit the cables and crashed into the Rainmaker Hotel below. All six naval personnel aboard were killed, as were two guests of the hotel. The monument commemorates those who died in the disaster. Around the corner is the cable-car terminal.

Having said all that, the cable car ceased operations several years ago and has been allowed to go to seed and, from the looks of things, it will never run again without complete refurbishing. If you want a look at it anyway, go to the lower terminal on Solo Hill. To get there, turn right at the first street past the Rainmaker Hotel (heading away from Pago) and follow it around the H Rex Lee Auditorium and some school buildings until another road leads away uphill. Follow it for about 250 metres to the monument. Just beyond it around the corner, there's a gazebo and a pleasant garden with a view.

On top of Mt 'Alava is a similar set-up, which affords spectacular views of nearly all of Tutuila Island and beyond to 'Upolu in Western Samoa and the Manu'a Islands 100 km east of Tutuila. It is accessible on foot from the crest of the hill between Pago Pago and Fagasa. For the best and clearest possible view, go early morning.

It is possible to walk to Mt 'Alava from Pago Pago along the good but sometimes muddy and slippery clay track leading up the ridge from the pass on Fagasa Rd. It's a ridge walk with lots of jungle and heavy vegetation, but views open up from time to time. Carry water – the sun beats down and will quickly dehydrate walkers.

Kirwan Studios

The Michael J Kirwan TV studios are in the village of 'Utulei, behind the Lee Auditorium. It was here that the pioneer program of broadcasting school lessons to elementary and secondary students began during the modernisation rush of the Governor Lee era. With more teachers and schools in the territory these days, the emphasis has shifted to public programming and commercial TV from Hawaii.

The studio used to conduct guided tours of the facility but operations seem pretty disorganised of late. If you're interested, there's no harm in trying anyway.

Governor's House

This two-storey wooden colonial mansion atop Mauga o Ali'i (the chief's hill) was built in 1903 and served as the home for all of American Samoa's naval commanders until the Department of the Interior took control of the place in 1951. Since then, all the territorial governors have used it as a residence. You can't go inside the building, but it is possible to stroll around the gardens on the grounds. On my last visit there, however, they had fallen into an extremely unkempt state.

To get there, climb the road leading uphill across the street from the entrance to the Rainmaker Hotel.

Net Repair Facility

Beneath a large sign stating that Pago Pago is the purse-seining capital of the Pacific, is the fleet net repair facility. Most of the time you'll be able to watch the men darning the nets and they're always happy to stop and chat with visitors about their tedious work and about the fishery in general.

Jean P Haydon Museum

Beside the fono buildings in Fagatogo is the Jean P Haydon Museum, named for its founder, the wife of Governor John Haydon, who devotedly saw the project through to completion. The building itself has an interesting history. It was constructed in 1917 to house the original naval commissary, after which it served as the main post office.

The museum houses numerous artefacts of early Samoa, including the *va'a* and *alia*

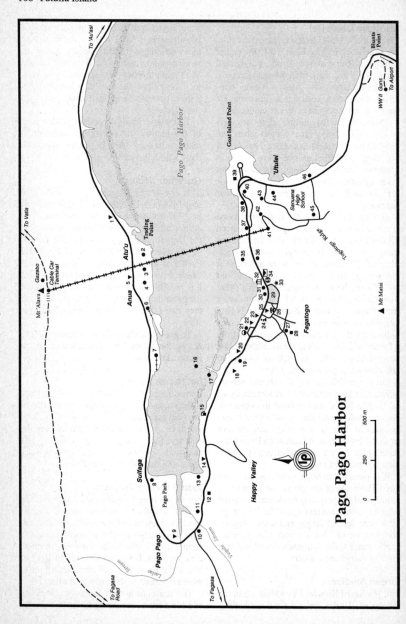

Pago Pago Harbor

PLACES TO STAY		American Samoa National Park Headquarters)
12	Motu-o-Fiafiaga Hotel	12	Evalani's Cabaret & Disco
28	Herb & Sia's Motel	13	Senior Citizens' Handicraft Fales
39	Rainmaker Hotel	15	Haleck's Petrol Station
		16	Yacht Anchorage
PLACES TO EAT		17	Dinghy Dock
		19	Malaloa Duty Free
1	Ramona Lee Restaurant	21	Fagatogo Market & Bus Station
5	Seoul Restaurant	23	Tedi of Samoa Shopping Center
9	Korean Food Kiosks	24	Tourist Office
14	Soli & Mark's Restaurant	25	Courthouse
18	Sadie's Restaurant	26	Telephone Office
20	Icewich Fale	27	Mary's Laundrette
22	Te'o Brothers Kitchen & Milovale's Drive-In	29	Malae o Le Talu (Town Square)
		30	Fono
23	Pizza Time	31	Handicraft Fale
25	Pele's Place	32	Jean P Haydon Museum
36	Pinoy's Fast Food	33	Police Station
		34	Bank of Hawaii & Post Office
		35	Container Dock & Ferry Dock
OTHER		36	Wesley Bookshop & Luana's Handicrafts
		37	Net Repair Facility
2	Samoa Packing	38	Feleti Pacific Library
3	American Can Company	40	Mauga o Ali'i & Governor's House
4	Starkist Samoa, Inc	41	Solo Hill Cable Car Terminal
6	Marine Railway	42	Air Disaster Memorial
7	Dry Dock	43	Michael J Kirwan TV Studio
8	Korea House	44	H Rex Lee Auditorium
10	Spencer's	45	Public Library
11	Pago Plaza (Paisano's Pizzeria Deli &	46	Pago Pago Yacht Club

(bonito canoes and war canoes) that inspired the old name for Samoa, the Navigator Islands. There are also other items in common use in early island life, such as coconut-shell combs, seashell and whales' teeth necklaces, fruit and seed jewellery, pigs' tusk armlets, fly whisks, bamboo pan-pipes (strikingly similar to the South American variety), siapo cloth, stone tools and an impressive variety of weapons. Also fascinating is the display of native pharma-copoeia used by the early Polynesians.

The museum is open from 10 am to 3 pm daily except Sunday. Admission is free.

The Fono

The large and impressive group of buildings beside the museum is the fono (legislature), where American Samoan law-makers convene and legislate during the months of January and July. It was completed in October 1973, at a cost of US$1 million.

Traditional Samoan architecture and building styles were integrated into the structure, including the *fale afolau* style, which may be seen as the primary home design in Western Samoa, and the *fale tele* (meeting house) design.

Courthouse

The two-storey colonial-style courthouse was built at the minuscule cost of US$46,000 between 1900 and 1904. Its original purpose was to contain the territorial executive and naval offices but it now houses the judiciary. It was expanded in 1929 and underwent total renovation in 1975. It is listed on the US National Register of Historic Places.

Market

The market and aiga bus terminal is found near the western end of Fagatogo village. Here, local growers come to sell their produce. Taro, bananas, coconuts, breadfruit and occasionally a few other things are available here at low and sometimes negotiable prices. The big market day is Saturday, but arrive before 7 am if you want to get the pick of the produce.

On weekday evenings the market serves as a bingo hall and the turn-out is phenomenal!

Sadie Thompson's

All American Samoans will assure you that Sadie Thompson is an historical figure, and the account they provide of her antics is far more involved than the Somerset Maugham classic *Rain* ever was.

The tale of Sadie Thompson was written after Maugham paid a brief visit to Pago Pago and was delayed there in the rain by an outbreak of measles while en route between Honolulu and Papeete on the steamship *Sonoma*. It is assumed that he stayed at the old Rainmaker Boarding House with his American lover Gerald Haxton, but there seems to be some dispute over just where that was.

Many sources believe it was on the main street in Fagatogo in the building now occupied by the Reid Company Store. Others (particularly the owners of Sadie's Restaurant) maintain that it was in the same building as Sadie's is in today. It would be nice to believe the latter claim, because that building's style and atmosphere certainly reflect the mood in the story better than the other building does. The building was bought by shopkeeper Max Haleck in the late 1940s and has since changed hands a couple of times.

Samoans say that the historical Sadie Thompson, who lived upstairs in this building, was a laundress by day and practised her trade by night.

We may never know her real name, but the woman Maugham called Sadie Thompson had been evicted from the Honolulu red-light district and travelled south in hopes of finding a new market for her goods. However, the ship was detained in Pago Pago and while the passengers were holed up, the Reverend Davidson, a holier-than-thou missionary who also happened to be holed up in the same hotel, took more than a passing concern for Miss Thompson's immortal soul. He set about changing her ways and persuaded her to repent. In the end, however, it was she who changed *his* ways (or at least brought out the human and humane in him).

Maugham's story more or less ends there, but the Samoans go on to say that Sadie stayed on in Pago and continued her chosen profession there until one night she was found drunk in the rain somewhere in Fagatogo. A police officer gathered her up and placed her, unconscious, on an Australia-bound steamer.

You can still see the building where it all took place (though there's not much to see), but it's better to just read the short story and wonder at the amount of rain that must have fallen on Pago Pago since it was written.

Pago Pago Village

There's really not much to the village itself which has given its name to the entire harbour area. At the head of the harbour (the area the yachties call the 'low rent district') is a large reclaimed area called Pago Pago Park (the tongue-tied use just one 'Pago' and are still understood). In Pago Park are basketball and tennis courts, a football field, a gymnasium, a bowling alley and a series of Korean food kiosks. The impressive Korea House was built as a social centre for fishermen from that country.

The cheapest shoes, clothing (US$1 T-shirts) and household goods in the territory can be found at the several Korean-owned shops in Pago village. If you're interested, the large blue building that appears to be constructed of bathroom tiles, is the territory's only shopping mall. Inside, there is a shop that will process film in 24 hours.

Tuna Canneries

The two tuna canneries, sources of most of the ever-present stench that pervades the harbour area, are found in the km-long industrial complex on the north coast. Nearest to Pago Pago is Starkist, the home of 'Charlie Tuna'. The other – the smaller of the two – is Samoa Packing (formerly Van Camp's) which makes 'Chicken of the Sea'. It has now passed into the hands of an Indonesian firm.

Charlie wouldn't want to be 'Starkist' if he knew what went on there. It is estimated that US$250 million worth of tuna per year is caught, killed, cut up and crushed or canned in American Samoa, which amounts to 9.7 million cases (at 48 cans to a case) of tuna per year.

Most of the workers relegated to the unpleasant task of cutting and cleaning the fish (yes, it is done by hand) are Western Samoans and Tongans earning a meagre US$2.92 per hour, a wage unheard of in their home countries.

To arrange a tour of the canneries (Samoa Packing is more amenable), go to the personnel office and ask if they're conducting tours. They may question your motives in order to ascertain that you're not a corporate spy from the other cannery. Chances are you won't be conducted through alone or even in a small group, but if you can muster a group of 10 or more (and your politics check out, of course), your chances of getting in to see all the blood, guts and general carnage involved in the tuna industry are better.

If you're in the area between August and October and don't feel that you can leave Pago Pago without viewing some tuna carcasses, talk to the yachties and see if they'd be interested in forming a tour group.

Fatumafuti

Fatumafuti, also known as the Flowerpot Rocks, are found along the highway, near the village of Faga'alu. The legend says that Fatu and Futi were lovers living on the Manu'a Islands. They wanted to marry but were forbidden to do so because tradition prevents members of the same aiga marrying. Fatu, the woman, built a coconut raft and set off for Tutuila. When Futi learned that she had gone, he was distraught and set out after her. Both their boats were destroyed by a tidal wave as they approached Tutuila and the two lovers were stranded on the reef where they have remained to this day.

The area around Fatumafuti is nice for picnics and reef walks at low tide.

Places to Stay – bottom end

Unfortunately for budget travellers, there is no longer any inexpensive formal accommodation in American Samoa. If you'd like to stay with a family, however, it's fairly easily arranged. Ask around shops and restaurants in town for news of anyone who'd like to take in a short-term guest for a little extra cash – again, perhaps US$15 to US$20 per day.

If you'd like to spend more than a couple of weeks in American Samoa, consider renting a flat or a room. There are always columns in the classified section of the paper and the *Pacific Hotline* advertising rooms in private homes or small flats for as little as US$150 per month.

Places to Stay – top end

Herb & Sia's Motel (☎ 633-5413), on the hill above Fagatogo, is a family outfit run by a New Zealander and his chiefly Samoan wife. Although they advertise air-conditioning, none of the units are working, so ask for a room without air-conditioning and you won't pay extra for the privilege of complaining about it. The biggest problem is the lack of hot water, which is essentially unacceptable given the price range.

For single/double/triple rooms with shared facilities, the charge is US$35/40/60. For a private bathroom (still no hot water), add US$5 per night to the previously listed prices. Weekly rates are US$210 with a private bathroom and US$180 with a shared bathroom.

There used to be a fiafia night once a week, but it was cancelled due to lack of interest. On Sunday after church they prepare a free feast for their guests; apart from the owners' affability, this is perhaps the only positive thing about the place.

A note of caution: when I last stayed at Herb & Sia's, one of the cleaning staff awoke me from a nap and trundled over to the far wall to spend the next few minutes watching a romantic liaison in the room next door through a peephole in the wall. If you don't want to be part of a free show, check the walls carefully and stuff up any holes with bits of paper before doing anything that may interest the staff!

Motu-o-Fiafiaga Hotel (☎ 633-7777; fax 633-4776) at Pago Pago beside the sometimes sleazy Evalani's Cabaret, is a new place with high hopes. Although it's probably the nicest place to stay in the harbour area, the building isn't as clean or tidy as it could be – and its position beside Evalani's gives it a sort of guilt-by-association problem – so it's off to a poor start. Single/ double rooms with air-conditioning and private facilities cost US$50/60, including breakfast.

The *Rainmaker Hotel* in 'Utulei, named after the famous mountain across the harbour, was built in the early 1960s to give island tourism a kick start. It failed miserably. Now government-run, the hotel has been expanded to 181 rooms and fales, many of which sit empty most of the time and some of which are aesthetically uninhabitable thanks to the crop of mould growing in the carpets.

This may be American Samoa's only resort, but in all my travels, it's the worst hotel of its class and price range that I've ever run across (but then, I haven't been everywhere, so who knows?). The biggest problem is the attitude. For example, arriving guests must pay a substantial 'deposit' against the price of the room as well as possible meals, drinks, damage and items they may be inclined to steal from the rooms (they don't take any chances with the TVs, however, which must be hired for an additional fee!) Then there's the pool, which manages to combine a stark concrete environment with a host of bizarre restrictions: no running, no jumping, no diving, no food, no beverages, no noise, no splashing and so on (presumably you're allowed to swim!) to yield a decidedly unpopular amenity. Some business travellers I met suggested that the whole hotel be demolished and turned into a park.

Without elaborating on the complicated pricing scheme, fales cost between US$80 and US$150, depending on their location, and room prices begin at US$60 a single or double without a view and climb to US$90 for double 'VIP rooms'. Residents of American Samoa receive substantial discounts.

Every Friday at 8.30 pm, they stage a fiafia with traditional foods and dancing by the Samoan staff. On Tuesday and Sunday there's live music in the Sadie Thompson Lounge.

Places to Stay – out of town

In a private residence in Leone village is *Barry's Bed & Breakfast* (☎ 699-5113; fax 633-9111). It's a long way from the harbour and difficult to reach after 6 pm when the buses stop running, but of the choices available, it's probably the best. Rooms cost US$35/40 a single/double.

The *Apiolefaga Inn* (☎ 699-9124), at Masepa near the American Samoa Community College, has gone downhill in recent years and is now rather grungy around the edges. However, it's quieter than the places in town, its location beneath the green peaks is quite pleasant and there's not a whiff of tuna on the air. Basic single/double rooms with shared facilities cost US$50/60.

Places to Eat

Most of the restaurants and shops on Tutuila are concentrated in Fagatogo and Pago Pago, but there is a growing number outside the harbour area which are also covered in this section (see Out of Town).

Breakfast The highlight of most breakfasts in American Samoa is the coffee, featuring the US-style 'bottomless cup'. If you're up for a caffeine buzz to start your day, this is the place to be!

For a leisurely breakfast, you can't beat the coffee shop at *Soli & Mark's* in Pago Pago, where you'll find American breakfast specials – bacon, eggs, toast and coffee – for US$5.99. Another popular breakfast option is the ambitiously-named *Pago Pago International Airport Restaurant* at the airport in

Tafuna. Full cooked breakfasts will cost from US$4 to 5. They serve hot cakes, sausage, fried rice, sai-min, etc, and a very good cup of coffee.

Another place for breakfast (locals swear by it) is *Pele's Place* on the malae in Fagatogo. It opens at 7 am. Further out, beyond the tuna canneries in Leloaloa, is *Aggie's*. This former snack bar which became so popular that Aggie expanded it into a great place for homemade breakfasts and lunches.

Snacks & Lunches The line between snacks and meals in American Samoa is a thin one; for some Samoan-sized snack suggestions, see under Full Meals later in this section.

One of the friendliest and best value places to grab a quick meal on Tutuila is *Te'o Brothers Kitchen*, near the market in Fagatogo. They have all the standard fare – curries, barbecue lamb and chicken, hot dogs and sausage, taro and chop suey – and it's well prepared. You'll pay about US$3 for a heaping plateful. It's open from 5.30 am to 10 pm daily, including Sunday. Just beside it, *Milovale's Drive-In* serves pseudo-Chinese and Samoan buffet-style meals. It's very popular with local people. They also have a branch in Nu'uuli.

Icewich Fale, just down the street, sometimes lives up to its name and serves ice cream and milkshakes, but most folks go in for greasy hamburgers, fish & chips, steaks, and chicken that cost from US$3 to US$5. Large pizzas cost US$9.75. It's open from 6.30 am to 4 pm Monday to Friday and 6.30 am to 1 pm on Saturday.

Behind Tedi of Samoa, the air-conditioned fast-food joint *Pizza Time* (☎ 633-1199) sells not only pizzas but tacos and hamburgers as well. If temperatures outside are too hot to handle, come in for a meal and a session watching recent films on the video screen. If it's too hot to budge at all, they also do pizza delivery.

On the malae in Fagatogo, try the very popular *Pele's Place* which is known for its delicious and original homemade burgers and other light meals. It's open Monday to Friday from 7 am to 4 pm, on Saturday from 7 am to 2.30 pm and on Sunday for ice cream from 10 am to 5 pm. In the same area is the *Hot Pot*, an option for quick and nasty Chinese takeaways. For Filipino-style takeaways, there's *Pinoys* in the Samoa News building between Fagatogo and 'Utulei.

In Pago Park at the head of the harbour are the bargain basement down-and-dirty Korean food stalls where you'll find all sorts of Oriental and pseudo-Samoan dishes. US$2 will buy you a plateful of food big enough for a Samoan football player (in fact, quite a few do take a break here from practice in the park). The kiosks normally run out of food around 2.30 or 3 pm.

Further out in Leloaloa, you'll find *Ramona Lee's*, which serves recommended Chinese takeaways. According to a reader who spent a year in American Samoa, it's the best Chinese food in the territory.

Another option is the *Pago Pago Yacht Club* in 'Utulei, which serves lunch from Monday to Friday, starting at 11.30 am. For about US$2.50 you'll get a burger or hot dog, chips and coleslaw. On Friday nights during happy hour (5 to 7 pm), they serve similar fare.

For the best ice cream on the island, go to *JMPL's Laundrette* in Fagatogo, which charges only 50 cents for a double scoop; it can become addictive.

Full Meals Repeatedly recommended is the unassuming *Seoul Restaurant*, on the mountain side of the main road beside Samoa Packing. It's an unfortunate location for a restaurant, to be sure, but if you can ignore the fishy smell this close to its source, you'll find this Korean restaurant to be among the best in the territory. The same cannot be said, however, for the *Korean Barbecue* across the harbour in Malaloa, which probably should be avoided.

Evalani's Cabaret & Lounge, between Fagatogo and Pago Pago, is probably the favourite adult disco/karaoke bar in the territory and serves pizzas, burgers and Mexican food as well. Friday night is the busiest and a video machine ensures that no one goes without entertainment. For more information, see under Entertainment later in this chapter.

Just down the road at Pago Plaza is the Italian-American run *Paisano's Pizzeria Deli*, a low-key, excellent-value Italian restaurant with a fast-food twist. The menu is heavy on the pizza and spaghetti but you can also get immense submarine sandwiches which are popular with hordes of hungry sailors.

With its period decor and atmosphere, its comfortable lounge, and tasteful live entertainment, *Sadie's* is the most elegant and expensive restaurant in the territory. It's very popular with expats, yachties and business people but travellers and tourists will also appreciate the option. Because everything is imported from the mainland, dinners will average from US$12 for chicken up to US$25 for anything more interesting. Soups, salads, desserts and drinks are all separate, so you can run up a substantial tab quite quickly. On the average, expect to pay about US$30 per person for a meal with wine.

The dining room at the *Rainmaker Hotel*, which is open from 6.30 to 10 pm Monday to Saturday, serves seafood or beef dishes for US$12 to US$15 while Samoan and Oriental cuisine costs as little as US$4. However, as with everything else about the Rainmaker, the food is marginal at best. On Tuesday and Sunday from 4 pm to midnight there's live music in the Sadie Thompson lounge and on Fridays at 8.30 pm, Samoan hotel employees stage a Polynesian fiafia with local dances and music.

Another up-market restaurant is *Soli & Mark's* in Pago Pago village. It overlooks the water and is a favourite with yachties. A well-prepared seafood or steak dinner costs US$9.95, and it is the only place in American Samoa that has a salad bar. They charge US$2.75 to US$5.50 for a self-serve salad, and after living on the cheap and greasy fare so typical of the territory, it's worth it!

Out of Town The *Pago Pago International Airport Restaurant* at the airport in Tafuna is a bit expensive when compared to places in town but it's a relaxing place, reminiscent of a small-town truck stop diner in the USA. To add interest, they've taken to thematic evenings: Tuesday is Western night with baby back ribs; on Thursday, they serve a Mexican feast; Friday is kung-fu night with Chinese cuisine; and Saturday is King's Night, with prime rib. These are especially good value at US$12.50 per person and they're especially popular with foreigners. Currently, the restaurant is open Sunday, Monday and Wednesday from 6 am to noon and on other days from 6 am to 9 pm, but that will probably change as flight schedules are altered. For something lighter in Tafuna, try the snack bar at *Luisa's Laundromat!*

Another option is *Katy's Kitchen Restaurant* on the mountain side of the road in Nu'uuli, which was once a health food shop and vegetarian restaurant. As one reader put it 'Health food restaurants can't survive on an island where turkey tails and canned corned beef are staple diet.' Katy's is still a bit pricier than the greasy-spoon places in Pago Pago but it isn't bad. It's open Monday to Friday from 7 to 11 am for breakfast and 11 am to 5 pm for lunch. On Saturdays, it's open only from 11 am to 2 pm.

Nearby is the new *Le Tausala*, which specialises in European-style fare in an up-market atmosphere. It's open daily for lunches and dinners.

Matai's Pizza Fale on the airport road near the intersection has a nice bar and juke box music. It's always crowded, mostly with local teenagers. Pizzas cost about US$5 to US$13, depending on the size and toppings. Hamburgers and other fast foods are available, too. A short distance down the road is the *Powerhouse Bar & Grill*, which is mostly for the benefit of lunch customers from the Tafuna Industrial Park.

In the same area, *Taima's Palace*, 100 metres west of the airport turn-off on the mountain side of the road, has Oriental and Samoan food, including great fish dishes, plantains, taro, curry and the like. For comfortable dining there's air-conditioning and a breezy terrace outside, and on Friday nights there's a Polynesian dance show. Best of all, it's good value.

The friendly and well-meaning *Smile Samoa* in the Nu'uuli Shopping Center is open from 8 am to 3 pm daily and offers inexpensive breakfasts. However, coffee fans may want to look for something else. It's run by Seventh-Day Adventists who rue the invigorating brew so the best you can do here is a cup of barley-based Postum. In the same complex you'll find *TJ's Restaurant & Cocktail Lounge*, with a seedy atmosphere that would appeal to North American lounge lizards.

At *Krystal's Burger* just east of Leone, you'll find some of the best burgers in the territory as well as fish & chips and other snacks. For a good value fast-food meal, you'll pay from US$2 to US$3 per person. It's open Monday to Thursday from 10 am to midnight, Friday and Saturday from 10 am to 3 am and on Sunday from 2 to 11 pm.

A new concept for the South Pacific is the drive-through and it seems that American Samoa is at the cutting edge with *A & A Pizza Mac's Drive-Thru* in Male'imi west of Nu'uuli. They serve everything from pizza and teriyaki sandwiches to burgers and – if you can believe it – 'pasta by the quart'.

At *Tui's Market* in Male'imi village, beside the Mormon church, is a new Kentucky Fried Chicken clone – *Flavor-Crisp Chicken*, which serves chicken by the bucket for about US$1 per piece. It's open Monday to Thursday from 11 am to midnight, Friday and Saturday from 11 am to 4 am and Sunday from 11 am to 10 pm.

Alternatively, there's *Ifo's Burger* in Pava'ia'i which offers 99-cent tacos; *Chicken Out* with (you guessed it) 'chicken in a basket', just east of Faganeanea; *Sugar & Spice Fast Food* east of Nu'uuli; the *Powerhouse Bar & Grill* on the airport road; and *EC Lynn Bakery & Fast Food*, selling curry, rice, sai-min, meat pies and doughnuts, just opposite American Samoa Community College.

For something slightly more elegant but not overly expensive, go to *Leala'ea Sliding Rock* near the sliding rock on the Vailoa road, which serves lunches and dinners Tuesday to Saturday. On Friday nights, they stage a Polynesian dance show and a Samoan buffet.

Self-Catering There are quite a few supermarkets on Tutuila that sell more or less the same fare available on the mainland for only slightly higher prices. For yachties provisioning in American Samoa, they offer discounts and delivery on bulk orders. Other favourites for provisions are Kruse at Leone village and Haleck's, with one store between Fagatogo and Pago Pago (formerly Burns-Philp) and another at Pavai'ia'i. For local shoppers, *Tom Ho Ching*, near the hospital in Faga'alu, is popular due to its convenient opening hours: 7 am to 9 pm Monday to Saturday and 7 am to 7 pm on Sunday. Another option is *Aiga Basket* in Nu'uuli. Alternatively, a number of small grocery shops and bush stores with limited supplies are dotted around the island.

For produce, however, avoid the supermarkets or a salad will become a luxury item and a melon will be worth its weight in silver! The best source for fresh produce will be the Fagatogo market, but unfortunately, there's little variety. From 5 am on Saturday morning you'll sometimes find eggplant (aubergine), tomatoes, cabbage, peppers (capsicum), green beans, carrots and the like, but most of the goodies are gone before 9 am, so go early. Fresh fish is available at *Star of the Sea* fish market, near the shore behind the main market.

Entertainment
Just about every place with a bar and music in American Samoa also has a dress code: patrons must be neatly dressed, with no dirt or grime.

If you're hoping to crew on to a yacht or would just like to meet and associate with yachties, the best time and place to do so would be during the Friday night happy hour from 5 to 7 pm at the *Pago Pago Yacht Club* in 'Utulei. During the cruising season, it's usually packed. Light meals are available, drinks (albeit weak ones) cost only US$1 and popcorn is free. Free hot showers (ahhh!) are also available, but plan on long queues, especially on Friday nights. Also on Fridays, locals hold rowing practice in the fautasi (longboats) stored in sheds outside. The yacht club is open until 8 pm (last call at 7.30 pm) Monday to Thursday and until 10 pm on Friday and Saturday.

If you're up for some active nightlife, *Evalani's Cabaret & Lounge* is *the* adult hangout in Pago Pago. Although it's generally friendly and above board, Evalani's does have a reputation as Pago Pago's red-light district, so in the evenings, unaccompanied female travellers may want to be on their guard.

The most casual night spot is the *Welcome to Pago Bar*, normally known as just Pago Bar, which is popular with locals as well as visitors. You don't need to wear your best clothes, but grunge isn't appreciated either. From Thursday to Saturday, there's live music and dancing in the evenings.

The nicest and most elegant place for a drink is the bar at *Sadie's Restaurant*, which is a classy pub. They occasionally have live music and it makes a worthwhile break for those wanting to treat themselves. This is not to be confused with *The Sadie Thompson Lounge* in the Rainmaker Hotel, which provides further evidence that the Rainmaker has a hard time getting its act together. When I last stopped by, there was no place to sit; every table was occupied by inert staff ogling the TV over the bar!

Near the tennis courts on Ottoville Rd is the *Player's Sports Club*, with a bar, pool tables, dart boards and rugby tapes showing on a giant-screen video. It's sleazy in typical US style.

For something entirely different, there's *Tisa's Barefoot Bar* at Alega village between Ma'a Kamela and the Masefau road. This lovely open fale bar is situated on what could well be the best beach on Tutuila and it's fine for snorkelling and swimming. Access to the beach costs US$2 person. Best of all, it's open on Sundays.

Around the Island

Upon leaving the Pago Pago Harbor area, you'll feel as if you've entered a different world. In rural Tutuila, everything moves at more of a Polynesian pace than in the capital. Around the island there is quite a lot to see and do – nice walks, white beaches, archaeological and historical sites, waterfalls and the like. Because the island is so small and the public transport so frequent, everything is fairly near at hand.

EASTERN DISTRICT

The eastern district of Tutuila includes the harbour area and everything east. Less populated and more rugged than the western half of the island, it is also less congested with traffic and commerce.

Fagasa

Fagasa ('sacred bay') the village over the pass from Pago Pago has an interesting legend associated with it. A group of three men and three women sailed from the western end of Tutuila in search of better fishing grounds and a place to start a new village. At dusk, they passed the mouth of a strange bay and in it saw a circle of mysterious lights. They panicked, believing that the aitu (spirits) had thrown down stars from the sky to prevent them from entering the bay because it was a sacred and forbidden place.

As the lights approached, it became apparent that they were merely the eyes of dolphins sent by the voyagers' ancestors to light their way and lead them into this ideal spot.

Today, the people of the village revere dolphins which shelter there on their annual migrations. The people believe that Tuiatua, the spirit of the elements, guards their bay and protects the dolphins.

Matafao Peak

It is possible to climb 653-metre Matafao Peak, the highest point on Tutuila, along the ridge from the high point of the Pago Pago to Fagasa road. The peak itself, like Rainmaker Mountain across the harbour, is a remnant of the great volcanic plug and more evidence of the origins of Tutuila Island. Above the 350-metre level, the peak area is designated a national landmark site.

Getting started on the climb is the most difficult part, since walkers must scramble up a steep cliff to get onto the ridge. The most accommodating place seems to be about 30 metres below the pass on the Pago Pago side. The view from the top is, of course, excellent, but the trail can be very muddy and overgrown. Plan on a full day for the trip up and down, and be sure to carry water and sunblock cream.

Rainmaker Mountain

Also known as Mt Pioa, this 524-metre mountain is the culprit that traps rain clouds and gives Pago Pago Harbor almost perpetually wet weather. It is Tutuila's best example of a volcanic plug associated with the major fissure zone that created the island. Although it appears as one peak from below, the summit is actually three-pronged. The separate peaks are known locally as North Pioa, South Pioa and Sinapioa. Rainmaker Mountain and its base area are designated a national landmark site due to the pristine nature of the tropical vegetation on its slopes.

From the village of Aua on the north coast of the harbour, a surfaced road switchbacks steeply up to Rainmaker Pass and continues equally steeply down to Afono and beautiful Vatia on the north coast. The views from the pass down to either side of the island are spectacular.

I've read in numerous places that it's possible to climb Rainmaker Mountain from the pass, but I've searched and never been able to find a route up it. It's extremely steep and the bush cover is dense. If you want to have a go at climbing the ridge, good luck and if you're successful, please let us know about it!

Vatia

Vatia is a charming and friendly village untouched by the mayhem and the grime just over the ridge. Strewn all along the idyllic beach are concrete bunkers from WW II. The village is neatly groomed and the road between Afono and Vatia is lined with gardens of flowers and ornamental plants.

At the end of the road is the school, and beyond is a short trail leading into the new national park. It ends at the rocky cliff that points across Vaiava Strait to magnificent Pola Island, which is, in the estimation of many who've seen it, the most beautiful natural feature of Tutuila. Also known as the Cockscomb, it's a real landmark and appears in most of American Samoa's tourist literature. Its dramatic and inaccessible 100-metre cliffs serve as a sanctuary for nesting sea birds.

Aiga buses go to Vatia several times daily. Since so many of the village's residents are Western Samoans who work at the canneries, the runs coincide with the shift changes there. Vatia can also be reached by scrambling down the ridge from Mt 'Alava. Walk from the Pago Pago to Fagasa road up to a point about 800 metres along the ridge beyond the cable-car terminal. There you'll come to a steep trail leading down to your left. It is infrequently maintained and is often badly overgrown, so look carefully. From the ridge to Vatia is about two km.

Don't go to Vatia on Sunday, however, as Samoans feel that the presence of visitors is disruptive.

Ma'a Kamela

The Ma'a Kamela, or Camel Rock, will be unmistakable as you pass it on the highway east of Breakers Point at Lauli'i. The Samoans say that the Chinese emperor set a young man adrift for inappropriate behaviour with the emperor's sister-in-law, and for some unfathomable reason, he was required to carry a camel with him. The young man's elder brother, Ah Chi Sun, set out in search of him. After travelling all over the Pacific, he found his brother's camel off the south coast of Tutuila and learned from it that the young man had been eaten by sharks. And of course the camel remains to this day.

On the shore around the Ma'a Kamela are

quite a few more WW II concrete bunkers. Not far to the east you'll find *Tisa's Barefoot Bar* where you can have a drink and swim or snorkel on one of Tutuila's finest beaches. Access to the beach costs WS$2 per person.

Masefau Rd

Near the village of Faga'itua, another cross-island road goes over to the north coast. At the pass, this one splits. The left fork leads down to the beautiful bay and village of Masefau. The right fork goes to the tiny settlement of Masa'usi and then through dense forest to Sa'ilele, which has what is undoubtedly the nicest beach on the entire island. The sandy area below the large rock outcrop at the western end provides an excellent place for a barbecue or camping. (First ask permission in the village, of course.)

On a track east of the village of Sa'ilele is a burial ground of reasonable interest where some *ali'i* (high chiefs) are interred. Don't go too far out of your way to see it though.

Shipwreck

Near Amouli is an impressive shipwreck right beside the road. The locals say that for them the disaster was like Christmas. The vessel ran aground with a full load of fish, and when it overturned, it spilled its yummy cargo within reach of anyone who cared to gather it.

'Au'asi Falls

Above the village of 'Au'asi is a pleasant waterfall, a nice place to cool off on a hot day. It can be reached by walking up the stream for about half an hour. If it's raining, the falls will be especially impressive.

'Aoa

Although the road between Amouli and 'Aoa is scenically rather uninteresting, more than 40 ancient star mounds have been discovered in the bush near the spine of the island but haven't yet been excavated.

Archaeologists and matais differ in their explanations of the origins of these elevated stone platforms which are filled with dirt or gravel and with stone protrusions radiating from a round or square base. The local chiefs, who admit they're not really sure, guess that the mounds were used in the ancient chiefly sport of pigeon-snaring. Due to their placement at strategic vantage points, many archaeologists believe that they served as military lookouts, perhaps for the observation of enemy canoes.

In addition to the star mounds, lapita pottery has been found in the 'Aoa area. Some estimates date the potshards found here from as early as 2000 BC, but the figure currently accepted by the scientific community is 500 BC. The most interesting aspect of the lapita finds is that the pottery in question became less and less intricately decorated until it disappeared from usage altogether. The Samoan elders of today have no recollection or knowledge of the historical use of pottery by the culture, nor are there any legends pertaining to it.

The Department of Tourism once maintained very rudimentary beach fales in 'Aoa, as well as camping sites, showers and barbecue facilities, but everything has now fallen into disrepair. The situation is unlikely to change, but you never know.

Tula

Tula, the easternmost village on Tutuila, is a quiet and laid-back place with a pleasant white beach. It is the end of the bus line east, but if you have a reliable vehicle or feel like a nice walk, you can continue around the end of the island to Cape Mata'ula and Onenoa, a beautiful area of high cliffs, small plantations and forested slopes. Again, it's a good idea not to wander into the more traditional area of Onenoa on Sunday, but the area between the villages has plenty of places to picnic or even camp, especially above the cliffs.

WESTERN DISTRICT

Although the western end of Tutuila sees much more activity than the area to the east of the harbour, primarily due to the placement of the airport, shopping areas and the Tafuna Industrial Complex, it still has numerous points of interest and secluded beaches and walks. If you have a vehicle, allow at least two days to explore this end of the island. Those relying on public transport should plan on at least twice that.

Virgin Falls

A one-km walk past the LBJ Tropical Medical Center in Faga'alu leads to a small rock quarry. From there, a rough trail climbs past a series of waterfalls. Some of the pools beneath the falls are suitable for bathing. The surrounding vegetation is beautifully lush so you may have to make your own trail in some sections. Watch for sudden rock slides as the ravine is quite steep in areas. Allow a couple of hours for the return walk if you plan to climb all the way to the top fall.

Nu'uuli

Nu'uuli is primarily a loosely defined shopping area along the main road between the Coconut Point and airport turn-offs. South Pacific Traders, the island's largest but most poorly stocked department store, is located here, as is Nu'uuli Shopping Center, Aiga Basket Supermarket and a number of trendy clothing shops. For information on restaurants, see under Places to Eat – Out of Town earlier in this chapter.

American Samoa Community College

American Samoa Community College is the territory's only tertiary-education institution. The main campus at Mapusaga has a variety of two-year programs. Also associated with the college are a nursing school at the hospital and vocational facilities in the Tafuna Industrial Complex.

Freddie's Beach & Ottoville

This lovely beach is marred only by the palagi condominium development behind it, which has put up signs reading 'Ua Sa – Samoan for 'Keep Out'. There are, incidentally, no such signs in English. If you'd still like to have a look, continue down the road that turns sharply to the right at the airport and follow it to the first left turn. The beach

is two km from this intersection, at the end of the road.

On the right, along the long, straight road between the airport and the Freddie's Beach turn-off, is the Ottoville turn-off. Ottoville is a sterile government compound apparently built under the assumption that government workers from the USA should live in barracks-like housing and be segregated from the population at large. The Samoans in general don't think much of Ottoville or its distinctly uninteresting architecture. Near the Catholic church is an archaeological park which contains a well-preserved ancient Polynesian mound and a small but lovely rainforest reserve.

On towards the small village of 'Ili'ili is the Lava Lava Golf Course (☎ 699-9366), the only one on the island. It's open seven days a week and equipment may be hired at the club house.

Turtle & Shark Point

In the picturesque village of Vaitogi along a scenic stretch of black lava coast, the most famous of Tutuila's legends is set. Unfortunately, there are so many versions of it that it's difficult to choose one that relates here! The two that follow are the ones that most often surface, but I suspect that you could ask five Samoans to relate the legend and get five completely different tales!

According to one explanation, a young husband on 'Upolu was selected as the 'guest of honour' at a cannibalistic feast to be given by King Malietoa Faiga. He chose, understandably, to decline the invitation. The man and his wife set out in a canoe, but while attempting to escape there was a storm and they were blown to Tutuila where they were put up by Letuli, the pulenu'u of 'Ili'ili.

When the practice of cannibalism fell into disfavour, Letuli offered them a free trip home, but they refused. Instead, as repayment for his kindness, they jumped into the sea. The husband became a shark and his wife a turtle. The husband told the chief that any time a gathering of children sang from the shore at Vaitogi, a turtle and a shark would appear to greet them.

Another version relates that the turtle and shark are an old blind lady and her granddaughter who jumped into the sea after being turned out of their village on Savai'i. It was during a time of famine and the two were incapable of providing for themselves. When their family learned what they'd done, they went to the shore, guilt-ridden, and called the pair by name. When the turtle and shark appeared, they knew that their family members were all right.

If you visit the site on a tour, you'll have the opportunity to watch a group of children singing to call the turtle and the shark. According to local sources, the shark will always turn up if given sufficient time. The turtle, unfortunately, isn't quite so reliable.

Even if the turtle and shark have taken the day off, you'll enjoy the solitude of the place, with its black lava cliffs, heavy surf, tide pools, blowholes and sandy beach. The walk up the road west to Sail Rock Point, through pandanus and coconut groves, is also nice.

Fagatele Bay

Fagatele Bay is a submerged volcanic crater surrounded by steep cliffs. The area contains the last remaining stretch of coastal rainforest on the island. If you'd like to walk along Matautuloa Ridge to the lighthouse on the headland at Steps Point for a look at this dramatic natural feature, you first need permission from locals. There are also two locked gates to get around. Otherwise, the only approach is from the sea.

Sliding Rock

The sliding rock, near Leone on the side road between Taputimu and Vailoatai, is on an interesting coast of black, table-flat volcanic terraces. The tilted one farthest from the road is the sliding rock. It's nondescript when dry, but when it's wet, local children use it as a slippery slide.

Leone

The village of Leone is the second-largest settlement on Tutuila and served as the Polynesian capital of the island. It was also the landing site of the first missionary, John Williams, who arrived on 18 October 1832 after spending two years in Western Samoa.

One product of his work is the imposing church in Leone, which was the first church in American Samoa. There is a monument to Williams' efforts in front of the building. It is well maintained, and if it's open, the interior is worth a look – it has nice stained-glass windows and beautiful woodwork on the ceiling. Also, if you're heading west from Leone, take notice of the tiny rocky islet across the bay which supports just a single coconut tree – the stuff of desert island cartoons!

Leone village also has a post office, and a bakery that is a nice place to stop for something gooey. Aiga buses direct to Leone leave every couple of minutes from the main terminal in Fagatogo, but Leone is the turnaround point. If you'd like to travel beyond there on the main road, you'll have to wait in front of the church for a westbound bus.

The Kruse Supermarket just east of Leone is popular with yachties because it gives them a 10% discount and delivers orders to the wharf.

Leone Falls

Go up the road past the grey Catholic church near the town centre to the end of the pavement, then follow the short walking track to the head of the valley, where a ribbon-like waterfall plunges into a moss-covered basin. The view has been 'enhanced' by a rusty water pipe down the side of the falls and an artificial catchment barrier that creates a freshwater pool at the bottom. It's a cool and pleasant spot, but wear strong footwear for the brief walk as the track can be extremely muddy.

For photographs, the light is best between noon and around 2 pm. It's a fine spot for a swim if there's enough water, but it's closed on Sunday.

Leone Quarry

The basalt quarry above Leone is the most important archaeological site in American Samoa. Artefacts made of stone from this

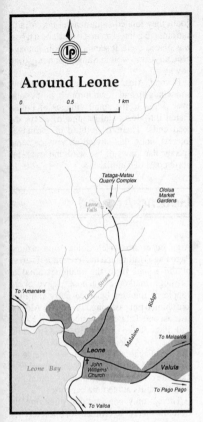

Around Leone

0   0.5   1 km

Tataga-Matau
Quarry Complex

Ololua
Market
Gardens

Leone
Falls

To 'Amanave

Leifu Stream

Ridge

Malaloto

To Malaaloa

Leone

John
Williams'
Church

Valula

Leone Bay

To Pago Pago

To Vailoa

quarry have turned up as far away as Micronesia.

In 1985, archaeologists Helen Leach and Dan Witter, with the help of some local villagers, set about investigating the quarry. Near Leafu Stream, they found numerous finished basalt adzes and cutting tools as well as 'pre-form' tools. Pre-form tools are those that have been excavated, chipped and worked on a bit, and then discarded before they have actually been finished. The finishing process of the day involved grinding the tool on a whetstone to a fine point or edge. There's also a star mound at the quarry

similar to those found at 'Aoa near the eastern end of Tutuila.

If you'd like to see the basalt quarry which is known as *Tataga Matau* ('hit the rock'), go to the end of the pavement near Leone Falls. The last house on the left belongs to Tony Willis, who also owns the trail leading up to the quarry. Although the site itself lies on community land, you need to ask Tony's permission, which is normally happily granted, to gain access to it. Follow the steep track up to the ridge on the right side of the road; after about 20 to 30 minutes, you'll arrive at the quarry.

Aasu Walk

The hiking trail down to Aasu at Massacre Bay leaves from the village of A'oloaufou, high on the spine of Tutuila, above Pava'ia'i on the main road. Massacre Bay is the site where, on 11 December 1787, 12 men from the crew of La Pérouse' ships *La Boussole* and *Astrolabe* and 39 Samoans were killed in a skirmish. There is an obscure monument in Aasu commemorating the European crew members who died there.

To get to A'oloaufou, take a Leone-bound bus from the market in Fagatogo to Pava'ia'i (75 cents) and wait on the corner there for one headed up the hill.

Across from the large park in A'oloaufou is the colourful garden that began life as an attempt by the Department of Tourism to create sites of interest on Tutuila. The trail to Aasu takes off downhill just east of that garden and continues for four km to the beach.

The first km of the track is a little intimidating; it's a veritable mudhole, and you'll be slogging in slippery, shoe-grabbing, ankle-deep ooze, so lace up your shoes tightly or remove them altogether. In the dry season, you can relax because you can be sure the trail will improve further on and will remain that way until just before the beach. Even so, most of the way down, the trail base is volcanic clay that turns waxy and treacherous when wet, which it is most of the time, and due caution should be exercised.

There are only several families living in

the near-abandoned village of Aasu, but they're quite friendly and their beach is like one of those out of a travel brochure. If you'd like to camp, you'll need permission; the worn-out admonition not to go on Sundays again holds.

For this or any other hike in Samoa, wear long trousers since weeds grow close to the trail and thorns and sharp grasses can slice unprotected shins to ribbons. For this trip, strong hikers should plan on an hour to walk the four km down and half again as long for the climb back up. There is no road outlet from Aasu.

Also from A'oloaufou (which means 'new A'oloau') there is a trail to the abandoned village of A'oloautuai (meaning 'old A'oloau') and another down the ridge to Fagamalo, where there are infrequent buses back to town. Most of the time both these trails are muddy and badly overgrown, so if they become particularly difficult it's probably best to turn back rather than press on in the hope that things will improve.

If you really enjoy walking, though, don't allow yourself to become discouraged by locals. Most of them have lived beside the tracks all their lives and never set foot on any of them. Most Samoans won't be able to fathom why anyone would want to do such a thing without some very good reason...and even if you can provide a good reason, they'll normally recommend you do it 'tomorrow'.

Cape Taputapu

The village of 'Amanave lies at the end of the beaten path. A short distance beyond the village on Loa inlet is a great white sand beach. It's just east of Cape Taputapu, which is Tutuila's westernmost point. If you're in a rental vehicle, go to the bush store in 'Amanave and ask for a safe place to leave it while you walk out to the beach and the cape.

Taputapu means 'forbidden' (taboo-taboo), and the cape was so named because it was the only source of paper mulberry trees on the island. The discoverers wanted to keep the bark for themselves so they could sell it to folks on other parts of the island. No

doubt they related some fearful tale of aitu and strange goings-on in the area and a taboo was placed on it. It seems that politics have been alive and well in Samoa for some time now!

Beyond 'Amanave, the road climbs steeply and winds up and down through valleys and over ridges to the small villages of Poloa, Fagali'i, Maloata and Fagamalo, where the road ends. There is nothing of particular interest along this stretch except for some spectacular views of the wild and trackless north coast of Tutuila.

Getting Around

Bus

Aiga buses do unscheduled runs around Pago Pago Harbor and the more remote areas of the island from the main terminal at Fagatogo market. Aiga buses leave every couple of minutes between early morning and about 6 pm eastbound for Avaio, Alofau, 'Au'asi and Tula, and westbound for Leone and Pago Pago International Airport at Tafuna. For A'oloaufou change at Pava'ia'i, and for Fagamalo (infrequent) change at Leone. To Vatia, over the Rainmaker Pass, there are only three buses per day, coinciding with the shifts at the tuna canneries.

There's only one bus that goes directly from the market to 'Amanave, but it's fairly easy to get there by going to Leone and changing buses there. It is also possible to find a bus from Fagatogo to Pago Pago International Airport at Tafuna. Another regular run is from Pava'ia'i up to A'oloaufou on the centre ridge.

Infrequently, buses go to Afono over the Rainmaker Pass, to Fagasa and to Fagamalo in the far north-western corner of Tutuila.

Any trip between the tuna canneries and the hospital in Faga'alu will cost 25 cents; between Faga'alu and Nu'uuli it is 50 cents. For anywhere along the road between Tafuna Airport and Leone, you'll pay 75 cents. To Fagasa, Tafuna or Pava'ia'i, or east as far as Ma'a Kamela is 50 cents. From Pava'ia'i, it's an extra 25 cents up the hill to A'oloaofou. It will cost 75 cents west to Leone or east to Faga'itua and US$1 to 'Amanave, 'Au'asi or Tula. The fare to 'distant' Poloa, Fagali'i and Fagamalo in the west and Onenoa, 'Aoa, Masa'usi and Sa'ilele in the east is US$1.25. The most expensive place to reach, however, is Vatia, which costs US$1.50.

Taxi

In American Samoa, expect to pay about 16 times the bus fare, or about US$1 per mile for a taxi to a particular destination on Tutuila. This works out to US$9 from the harbour area to Pago Pago International Airport at Tafuna, US$13.50 to Leone, US$3 to the tuna canneries and US$15 to Au'asi. Between the Tafuna Airport terminal and the Rainmaker Hotel is US$7.50. There are taxi stands at the international airport and local taxi companies have booths beside the market in Fagatogo.

The government issues strong directives against overcharging by taxi drivers, but foreigners still have problems. Your only recourse is to take down the number plate of the taxi and report the incident to the American Samoa Commerce Commission (☎ 633-5155).

Car

The following is a list of car hire agencies on Tutuila:

Avis Car Rental, PO Box 1858, Pago Pago (☎ 699-4408; fax 699-4305)
Kent Samoa Rent-a-Car, PO Box 4047, Pago Pago (☎ 699-1520)
Pavitt's U-Drive, PO Box 3255, Pago Pago (☎ 699-1456)
Purse Seiner Services Rent-a-Car, PO Box 3204, Pago Pago (☎ 633-2265; fax 633-2953)
Royal Samoan Rent-a-Car, PO Box 727, Pago Pago (☎ 633-2017; fax 633-1311)

Bicycle

As far as I'm aware, there are no motorbikes or bicycles for rent in American Samoa, and given the traffic situation, it's probably best not to venture onto the roads without more protection than a bike would offer, anyway.

Hitching

Hitching is possible all over the island and there are lots of pick-up trucks full of Samoans doing just that. Feel free to do the same and perhaps offer the equivalent of a bus fare for the service. It will probably be refused, but the offer will be appreciated.

'Aunu'u Island

Tiny 'Aunu'u Island, only three sq km in area, lies off the south-eastern end of Tutuila. It is a treasure house of natural phenomena and serves as a tranquil and pristine place to spend a day, if not longer. The waters around the island are clear and blue and the one village is spacious and unspoilt.

What's more, with no vehicles on the island and the traffic-choked south coast of Tutuila far away, you'll appreciate the silence and solitude. Since it's only a couple of km from end to end, the island can be quickly and easily explored on foot in a day, with plenty of time left over for a picnic at churning Ma'ama'a Cove, looking for shells on the beach and a swim in the harbour.

As usual in Samoa, Sundays in 'Aunu'u are only for sleeping, eating, visiting and attending one of the three churches serving the village of 400 people. Outsiders are not welcome on Sunday and the villagers will let such trespassers know it. However disagreeable that may seem, it's a fact of life in the Samoas, and visitors may as well learn to deal with it. At other times, however, they're a friendly lot, and most enjoy the diversion provided by the presence of visitors.

Pala Lake

Heading north from the village, you will arrive at Pala Lake after walking about 700 metres. This beautiful and deadly-looking expanse is a sea of fiery red quicksand, and it's a safe bet to say you'll never have seen anything like it before.

During the rainy season, the sand thins out and is inhabited by ducks that are shot by locals, who actually swim out to retrieve the

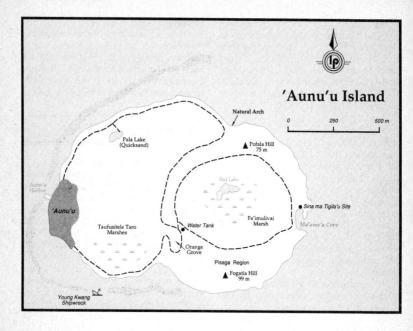

'Aunu'u Island

Natural Arch

Pala Lake
(Quicksand)

Pofala Hill
75 m

Red Lake

'Aunu'u
Harbor

'Aunu'u

Taufusitele Taro
Marshes

Water Tank

Fa'imulivai
Marsh

Sina ma Tigila'u Site

Ma'ama'a Cove

Orange
Grove

Pisaga Region

Fogatia Hill
99 m

Young Kwang
Shipwreck

0   250   500 m

carcasses. To avoid being sucked down into sandy doom, swimmers must remain horizontal at all times and propel themselves only using their arms.

Red Lake

Red Lake lies in the middle of Fa'imulivai Marsh, which, in turn, lies in the middle of 'Aunu'u's pronounced volcanic crater. It is filled with eels and tilapia fish. They are sometimes caught with a hook, but thanks to the lake's frequent level changes, there is an easier method.

When the water is high, the eels move out to the lake's margins in search of food in the newly flooded areas. When the water drains, it does so quickly, leaving the eels stranded around the edges. The people consider them good eating, and at this point all they have to do is gather them up.

'Aunu'u has water wells but Public Works currently has plans to pump and purify Red Lake water for use in the village.

The water of Red Lake really is reddish – the colour of weak tea. If you want to get a look at it and the eels, you can walk out to the edge on the sedges that surround the marsh. To get there, follow the track past Pala Lake and up the hill to the crater. There is a well-groomed track around the crater, but access to the lake is a little tricky, since it will require a bit of bushwhacking on the approach. The best place to have a go at it is from the western side of the crater north of the intersection of the village trails.

Ma'ama'a Cove

The word 'cove' may normally conjure up visions of a peaceful inlet, but this place is not what its name implies. This bowl in the rocks is actually more of a cauldron of surf that boils, pounds and sprays dramatically over, through and around the rocks. The wave action here seems to be completely random and is good for hours of entertainment, but don't venture too close to the edge.

Stray and completely unexpected waves appear out of nowhere and will wash away forever anything in their path.

Legends say that this is the site of *Sina ma Tigila'u* (Sina and Tigila'u), two lovers who were shipwrecked here. You will still be able to make out bits of crossed 'rope' and broken 'planks' embedded in the rocks around the cove.

There is also a powerful blowhole not far from the edge. There is never any water blown out of it but sand thrown into it will be blown back out.

Pisaga

The Pisaga is a region just inside the crater, below Fogatia Hill. Here people are forbidden to call out or make loud noises lest they disturb the aitu that inhabit this place. The Samoans believe that those who make noise may be answered by an irritable spirit.

For a superb view over Red Lake, as well as Aunu'u village, climb up past the water tank on the slopes of Fogatia Hill.

Other Attractions

The western slope of the crater is planted with an orange grove, a new crop diversification project in American Samoa. Below that, along the trail, are the Taufusitele Taro Marshes, which are planted Hawaiian-style with swamp taro, a rarity in this part of Polynesia.

On the reef just south of town is the wreck of the Korean tuna boat *Young Kwang* (interestingly enough, a ship of the same name lies on the reef off Niuatoputapu Island in Tonga). It was empty when it became lodged here while on a test-run in the early 1980s.

The harbour in the village is safe, calm and great for a refreshing swim. There is also a nice bit of coral nearby and excellent underwater visibility making for good snorkelling.

Places to Stay & Eat

There is no formal accommodation available on 'Aunu'u. If you'd like to stay with a family, you'll need to have a Tutuila connection beforehand – a 'sponsor' if you will – who can ensure that your activities on the island aren't disruptive. This is one place where you can't just turn up and hope to find something. If you'd like to camp in the bush somewhere, you'll still have to ask permission in the village and let them know where you'll be staying. There should be no problem as long as you don't stay over on a Sunday.

There is a bush store in the village where you can buy soft drinks and basic supplies, but they'll naturally be a bit more expensive than on Tutuila.

Getting There & Away

Getting to 'Aunu'u is fairly straightforward. Take the bus to the harbour at 'Au'asi (fare US$1 from Pago Pago). From here, a ferry travels frequently to and from 'Aunu'u Harbor for US$2 per person. If you can't be bothered waiting for the ferry, you can charter a boat in the bush store at 'Au'asi for US$10 each way for as many people as will fit. The trip takes about 15 minutes, harbour to harbour, and can get a bit hairy through the strait, especially if the wind is blowing.

Swains Island

Swains Island is not geologically part of the ridge that forms the other Samoan islands. Situated about 350 km north-north-west of Tutuila, it consists only of a 3¼-square-km ring of land surrounding a brackish lagoon to which there is no entrance from the sea. Both culturally and geographically it belongs to the Tokelau Islands.

In 1606 the Spanish explorer Quiros happened upon a fragment of land which he named Gente Hermosa because he thought the local people were very attractive. For many years it was thought that Gente Hermosa was in fact Swains Island, but recently the island of beautiful people has been identified as Rakahanga in the Cooks.

Swains Island was 'discovered' in 1841 by an American, W L Hudson, who learned of its existence from a whaler by the name of Swain. It was soon colonised by some

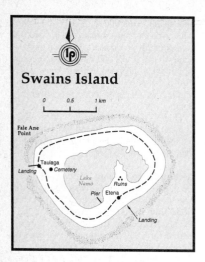

Tokelauans, who had long known it as Olohega, and some French entrepreneurs who saw its potential as a copra plantation (and incidentally impressed the Tokelauans into service there). The whole operation was taken over by an American named Eli Jennings and his Samoan wife in 1856 and has been private property of the Jennings family ever since.

When Britain formed the colony of the Gilbert and Ellice Islands in 1916, Swains was included in the Union Group (later to be known as Tokelau). In 1925, however, Tokelau was transferred to the New Zealand administration. Pressure from the Jennings family, who wanted to see their island under American jurisdiction, persuaded the USA to annex the island as part of American Samoa. US control really wasn't much of an issue, though, until 1953, when labour disputes between the Tokelauan workers and the Jennings family brought a US government representative to oversee the political affairs there and maintain 'law and order'.

In 1983 the USA and Tokelau signed the Treaty of Tokehega, which gave sovereignty over the island to the USA in exchange for US recognition of Tokelauan fishing rights. Culturally, however, the island remains Tokelauan. Renewed disputes in the mid-80s caused the Department of Public Works to discuss the building of an airport on the island. This would not only provide easy access to the island but would also ensure continued US sovereignty there. The problem would be that an airport would cover a good percentage of the land and would severely cut into the island's copra production, its economic mainstay, which is currently estimated to be 200 tonnes annually.

In the early 1990s, the Treaty of Tokohega was again challenged when Tokelau's Director of Agriculture & Fisheries, Foua Toloa, said that the treaty had been unfairly explained to the Tokelauan leadership and that he'd take the issue to the United Nations. He warned that the Tokelauan people were prepared to 'declare war on the US' and launch a canoe invasion of Swain's Island. As yet, the USA hasn't budged and nothing has come of the threat.

Getting There & Away
It is possible to visit Swains Island without any sort of permit, but transport there is infrequent and difficult to arrange. If you're interested in trying, ask at the wildlife office behind the market in Pago Pago. They keep pretty close tabs on the island and will probably be able to tell you if anyone will be going in the near future. In addition, there is an infrequent supply barge that occasionally does the run.

Getting Around
Your only option on Swain's Island will be to walk, but the size of the island lends itself well to getting around on foot. The main landing is at the tiny settlement of Taulaga and on the north-eastern side is another small hamlet of Etena. The two are connected by the six-km track that encircles the island.

The Manu'a Islands

The three small islands of the Manu'a group – Ofu, Olosega and Ta'u – lie only 100 km east of Tutuila, but in many ways, they are also 100 years away. As you arrive at Ofu, prepare for a jolt from both the time warp and the sensory overload you're certain to experience. Offering what is unquestionably the most stunning scenery in either Samoa, they are unspoilt by the outside influences that have so altered Tutuila and much of 'Upolu.

Geologically, the Manu'a Islands are, of course, of volcanic origin. Ofu and Olosega, just a few metres apart, are a complex of volcanic cones that have been buried by lava from two merging shield flows. During a long period of dormancy, deep valleys were carved out, leaving 90-metre cliffs around the islands. The bight along the south coast of the islands was caused by the collapse of one wall of the caldera. Ta'u Island, on the other hand, is a hulking shield volcano, half of which has fallen away in the south, leaving an island that really looks like half an island. On the south coast, the cliffs rise to a dramatic 365 metres and the entire surface is dotted with inactive cones and craters.

History

Many Samoans believe that Manu'a was the first creation, the first land to emerge at the hands of the god Tagaloa.

With the islands so favoured by Tagaloa, the Tu'i Manu'a, any chief of these islands would certainly have been held in high esteem by the Samoans, and indeed, many supernatural powers have been ascribed to holders of the title down through history. Certain *tu'is* were credited with the ability to fly and to become invisible. All, of course, had exceptional prowess at war.

Many believe that, directly and indirectly, the Tu'i Manu'a was revered as the sovereign of all Polynesia. Although wars and fragmentations split the islands, he was still a proud and powerful figure at the time of cession to the USA. The last Tu'i Manu'a ceded the islands in 1904, but in his will stipulated that the title would die with him. By allowing themselves to come under the jurisdiction of a foreign power, the islanders at the centre of the Polynesian world lost much of the respect they had once been accorded and the revered chief apparently decided that such a title would thereafter be superfluous.

The last Tu'i Manu'a died on 2 April 1909, and since then, Manu'a has been little more than the American Samoan backwater as far as the government is concerned. Many American Samoans, however, whether they live on Tutuila or abroad (even those who have never set foot in the Manu'a Islands), give their official address as Manu'a out of respect to the place that Tagaloa created before all others.

In January 1987, Manu'a was hit by Cyclone Tusi, one of the worst storms in their recorded history. Ofu and Olosega suffered badly and many buildings were destroyed, but Ta'u was the hardest hit. All three villages on the island were reduced to heaps of rubble, coconut trees were decapitated and crops ruined. Thanks to a shortage of supplies, proper equipment and reliable transport, as well as political disputes, contract squabbles and bureaucracy, reconstruction wasn't completed for at least three years. In the meantime, schools met in temporary shelters with leaky roofs, and on Ta'u, classes had to be dismissed whenever it rained!

To compound matters, in early 1990 and late 1991, Cyclones 'Ofa and Val also ploughed through the Manu'a Islands (they struck with far less force here than on Savai'i) but the cleanup was thwarted by tangles of US bureaucracy and local scamming. Numerous false claims were filed for government compensation, especially on Ta'u. These included buildings destroyed by Tusi which had already been paid off by previous compensation! The mess – both literal and figurative – is still being sorted out.

Orientation & Information

If at all possible, don't miss Manu'a, which is worth two days or two weeks, depending upon your interests and available time. If you want to see the sights quickly and move on, a couple of days will be sufficient. The islands aren't full of 'must-see' items; in fact, the only thing that qualifies for must-see status is the beach on Ofu's south coast. Although the lack of transport will slow you down considerably, that's just what the Manu'a Islands do best.

If you're not pressed for time, Manu'a can absorb a lot of it. You can sit for hours relaxing or reading on a four-km-long deserted white beach, go snorkelling over the reefs, gaze at sea birds riding thermals over unimaginable cliffs, climb to the prehistoric-like cloud forests on the towering peaks and meet the people in the tiny, still traditional villages. Manu'a is American Samoa at its best, and it promises to remain that way for a long time to come.

The Islands

OFU ISLAND

Ofu is the most dramatic and beautiful of the Manu'a Islands, and it is the place most often seen by outsiders. It is also the easiest to visit, with a superb airstrip on Va'oto Marsh, the only available bit of flat land, and a clean, friendly and reasonably-priced hotel adjoining it.

The Beach

Ofu's crown jewel is the beach along the south coast. It is surely one of the finest in the South Pacific – four km of shining, palm-fringed white sand, and the only footprints to be seen other than your own are those of birds and crabs. This is the sort of place visitors to Waikiki and Surfers Paradise are actually dreaming of. Once you've seen it, you'll want to settle in for a few days and savour the good fortune of turning up in such a lovely spot.

With your own snorkelling equipment, parts of the stretch offshore are deep enough for some excellent viewing of coral and tropical fish – probably the best available from the shore anywhere in American Samoa.

The place is just as idyllic on a starry night, but the locals stay away because they believe the bush between the road and the beach is infested with devilish aitu. Therefore, someone may question your motives if you set up camp there.

If you're set up for camping, a better idea is to check out the beach on the northern shore near the bridge to Olosega. Although it's not as nice as the beach on the south coast, it isn't under the control of any village and is so secluded that no one is likely to realise you're there. Access will involve some climbing down through dense bush and banana trees at the bottom of the 'concrete' hill (see map).

Ofu Village

Just two km north of the airstrip is Ofu village, which was devastated by Cyclone Tusi and is still in the process of being rebuilt. All that remains of the former church is a foundation and a heap of concrete blocks. The storm, however, may have been a blessing in disguise. It caused the Department of Public Works to take notice of the place, and in recent years a new harbour with floating docks was constructed (and subsequently mangled by Cyclone 'Ofa), the airstrip runway has been paved and road access to the TV relay tower atop Mt Tumutumu has been greatly improved.

Along the shore is a calm lagoon for swimming (ask permission), but avoid the pass between Ofu and Nu'utele Island just offshore as the currents are powerful and dangerous.

Out beyond the small village of Alaufau and the former docks, a rough track leads out to Tauga Point. It is possible to walk out beyond there to the wild north coast but the going is over huge volcanic boulders and it's a very rough proposition.

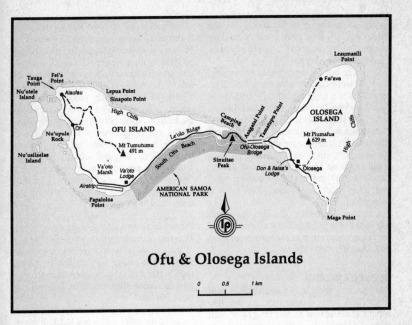

Ofu & Olosega Islands

0   0.5   1 km

Mt Tumutumu

The new road to the summit of 491-metre Mt Tumutumu leaves from Alaufau near the floating docks and twists and climbs up to the new TV relay tower atop the mountain. (The original tower, which was built to withstand winds in excess of 200 km per hour, was destroyed in the cyclone of January 1987).

The road can be negotiated in a sturdy 4WD vehicle, and occasionally you can hitch a ride up with Public Works. Most of the time, however, the trip to the top involves a hot and sweaty 5½-km climb but the vegetation and views from the top make it well worthwhile. Less than halfway up, look for the experimental garden project where temperate vegetables like cabbage, onions and carrots are being grown. If it's hot, allow a full day and don't forget to carry all the food and water you'll need as none is available anywhere above the village.

The altitude of the mountain gives it a

climate similar to that of northern New Zealand, and the flora found there is reminiscent of that in more southerly latitudes. Amazing cloud forests of tree ferns and wild coleus that appear to be straight out of a Dr Seuss fantasy cover the slopes and summit. Below, you can see the perpendicular cliffs of both Ofu and Olosega plunging into the sea.

Although it's often cold and windy, the summit of Mt Tumutumu offers a spectacularly scenic camping site but you'll need a sturdy windproof tent and sleeping bags.

Places to Stay & Eat

The only hotel on Ofu is the friendly *Va'oto Lodge* (☎ 699-9628), conveniently located near the beach, right between the airstrip and Va'oto Marsh (which is no longer apparent). It is run by a friendly couple from Tutuila, Tito and Margaret Malae. The rooms are clean and quiet, all with electric fans and private facilities. In the lounge, they keep a library of reading material and across the airport runway, they have a sort of outdoor lounge which consists of a circle of chairs overlooking the shore.

If you're not on the strictest of budgets, it's a perfect place to relax for a few days. Single/double rooms cost only US$35/40, with discounts for longer stays, and they do excellent family-style Samoan dinners – oka, palusami, taro, plantain, fresh fish and chicken – for US$6 per person. On weekends the owners return from Tutuila and put on a really big feed for themselves and guests. Lunch (US$2) and brekkie are also served if you book them in advance. Real brewed coffee costs US$1.

Camping is possible (see The Beach and Mt Tumutumu sections), but as usual, carry water since surface water is hard to come by on this nearly vertical island.

OLOSEGA ISLAND

Olosega, only three km square, is Ofu's twin island, and when viewed from the sea they appear to be almost mirror images of each other. Olosega lies only 137 metres or so from Ofu and is joined to it by a bridge. Strong winds and water currents are funnelled through this pass by steep cliffs on both islands. They are both encircled by the same reef.

Things to See

Olosega has a very nice beach along its south-west coast between the pass and the village. An interesting short walk is the trip to Maga Point on the southern tip of the island.

The road south-east of Olosega village leads out to the point above high and windy cliffs where you not only have a good view of the impossibly rugged east coast of Olosega, but a good view of Ta'u as well. There appears to have been an attempt at road-building beyond the point but the project looks fairly hopeless, as you'll see. Note that the cliffs are covered with the nests of brown noddies and white terns, which can be seen riding the thermals above.

Another possibility, but only for the hardy, is the climb to the summit of 629-metre Mt Piumafua. Be warned that it's not at all easy and toward the top, the trail is almost entirely overgrown and indistinguishable. Begin by following an easy trail inland from Olosega village, climbing up the mountainside to a water catchment which has constructed by the village. At this point, the trail disappears, so the rest of the way to the summit will involve heavy bush-bashing along a route that is marked only occasionally by ribbons tied to tree branches. On the summit, you'll find another of those prehistoric-looking cloud forests. Allow all day for the trip and carry food and water.

Places to Stay & Eat

Don & Ilaisa's Lodge (☎ 633-2304) in Olosega village is slightly less expensive than Va'oto Lodge on Ofu and is recommended for anyone looking for an even more remote setting than the 'airport hotel' can offer. No one is able to say exactly who Don & Ilaisa are or were, but that was the original name of the place and it has stuck. Pleasant rooms cost US$20/35 for a single/double, with meals available on site. There's no public transport available, but from the airport on Ofu, you can hitch a ride with one of the pick-up trucks which come to pick up cargo whenever a plane lands. Alternatively, make an advance booking and the hotel will send a truck to pick you up. Meals are available if ordered in advance.

Basic, albeit expensive, supplies – soft drinks and tinned foods – are available at the store in Olosega village, aptly marked 'Store', not far from Don & Ilaisa's Lodge.

Getting There & Away

Since there is no harbour or airstrip, access to Olosega is on foot or by vehicle from Ofu. To walk from Ofu village to Olosega village will take about two hours.

TA'U ISLAND

Mt Lata, the sacred mountain of Ta'u, is 995 metres high, the highest point in American Samoa. Although a better case is made for

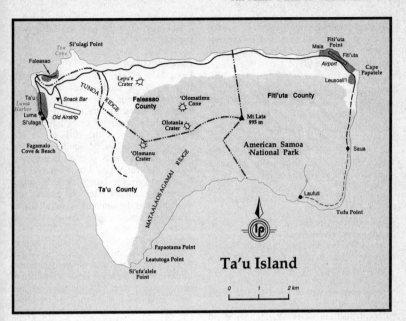

Ta'u Island

Savai'i in Western Samoa, some people believe that Ta'u is the ancient Hawaiki frequently referred to in Polynesian legend, the place from which the Maoris say they sailed to Aotearoa (New Zealand). Manu'a was the spiritual 'capital' of Polynesia, and Ta'u was the capital of Manu'a, and it was from here that the Tu'i Manu'a reigned. The last Tu'i Manu'a is buried in Luma, the northern section of Ta'u village on the west coast of the island.

Also in Luma, the young Margaret Mead researched and wrote her classic anthropological work *Coming of Age in Samoa* in 1925. These days, Ta'u and the island's other two villages, Fiti'uta and Faleasao, lie in ruin, devastated by the 1987 Cyclone Tusi.

Reconstruction, though constant, is moving slowly, but when all is said and done, Fiti'uta village has gained the most from the disaster. It now has the only hotel on the island, since the one in Ta'u was destroyed in the cyclone. (It was rebuilt with insurance money then suspiciously burned down a week later, only to be rebuilt and burned down yet again!)

The storm destroyed not only the villages but much of the island's beauty and left the place looking quite unappealing. Crops and bushland were flattened and trees blown over. Although it seems to be coming back now, it will be quite a while before the beauty of the island's natural lushness returns completely.

A new school and church have emerged in Fiti'uta to replace the tumbledown (literally) buildings that used to stand there. What's more, in the fury of reconstruction, the Department of Public Works decided on Fiti'uta as the site of the new airport, which has now replaced the disaster-prone airstrip on the ridge above Faleasao village.

Ta'u is lacking the spectacular beaches of Ofu and Olosega, but there are still a couple of nice ones and the island is certainly worth a day or two of exploring on foot. It's also fairly easy to hitch a ride between the eastern and western ends. Although traffic is sparse, if someone is going your way, they're sure to stop and offer a lift.

American Samoa National Park

The new American Samoa National Park, created in 1988, occupies 2000 hectares, comprising most of the uninhabited southern half of Ta'u and amounting to 40% of the island's total area. As would be expected, the protected area takes in some of American Samoa's most dramatic scenery.

As previously mentioned, Ta'u is a shield volcano that has undergone dramatic changes. The apocalyptic collapse of half its caldera left a spectacular 425-metre escarpment along the southern side and cliffs as high as 365 metres along the coast. On the northern slope, numerous craters and cones remained active after the big event and continued to build that side of the island.

However, it will still be several years before the island sees any park-related development. Such amenities as camping sites and hiking trails are still in the discussion stages, so if you want to see the place before tourism arrives, there's still time.

Ta'u Village

The main settlement on Ta'u consists of the twin villages of Luma and Si'ufaga. In Luma is the tomb of the last Tu'i Manu'a and the tombs of several other early politicians, but they're nothing earth-shattering. Everything in the village, including the tombs, was damaged by Cyclone Tusi and the whole scene remains fairly depressing.

There are a couple of brand new air-conditioned bush stores, where you can buy expensive soft drinks and supplies; occasionally they even have fresh bread. Faleasao village, over the ridge, has one small store.

Both Ta'u and Faleasao have lovely white sand beaches, but they're not ideal for swimming or snorkelling. Just offshore there is a lot of coral and stone that is exposed at low tide and lies just below the surface at other times.

At Luma is a new harbour with fairly good swimming.

Fagamalo Cove

From Ta'u village, the walk out past the harbour to the sandy beach at secluded Fagamalo Cove is a pleasant way to pass a couple of hours. The track along the west coast can be muddy at times but it offers some nice views of the cliffs above and pounding surf below. Mosquitoes, even at midday, are voracious, so don't forget some sort of repellent or you'll be miserable. The best time to go is in the cool of the morning, before the brilliant afternoon sun (if it's shining) turns the white sand into a furnace of reflected heat.

Agricultural Rd

Although it can be muddy, a stroll up the Agricultural Rd to Tunoa Ridge is pleasant. In the morning there are lots of birds active here. In the evening, look for barn owls and fruit-eating bats. If it's been cleared recently, you can actually walk all the way up to Mataalaosagamai Ridge for a view into the gaping caldera and along the south coast. It is likely that improvement of this route will be one of the first projects on the agenda when national park development funds are appropriated.

Fiti'uta

Between Ta'u and Fiti'uta, near the steep hill, is a black-sand beach. It's very nice to look at but the water is too rough for swimming and the locals may try to charge you a custom fee to sit there.

Three hours by trail beyond Fiti'uta is a very nice beach, secluded and good for camping. If you wish to walk further along this route towards Laufuti Stream and Falls, some bushwhacking will be necessary. It's a nice long day hike and the water is refreshing.

Places to Stay & Eat

The main place to stay is the *Fiti'uta Lodge* (☎ 677-3155) – also known as Ta'u Lodge or Ale's Lodge – near the airport in the village of Fiti'uta. Fairly basic rooms with private facilities cost US$30/40 a single/double. Next door is a shop that seems to be closed most of the time.

There was once another hotel, the Niumata, in Ta'u village, but it habitually suffered disaster. It was first destroyed by Cyclone Tusi, but was then rebuilt and burned down twice (with compensation, of course). It may be back again someday, but don't stay there without insurance against personal injury!

Most of the supplies on Ta'u now come in on a barge that lands at Luma Harbor when the water isn't too rough. If rough weather continues for a long period of time, which happens frequently enough to become a problem, the island has to go without anything that is too heavy to be brought in by plane – beer, for instance! It's a good idea to take any food or supplies you'll be needing from Tutuila.

There are no restaurants on the island, but a small snack bar operates on the road just below the former airstrip.

Getting There & Around

Air

Ofu Airport is a lovely 500-metre surfaced strip at Va'oto on the south coast of the island. Fortunately for travellers heading for Ta'u, the old 400-metre nightmare airstrip – which had a cliff on one end, a mountain on the other and lots of quirky air currents throughout – has been decommissioned and replaced by a flash new facility in a more suitable location at Fiti'uta, seven km east.

Samoa Air flies twice daily between Tutuila and the Manu'a Islands. The planes stop at either or both Ta'u and Ofu whenever there are passengers to be picked up or dropped off. Between Pago and either Manu'a airstrip, the fare is US$30 each way or US$56 return. Phone and make a reservation, then reconfirm the return flight upon arrival. The trip between Ofu and Ta'u is only US$15 each way.

Sea

Water transport to the Manu'a Islands is at present limited to private yachts, which very infrequently call in at Luma on Ta'u and at Ofu village. Cruising yachts arriving from the east must check into Pago Pago before they'll be permitted to land at Manu'a and once they've arrived in Pago Pago, they're facing a fierce beat into the wind to get back to Manu'a. Few people bother with it.

The harbours of both Ofu and Ta'u are marginal, and can prove disastrous in the event of any carelessness. There were once two weekly barges from Tutuila but one of them sank at Ta'u harbour and now, much of the cargo to Manu'a arrives on Samoa Air. In any case, the barges never accepted passengers.

Hitching

Much of your getting around on the Manu'a Islands will involve hoofing it. There are some vehicles on the islands, however, and few drivers will pass a walker without offering a lift.

Rose Atoll

Rose Atoll, 100 km east of the Manu'a Islands, is composed of two tiny specks of land and the surrounding reef. Rose Islet, only three metres above sea level at its highest point, has an area of five hectares. Sand Islet, soaring to an evalation of five metres, is only 2½ hectares in area.

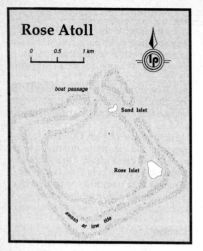

Rose Atoll

0   0.5   1 km

boat passage

Sand Islet

Rose Islet

awash at low tide

Geologically, the atoll was probably once a shield volcano (like Manu'a) that has completely eroded away since the Pleistocene era. Coral reefs have built up on the remnants making the island visible today.

Rose Atoll is designated a US national wildlife refuge, and permission to visit, which is very difficult to obtain, must be secured from the controlling agency in Hawaii. The refuge exists primarily to protect the black turtle, which lays its eggs in the sand here, as well as the extremely rare and endangered hawksbill turtle. Numerous species of seabirds nest on the atoll, including the sooty tern (whose presence on Rose Atoll represents 85% of the total seabird population of American Samoa), and a variety of other terns, tropical birds, noddies and boobies.

Index

PLANET TALK
Lonely Planet's FREE quarterly newsletter

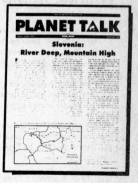

We love hearing from you and think you'd like to hear from us.

When...is the right time to see reindeer in Finland?
Where...can you hear the best palm-wine music in Ghana?
How...do you get from Asunción to Areguá by steam train?
What...is the best way to see India?

For the answer to these and many other questions read PLANET TALK.

Every issue is packed with up-to-date travel news and advice including:

- *a letter from Lonely Planet founders Tony and Maureen Wheeler*
- *travel diary from a Lonely Planet author - find out what it's really like out on the road*
- *feature article on an important and topical travel issue*
- *a selection of recent letters from our readers*
- *the latest travel news from all over the world*
- *details on Lonely Planet's new and forthcoming releases*

To join our mailing list contact any Lonely Planet office (address below).

LONELY PLANET PUBLICATIONS
Australia: PO Box 617, Hawthorn 3122, Victoria (tel: 03-819 1877)
USA: Embarcadero West, 155 Filbert St, Suite 251, Oakland, CA 94607 (tel: 510-893 8555)
TOLL FREE: (800) 275-8555
UK: 10 Barley Mow Passage, Chiswick, London W4 4PH (tel: 081-742 3161)
France: 71 bis rue du Cardinal Lemoine – 75005 Paris (tel: 1-46 34 00 58)

Also available: Lonely Planet T-shirts. 100% heavyweight cotton (S, M, L, XL)

Guides to the Pacific

Australia – a travel survival kit
The complete low-down on Down Under – home of Ayers Rock, the Great Barrier Reef, extraordinary animals, cosmopolitan cities, rainforests, beaches ... and Lonely Planet!

Bushwalking in Australia
Two experienced and respected walkers give details of the best walks in every state, covering many different terrains and climates.

Bushwalking in Papua New Guinea
The best way to get to know Papua New Guinea is from the ground up – and bushwalking is the best way to travel around the rugged and varied landscape of this island.

Islands of Australia's Great Barrier Reef – Australia guide
The Great Barrier Reef is one of the wonders of the world – and one of the great travel destinations! Whether you're looking for the best snorkelling, the liveliest nightlife or a secluded island hideaway, this guide has all the facts you'll need.

Melbourne – city guide
From historic houses to fascinating churches and from glorious parks to tapas bars, cafés and bistros, Melbourne is a dream for gourmets and a paradise for sightseers.

Sydney – city guide
From the Opera House to the surf; all you need to know in a handy pocket-sized format.

Victoria – Australia guide
From old gold rush towns to cosmopolitan Melbourne and from remote mountains to the most popular surf beaches, Victoria is packed with attractions and activities for everyone.

Fiji – a travel survival kit
Whether you prefer to stay in camping grounds, international hotels, or something in-between, this comprehensive guide will help you to enjoy the beautiful Fijian archipelago.

Hawaii – a travel survival kit
Share in the delights of this island paradise – and avoid some of its high prices – with this practical guide. It covers all of Hawaii's well-known attractions, plus plenty of uncrowded sights and activities.

Micronesia – a travel survival kit
The glorious beaches, lagoons and reefs of these 2100 islands would dazzle even the most jaded traveller. This guide has all the details on island-hopping across the Micronesian archipelago.

New Caledonia – a travel survival kit
This guide shows how to discover all that the idyllic islands of New Caledonia have to offer – from French colonial culture to traditional Melanesian life.

New Zealand – a travel survival kit
This practical guide will help you discover the very best New Zealand has to offer: Maori dances and feasts, some of the most spectacular scenery in the world, and every outdoor activity imaginable.

Tramping in New Zealand
Call it tramping, hiking, walking, bushwalking or trekking – travelling by foot is the best way to explore New Zealand's natural beauty. Detailed descriptions of over 40 walks of varying length and difficulty.

Papua New Guinea – a travel survival kit
With its coastal cities, villages perched beside mighty rivers, palm-fringed beaches and rushing mountain streams, Papua New Guinea promises memorable travel.

Rarotonga & the Cook Islands – a travel survival kit
Rarotonga and the Cook Islands have history, beauty and magic to rival the better-known islands of Hawaii and Tahiti, but the world has virtually passed them by.

Solomon Islands – a travel survival kit
The Solomon Islands are the best-kept secret of the Pacific. Discover remote tropical islands, jungle-covered volcanoes and traditional Melanesian villages with this detailed guide.

Tahiti & French Polynesia – a travel survival kit
Tahiti's idyllic beauty has seduced sailors, artists and travellers for generations. The latest edition of this book provides full details on the main island of Tahiti, the Tuamotos, Marquesas and other island groups. Invaluable information for independent travellers and package tourists alike.

Tonga – a travel survival kit
The only South Pacific country never to be colonised by Europeans, Tonga has also been ignored by tourists. The people of this far-flung island group offer some of the most sincere and unconditional hospitality in the world.

Vanuatu – a travel survival kit
Discover superb beaches, lush rainforests, dazzling coral reefs and traditional Melanesian customs in this glorious Pacific Ocean archipelago.

Also available:
Pidgin phrasebook.

Lonely Planet Guidebooks

Lonely Planet guidebooks cover every accessible part of Asia as well as Australia, the Pacific, South America, Africa, the Middle East, Europe and parts of North America. There are five series: *travel survival kits*, covering a country for a range of budgets; *shoestring guides* with compact information for low-budget travel in a major region; *walking guides*; *city guides* and *phrasebooks*.

Mail Order

Lonely Planet guidebooks are distributed worldwide. They are also available by mail order from Lonely Planet, so if you have difficulty finding a title please write to us. US and Canadian residents should write to Embarcadero West, 155 Filbert St, Suite 251, Oakland CA 94607, USA; European residents should write to 10 Barley Mow Passage, Chiswick, London W4 4PH; and residents of other countries to PO Box 617, Hawthorn, Victoria 3122, Australia.

Indian Subcontinent
Bangladesh
India
Hindi/Urdu phrasebook
Trekking in the Indian Himalaya
Karakoram Highway
Kashmir, Ladakh & Zanskar
Nepal
Trekking in the Nepal Himalaya
Nepali phrasebook
Pakistan
Sri Lanka
Sri Lanka phrasebook

Africa
Africa on a shoestring
Central Africa
East Africa
Trekking in East Africa
Kenya
Swahili phrasebook
Morocco, Algeria & Tunisia
Arabic (Moroccan) phrasebook
South Africa, Lesotho & Swaziland
Zimbabwe, Botswana & Namibia
West Africa

Central America & the Caribbean
Baja California
Central America on a shoestring
Costa Rica
Eastern Caribbean
Guatemala, Belize & Yucatán: La Ruta Maya
Mexico

North America
Alaska
Canada
Hawaii

Europe
Baltic States & Kaliningrad
Dublin city guide
Eastern Europe on a shoestring
Eastern Europe phrasebook
Finland
France
Greece
Hungary
Iceland, Greenland & the Faroe Islands
Ireland
Italy
Mediterranean Europe on a shoestring
Mediterranean Europe phrasebook
Poland
Scandinavian & Baltic Europe on a shoestring
Scandinavian Europe phrasebook
Switzerland
Trekking in Spain
Trekking in Greece
USSR
Russian phrasebook
Western Europe on a shoestring
Western Europe phrasebook

South America
Argentina, Uruguay & Paraguay
Bolivia
Brazil
Brazilian phrasebook
Chile & Easter Island
Colombia
Ecuador & the Galápagos Islands
Latin American Spanish phrasebook
Peru
Quechua phrasebook
South America on a shoestring
Trekking in the Patagonian Andes

The Lonely Planet Story

Lonely Planet published its first book in 1973 in response to the numerous 'How did you do it?' questions Maureen and Tony Wheeler were asked after driving, bussing, hitching, sailing and railing their way from England to Australia.

Written at a kitchen table and hand collated, trimmed and stapled, *Across Asia on the Cheap* became an instant local bestseller, inspiring thoughts of another book.

Eighteen months in South-East Asia resulted in their second guide, *South-East Asia on a shoestring*, which they put together in a backstreet Chinese hotel in Singapore in 1975. The 'yellow bible' as it quickly became known to backpackers around the world, soon became *the* guide to the region. It has sold well over half a million copies and is now in its 7th edition, still retaining its familiar yellow cover.

Today there are over 130 Lonely Planet titles in print – books that have that same adventurous approach to travel as those early guides; books that 'assume you know how to get your luggage off the carousel' as one reviewer put it.

Although Lonely Planet initially specialised in guides to Asia, they now cover most regions of the world, including the Pacific, South America, Africa, the Middle East and Europe. The list of *walking guides* and *phrasebooks* (for 'unusual' languages such as Quechua, Swahili, Nepali and Egyptian Arabic) is also growing rapidly.

The emphasis continues to be on travel for independent travellers. Tony and Maureen still travel for several months of each year and play an active part in the writing, updating and quality control of Lonely Planet's guides.

They have been joined by over 50 authors, 60 staff – mainly editors, cartographers & designers – at our office in Melbourne, Australia, at our US office in Oakland, California and at our European office in Paris; another five at our office in London handle sales for Britain, Europe and Africa. Travellers themselves also make a valuable contribution to the guides through the feedback we receive in thousands of letters each year.

The people at Lonely Planet strongly believe that travellers can make a positive contribution to the countries they visit, both through their appreciation of the countries' culture, wildlife and natural features, and through the money they spend. In addition, the company makes a direct contribution to the countries and regions it covers. Since 1986 a percentage of the income from each book has been donated to ventures such as famine relief in Africa; aid projects in India; agricultural projects in Central America; Greenpeace's efforts to halt French nuclear testing in the Pacific and Amnesty International. In 1994 $100,000 was donated to such causes.

Lonely Planet's basic travel philosophy is summed up in Tony Wheeler's comment, 'Don't worry about whether your trip will work out. Just go!'.